LANGUAGE AND LITERACY SERIES

Dorothy S. Strickland, FOUNDING EDITOR
Celia Genishi and Donna E. Alvermann, SERIES EDITORS

ADVISORY BOARD: Richard Allington, Kathryn Au, Bernice Cullinan, Colette Daiute, Anne Haas Dyson, Carole Edelsky, Shirley Brice Heath, Connie Juel, Susan Lytle, Timothy Shanahan

ReWRITING the Basics:
Literacy Learning in Children's Cultures
ANNE HAAS DYSON

Writing Instruction That Works:
Proven Methods for Middle and High School Classrooms
ARTHUR N. APPLEBEE & JUDITH A. LANGER, WITH
KRISTEN CAMPBELL WILCOX, MARC NACHOWITZ,
MICHAEL P. MASTROIANNI, AND CHRISTINE DAWSON

Literacy Playshop: New Literacies, Popular Media,
and Play in the Early Childhood Classroom
KAREN E. WOHLWEND

Critical Media Pedagogy:
Teaching for Achievement in City Schools
ERNEST MORRELL, RUDY DUEÑAS, VERONICA GARCIA,
& JORGE LOPEZ

A Search Past Silence: The Literacy of Young Black Men
DAVID E. KIRKLAND

The ELL Writer:
Moving Beyond Basics in the Secondary Classroom
CHRISTINA ORTMEIER-HOOPER

Reading in a Participatory Culture:
Remixing Moby-Dick in the English Classroom
HENRY JENKINS & WYN KELLEY, WITH KATIE CLINTON, JENNA
MCWILLIAMS, RICARDO PITTS-WILEY, AND ERIN REILLY, EDS.

Summer Reading: Closing the Rich/Poor Achievement Gap
RICHARD L. ALLINGTON & ANNE MCGILL-FRANZEN, EDS.

Real World Writing for Secondary Students:
Teaching the College Admission Essay and Other
Gate-Openers for Higher Education
JESSICA SINGER EARLY & MEREDITH DECOSTA

Teaching Vocabulary to English Language Learners
MICHAEL F. GRAVES, DIANE AUGUST,
& JEANNETTE MANCILLA-MARTINEZ

Literacy for a Better World:
The Promise of Teaching in Diverse Schools
LAURA SCHNEIDER VANDERPLOEG

Socially Responsible Literacy:
Teaching Adolescents for Purpose and Power
PAULA M. SELVESTER & DEBORAH G. SUMMERS

Learning from Culturally and Linguistically
Diverse Classrooms: Using Inquiry to Inform Practice
JOAN C. FINGON & SHARON H. ULANOFF, EDS.

Bridging Literacy and Equity
ALTHIER M. LAZAR, PATRICIA A. EDWARDS, &
GWENDOLYN THOMPSON MCMILLON

"Trust Me! I Can Read"
SALLY LAMPING & DEAN WOODRING BLASE

Reading Girls
HADAR DUBOWSKY MA'AYAN

Reading Time
CATHERINE COMPTON-LILLY

A Call to Creativity
LUKE REYNOLDS

Literacy and Justice Through Photography
WENDY EWALD, KATHERINE HYDE, & LISA LORD

The Successful High School Writing Center
DAWN FELS & JENNIFER WELLS, EDS.

Interrupting Hate
MOLLIE V. BLACKBURN

Playing Their Way into Literacies
KAREN E. WOHLWEND

Teaching Literacy for Love and Wisdom
JEFFREY D. WILHELM & BRUCE NOVAK

Overtested
JESSICA ZACHER PANDYA

Restructuring Schools for Linguistic Diversity,
Second Edition
OFELIA B. MIRAMONTES, ADEL NADEAU, & NANCY L. COMMINS

Words Were All We Had
MARÍA DE LA LUZ REYES, ED.

Urban Literacies
VALERIE KINLOCH, ED.

Bedtime Stories and Book Reports
CATHERINE COMPTON-LILLY & STUART GREENE, EDS.

Envisioning Knowledge
JUDITH A. LANGER

Envisioning Literature, Second Edition
JUDITH A. LANGER

Writing Assessment and the Revolution in
Digital Texts and Technologies
MICHAEL R. NEAL

Artifactual Literacies
KATE PAHL & JENNIFER ROWSELL

Educating Emergent Bilinguals
OFELIA GARCÍA & JO ANNE KLEIFGEN

(Re)Imagining Content-Area Literacy Instruction
RONI JO DRAPER, ED.

Change Is Gonna Come
PATRICIA A. EDWARDS, GWENDOLYN THOMPSON MCMILLON, &
JENNIFER D. TURNER

When Commas Meet Kryptonite
MICHAEL BITZ

Literacy Tools in the Classroom
RICHARD BEACH, GERALD CAMPANO, BRIAN EDMISTON,
& MELISSA BORGMANN

Harlem on Our Minds
VALERIE KINLOCH

Teaching the New \
ANNE HERRINGTON, \

LANGUAGE AND LITERACY SERIES *(continued)*

Critical Encounters in High School English,
Second Edition
DEBORAH APPLEMAN

Children, Language, and Literacy
CELIA GENISHI & ANNE HAAS DYSON

Children's Language
JUDITH WELLS LINDFORS

The Administration and Supervision of Reading Programs,
Fourth Edition
SHELLEY B. WEPNER & DOROTHY S. STRICKLAND, EDS.

"You Gotta BE the Book," Second Edition
JEFFREY D. WILHELM

No Quick Fix
RICHARD L. ALLINGTON & SEAN A. WALMSLEY, EDS.

Children's Literature and Learning
BARBARA A. LEHMAN

Storytime
LARWRENCE R. SIPE

Effective Instruction for Struggling Readers, K–6
BARBARA M. TAYLOR & JAMES E. YSSELDYKE, EDS.

The Effective Literacy Coach
ADRIAN RODGERS & EMILY M. RODGERS

Writing in Rhythm
MAISHA T. FISHER

Reading the Media
RENEE HOBBS

teaching**media***literacy*.com
RICHARD BEACH

What Was It Like?
LINDA J. RICE

Research on Composition
PETER SMAGORINSKY, ED.

The Vocabulary Book
MICHAEL F. GRAVES

Powerful Magic
NINA MIKKELSEN

New Literacies in Action
WILLIAM KIST

Teaching English Today
BARRIE R.C. BARRELL ET AL., EDS.

Bridging the Literacy Achievement Gap, 4–12
DOROTHY S. STRICKLAND & DONNA E. ALVERMANN, EDS.

Out of This World
HOLLY VIRGINIA BLACKFORD

Critical Passages
KRISTIN DOMBEK & SCOTT HERNDON

Making Race Visible
STUART GREENE & DAWN ABT-PERKINS, EDS.

The Child as Critic, Fourth Edition
GLENNA SLOAN

Room for Talk
REBEKAH FASSLER

Give Them Poetry!
GLENNA SLOAN

The Brothers and Sisters Learn to Write
ANNE HAAS DYSON

"Just Playing the Part"
CHRISTOPHER WORTHMAN

The Testing Trap
GEORGE HILLOCKS, JR.

Inquiry Into Meaning
EDWARD CHITTENDEN & TERRY SALINGER, WITH ANNE M. BUSSIS

"Why Don't They Learn English?"
LUCY TSE

Conversational Borderlands
BETSY RYMES

Inquiry-Based English Instruction
RICHARD BEACH & JAMIE MYERS

The Best for Our Children
MARÍA DE LA LUZ REYES & JOHN J. HALCÓN, EDS.

Language Crossings
KAREN L. OGULNICK, ED.

What Counts as Literacy?
MARGARET GALLEGO & SANDRA HOLLINGSWORTH, EDS.

Beginning Reading and Writing
DOROTHY S. STRICKLAND & LESLEY M. MORROW, EDS.

Reading for Meaning
BARBARA M. TAYLOR, MICHAEL F. GRAVES,
& PAUL VAN DEN BROEK, EDS.

Young Adult Literature and the New Literary Theories
ANNA O. SOTER

Literacy Matters
ROBERT P. YAGELSKI

Children's Inquiry
JUDITH WELLS LINDFORS

Close to Home
JUAN C. GUERRA

Life at the Margins
JULIET MERRIFIELD ET AL.

Literacy for Life
HANNA ARLENE FINGERET & CASSANDRA DRENNON

The Book Club Connection
SUSAN I. McMAHON & TAFFY E. RAPHAEL, EDS., ET AL.

Until We Are Strong Together
CAROLINE E. HELLER

Writing Superheroes
ANNE HAAS DYSON

ReWRITING
the Basics

Literacy Learning in
Children's Cultures

ANNE HAAS DYSON

Teachers College, Columbia University
New York and London

Published by Teachers College Press, 1234 Amsterdam Avenue, New York, NY 10027

Copyright © 2013 by Teachers College, Columbia University

Cataloging-in-Publication Data is available from the Library of Congress

ISBN 978-0-8077-5455-9 (paper)
ISBN 978-0-8077-5456-6 (hardcover)

Printed on acid-free paper
Manufactured in the United States of America

20 19 18 17 16 15 14 13   8 7 6 5 4 3 2 1

For Celia Genishi,
in appreciation of years of friendship

Contents

Preface   xi

Acknowledgments   xv

1. The "Basics" and Society's Children:
   Cases of Classroom Writing   1

   On Metaphoric Mailboxes and Textual Playgrounds:
   Basic Critiques   4

   Neighborhood Drives:
   Places for Childhoods Past and Present   9

   PART I: BASIC LESSONS AND BASIC TENSIONS

2. Welcome to Writing Workshop   25

   The Classroom as Community:
   Working (and Playing) Together   26

   The Basics and the Official
   Writing Lives of Young Children   33

   Wide-Awake Children and Blinds-Shut Basics   41

3. Looking Good and Sounding "Right": Fix-Its   43

   Kindergarten Fix-Its:
   Where Do Written Stories Come From?   46

   1st-Grade Fix-Its: Whose Voice Is That?   59

   The Basics in a Symbol-Mediated, Voice-Filled World   67

4. **The Ethics of Writing: On Truth and Ownership**   **69**

"A Real Story About You"
(The You That Is Not Spider-Man)   70

Your Own Story (The One That Is Not Copied)   75

Writing a Life Story (Or Writing in a Social Life?)   78

A Change in Angle of Vision   80

PART II: WRITING "BASICS" IN CHILDHOOD SPACES

5. **Shifting Expectations and Differing Ethics:
Entering Childhood Cultures**   **87**

Relational Fix-Its: "Put My Name in There!"   89

Organizing and Enacting Relationships: "Can I Play?"   94

A Caution About Developmental Order   97

6. **Collegial Relations and Coordinated Actions:
Textual Handclaps**   **99**

Written Language and the
Mediation of Childhood Cultures   100

The Relational Landscape for Textual Play:
Situating Old Basics in Child Spaces   111

7. **Complementary Relations and Improvisational Play:
On Matters of Birthdays, Love, and War**   **113**

Complementary Relations and Birthday Parties   115

Complementary Relations and Their Lack:
The Complex Game of Love   122

From Complementary Relations to Collaborative
Improvisations: The Pine Cone Wars   135

The Basic Dramas of Children's Textual Play   142

8. **Performers on a Movable Stage:
On the Malleability of Voice and Image**   **143**

Storytelling: Communicative Resources and Social Stages   145

Rhyming and Singing:
New Written Venues for Play and Performance   157

On Child Performers   160

9. **Re-Imagining Writing Basics
    for Contemporary Childhoods**   **162**

Contextualizing the Basics   164

Toward a Re-Envisioned Basic Education   174

So, What Do You Think?   178

Appendix A. Reflections on Methods   **180**

Situating Teachers   180

Copying the Children   181

Constructing Analytic Narratives   183

Appendix B. Demographic Tables   **185**

Table B.1. Sex and Ethnicity of Mrs. Kay's Children   185

Table B.2. Sex and Ethnicity of Mrs. Bee's Children   186

References   **187**

Index   **197**

About the Author   **206**

Preface

The ABC's are supposed to be as easy as 1, 2, 3, as the Jackson 5 (1970) pointed out. Indeed, the ABC's of just about anything are the "basics"—the foundation for moving forward. In literacy education, the ABC's are taken quite literally. They come making sounds and bearing reams of rules about how they should be arranged on a page, decked out in CAPITAL or lowercase garb, phonologically linked in words, and grammatically laid out in sentences. Teeming with expectations for the proper learning child, there is nothing particularly easy about the ABC's.

Nor does their use, so to speak, necessarily make matters easier. Even in today's kindergartens and 1st grades, the subject of writing can be draped in a vocabulary all its own—young children are to "draft" and "revise," to "stretch words [to better hear their sounds]," indeed, to "stretch stories [to better fill the page]"; they must "sketch" (not "draw"), and "zoom in" to adorn their texts with "details." Their assumed aspirations are to be *real* writers, who shape individual experience on paper.

So it was in Mrs. Bee's kindergarten and Mrs. Kay's 1st grade (all names in this book are pseudonyms, except for those of certain kindergartners for whom I received permission to use their first names). As in many public school classrooms in city schools, the basics were considered especially important, because their students were deemed "at risk" of school failure—that is, they were from economically distressed neighborhoods and, also, disproportionately children of color. For children so designated, the earlier the basics are taught, the better, or so it is thought (Lonigan & Shanahan, 2010). In Mrs. Bee's and Mrs. Kay's rooms, the expected basics were clearly detailed, the language arts curricula mandated, individual progress regularly tested.

In the pages to come, the assumed basics are not dismissed, nor are the efforts of dedicated teachers like Mrs. Bee and Mrs. Kay. In fact, I complicate the basics, examining the values and beliefs—the ideologies—they embody about proper language and proper children. I ask, in a world—and among children—whose rhythms beat out in varied languages and vernaculars, whose landscapes are strewn with multimodal and rhetorically designed texts (e.g., *PiZZA, saveBIG*), is it sensible, or clarifying, to treat written language as a static set of rules?

Still, the goings-on in Mrs. Bee's and Mrs. Kay's classrooms had to do with more than official expectations. There were unofficial ones too, grounded in children's worlds. And in these worlds, individual achievement and singular selves were not the motivational fuel for writing time. As the curriculum marched each child forward to a benchmarked beat, children could take what the school had to offer—its times and spaces, its materials, and its symbolic resources—and construct more collective encounters with print. As those Jackson 5 lyrics rhymed out, you got to "spell me, you" and then "add the two." That is, written language is rooted in human relationships.

For example, even if they did not know "how to make the words," kindergartners could "play . . . on paper," as 5-year-old Willo said; they could draw themselves side by side and even write their names so close together their letters seemed to be holding hands. The more experienced 1st-graders could coordinate their composing to enact some jointly improvised event—a plan for a fun-filled birthday, a battle in outer space, or, more humbly, a joint trip to the grocery store or, maybe, the circus.

Composing time could yield new kinds of playgrounds and new kinds of childhood practices. Childhood relations and practices potentially made writing relevant—and easier if not easy; such relevance is necessary if children are to learn, not just the subject of writing, but a cultural tool for participation (Vygotsky, 1978).

Children's attunement to one another and the social ability to adapt relevant symbolic material, coordinate their actions, assume complementary roles, and thereby jointly construct a textual place are key to extending and re-imagining the basics, the fundamental work of this book. To capture the basic transformation I am after here, I turn to an excerpt from the novelist Andrea Levy's book *Small Island* (2004). In this scene, Queenie is searching for a metaphor to capture the essence of her father-in-law, Arthur. She finds one in an old basic, as it were:

> Early Bird, my teacher at Bolsbrooke Elementary School, taught us all in English grammar that an apostrophe is a mark to show where something is missing. And that was how I'd always seen Bernard's father, Arthur: a human apostrophe. He was there but only to show us that something precious had gone astray. (p. 238)

In that evocative passage, Levy moves from a graphic matter to a relational one, from a sound, a letter gone missing, to some fundamental responsiveness, some *there* there, gone astray. In a modest way, that is what I am attempting to do in this book. I aim to move from an individualistic conception of childhood-writing basics to one better suited to the sociability—the humanity—of our children, the diversity of their resources (including language), the multimodality of their play, and the malleability of this nimble medium, written language.

I begin in Chapter 1 by introducing both key concepts and key players in this book. The concepts have to do with our fundamental beliefs about—our ideologies of—childhoods and language; these fuel "basic" instruction. I introduce those key players by taking readers on a discursive drive with me through Mrs. Kay's school neighborhood and then Mrs. Bee's. I end each drive at the schoolhouse, pointing out to readers the teachers and the children who we will soon see grappling with the basics.

As the book unfolds, the textual spotlight will center on official worlds and traditional basics in Part I (Chapters 2–4). The spotlight will intermittently move to the children's unofficial worlds before settling there in Part II (Chapters 5–8). It will be important not to romanticize those worlds or to dismiss children's need for guidance from their caring teachers. But it will also be important to take the children seriously. It is, after all, their childhoods they are writing out, the foundation for their sense of themselves as intelligent, active agents in a world composed with others.

Finally, in Chapter 9, I provide a summary of the re-imagined basics and consider what they mean for day-to-day teaching and learning. The pedagogic goal is to take those ABC's and situate them in the social and intellectual lives of the very young.

Acknowledgments

"I'm writing all our names," Alicia told me one day, "so you remember us." She need not have worried. The children in this book, including Alicia, are etched in my mind. My memory is not what it once was, but still, at will, I can conjure up scenes from our lives together as if they happened yesterday. I am immensely grateful to the children, who allowed me into their worlds. I am fortunate too that they had teachers who warmly welcomed me as well. If not for the generosity of kindergarten teacher Mrs. Bee and 1st-grade teacher Mrs. Kay, and their patience with the attentive, smiling, but mighty quiet me, this consideration of "the basics" would never have come to be.

There are others too who must be remembered here. I moved to Michigan from California in the early 2000s, just as federal attention to schooling, literacy, and young children was materializing in standardized test requirements and curriculum-dependent funding. Mrs. Kay's school and her classroom were prime sites for examining the "basic education" imagined for the young. Yanan Fan, now a tenured professor at California State University-San Francisco, was my dependable (and very fun) assistant from the get-go, and we were joined by the energetic Tambra Jackson, now also a tenured professor, at University of South Carolina-Columbia. (Tambra's nephews, then quite young, also helped with information on children's references to popular media; a heartfelt thanks to Demetrius JaQuan Jackson and Kaliq Demetri Jackson).

No project of this complexity can proceed without funds for equipment, assistants, and, most precious of all, time; so the funders of this project are in no danger of slipping into the cracks of my memory. I warmly thank former Dean Carole Ames, of Michigan State University College of Education, for faculty funds that helped the project begin to take shape. And I cannot forget to give a huge hurrah for The Spencer Foundation, which was critical in providing funds to develop the project as its plot, and its analyses, thickened. (Although I am a huge fan of The Spencer Foundation, they are, of course, not responsible for my findings and perspectives.)

A move to Illinois accompanied my worries that I was missing some aspects of the "basics" story because of the intense curricular push-down from 1st grade to kindergarten. In search of a school where I could extend the basics work, my much-missed colleague Christina DeNicolo, now of Wayne State University, introduced me to Mrs. Bee's school and helped pave the way for my visits to her kindergarten. The University of Illinois College of Education, and former Dean Susan Fowler in particular, provided funds for this extension of the work. I am especially grateful to current Dean Mary Kalanztsis for the appointment as Vera Nofftz Early Childhood Fellow.

As I think of the work here in Illinois, my terrific research assistants come into view. Sophie Dewayani, now doing university teaching in Indonesia, was a diligent and compassionate assistant; her newness to American education kept me alert to the social and instructional choices being made. Sophie was my first and my long-term assistant in Illinois, but others played their roles as well. Sophie was joined by another hard-working assistant, Nikisha Blackmon, now completing her dissertation, and the two of them figured out which children's books about kindergarten—and what images of kindergarten—dominated local bookstore sales and library checkouts.

As the research project became a writing project, others joined the work. The multitalented, good-humored, and insightful Haeny Yoon (now a professor at the University of Arizona) took photos of images and print in the children's neighborhood, just as Yanan had done in Michigan; then Haeny pored over children's products, examining if and how those local sites (and graphic sights) took form on children's papers. Finally, now, as I move toward the finish line, doctoral student and classroom teacher Wendy Maa has labored over this book with me. A dependable and indispensable companion, she has read every page of this book repeatedly; she has found misplaced references, headings run amuck, and punctuation marks that don't know where they are supposed to be. Moreover, she has talked with me through every example in this book; as an active early childhood teacher, Wendy has helped me figure out how to make those vignettes, and the points they illustrate, clear. Most important, when I have become weary of the endless small tasks in preparing the manuscript, Wendy has become excited, envisioning how the basics book would come together in a grand finale.

I must admit that family and friends have heard more than they should have had to about this book. As I was despairing of ever finishing, my mother Athleen W. Haas, said she would pray for me (which prayers I needed), my sisters Ruth and Mary, my brother David, and brother-in-law Peter assumed I would finish (which was heartening), and my sister-in-law JoAnn early on planned to get a copy in the local book store, long before there was an actual book.

Throughout the whole process, I was privileged to work with the marvelous folks at Teachers College Press. Early on, I fed off the enthusiasm of Meg Lemke, who was acquisitions editor when I first proposed the book. More recently, I have needed the dependable responsiveness of Emily Spangler, who has ably slipped into the editor's role. Sue Liddicoat, development editor extraordinaire, helped me tighten up my prose, including my sometimes breathtakingly long clauses with parentheses to boot (kind of like this). And Karl Nyberg carefully shepherded the book through production to completion (Yay!).

Finally, I will not forget to thank my teacher, mentor (after all these years), frequent co-author, and forever fake sister Celia Genishi. She knows what's basic.

CHAPTER 1

The "Basics"
and Society's Children
Cases of Classroom Writing

Mrs. Kay's 1st-graders are discussing the post office, the delivery of mail, and their experience getting letters. Why, their teacher wondered out loud, do people send letters anyway? Although new technology has altered the place of written letters in societal lives, Mrs. Kay's children had nothing but good words for "you got mail" (in your literal mailbox):

SASHA: Because [letter writers] might be your friend. . . .
JANETTE: Some people write to their grandpas and grandmas because they live very very far away. Like my aunt lives down in Tennessee. . . .
TIONNA: My auntie—it was my great great grandma—she died. No she didn't die, that was my auntie. She got me a necklace in the mail. It was in a little square envelope.

As the social studies lesson draws to a close and writing time begins, Ezekial whispers to his friend Joshua, "I'm gonna write a letter to you. Joshua! I'm gonna write a letter to you."

A mailbox anchored to a front porch, one atop a post on a city street, another crowded next to others in a small village's post office or an urban apartment entry way, or one all alone at the end of a path on a rural route—mailboxes are located in particular kinds of spaces and places, in certain historical and technological times, but at the least, they are a metaphor for the physical and symbolic act of, and the human need for, communicative exchange.

In this book about schooling and the basics of child writing, the old-fashioned mailbox serves as a reminder of the human responsiveness that is at the heart of communication in any mode, through any means. In school, learning the basics means mastering the ABC's—the sounds emanating from this letter or that one, the ways they are arranged in grammatically "proper" sentences, and the little punctuation pets that mark

1

their textual territory. But, in children's everyday places, written language is tied to human relationships, social participation, and societal institutions, among them families, friendships, and neighborhoods themselves, with their signs on familiar street corners and pizza places, their labels on much used commodities, their material forms for worship in church or for long-distance kisses from grandma.

Moreover, the image of the located mailbox underscores the situated nature of schooling. It unfolds in particular neighborhoods in which socioeconomic circumstances and public services, educational politics and resultant policies, reigning ideologies and popular pedagogies all play out in the lives of particular children. In this book, "basic" writing dramas play out in Mrs. Bee's kindergarten and Mrs. Kay's 1st grade. Both classrooms were in schools that served neighborhoods whose children were glossed as "at risk" (i.e., from low-income homes) and in need of "the basics."

Finally, the mailbox situates schooling, not only in sociocultural sites, but also in historical times. Early in the last century, mailboxes in the urban United States were a new means of communicative exchange, more efficient than face-to-face delivery by postal workers (www.usps.com/postalhistory). In this century, mailboxes are an old means of exchange; electronic delivery through virtual mailboxes is increasingly dominant (but not, of course, when you want to send a gift, maybe in a little square envelope). As communicative means multiply and become increasingly multimodal (Bezemer & Kress, 2008), as home access remains economically stratified (Zickuhr & Smither, 2012), "the basics" of school writing hold firm.

In Mrs. Kay's and Mrs. Bee's schools, federal legislation reinforced those basics. School funds were linked to school accountability via standardized testing of basic skills. Both teachers' districts responded with standardized curricula focused on the identified basics; the ostensible aim was to lessen if not end class and racial disparities in achievement.

All this attention to "the basics" raises questions, among them, what *are* they? To answer that question, I spent an academic year in Mrs. Kay's classroom and, then, a year-and-a-half in Mrs. Bee's. In each of these case studies, I examined how writing basics were locally defined in district documents and in everyday practice. And I considered the ideologies, or values and beliefs, about language and childhoods that undergirded the institutionalized "basics."

Within each case, I also wondered, what did the children make of these "basics?" What aspects of their meaning-making were officially visible, and which were lost to the official world, focused, as it was, on the basics? Twice weekly in both projects, I observed children closely. Through field notes, children's products, and accumulated audiotapes, I documented how a curricular focus on "basic" skills played out in children's daily school lives and, especially, in their entry into school writing.

In the process, I also documented children's own relationships and their playful practices. I learned what expectations *they* had for one another's participation in writing time. In other words, in unofficial worlds, there were also basic competencies to be displayed, and these were not isomorphic with official ones. (For methodological details of my data collection and analysis, see Appendix A.)

Both classrooms had similar hybrid writing programs: They blended an emphasis on conventional basics (i.e., the assumed foundational skills, including knowing letter names and sounds, being able to sound out reasonable spellings, using punctuation marks and "standard" grammar) with an emphasis on the writing process and the production of real "life stories," as Mrs. Kay said (i.e., producing the basic text, as it were: brief but detailed and linearly linked sentences about the self).

Each classroom was its own *telling case* (Mitchell, 1984), that is, its own particular realization of the complexities of writing basics in regulated (test-monitored, curriculum-scripted) times. In this book, though, the participants in each classroom collectively *tell* about, problematize, and inform the re-imagining of the basics by situating them within the times and spaces, the relations and practices, of childhoods-in-formation.

I offer herein no list of substitute basics. Nor do I dismiss the traditional basics or children's need for teachers' support and guidance. But I do offer an angle of vision on the basics, one that situates the traditional basics in the voices and images, the symbolic stuff, of children's everyday worlds. From that vantage point, I give witness to how familiar symbolic material becomes communicative resources for children's relations and practices. In this way, I aim to stretch those basics to include the socially attuned and responsive skill evident in children's lives with other children. Thus re-imagined, the basics provide a foundation for children who can make socially astute choices from their symbolic repertoire, children who see themselves as participants in an ever-widening world.

Below I use the mailbox metaphor to introduce the ideologies of language and childhoods that played out in Mrs. Bee's kindergarten and Mrs. Kay's 1st grade. Then I take readers on two drives with me, one to the neighborhood of Mrs. Kay's school (now closed, a victim of a depressed economy) and then to that of Mrs. Bee's school (now demolished and reorganized, a benefit, perhaps, of litigation on racial disparities in her district). A drive through the neighborhoods will reveal something of the economic, demographic, and physical contexts of the schools as I knew them. It will reveal as well spaces and places transformed in the symbolic efforts and social play of the children who populate this book. As I wind up each drive, I will briefly introduce the teachers and children who will be featured in the chapters to come.

ON METAPHORIC MAILBOXES AND TEXTUAL PLAYGROUNDS: BASIC CRITIQUES

It starts when you say we *. . . (Piercy, 1994, p. 45)*

"And what about writing?" I asked the older gentleman, as he sat on a tired chair in my cramped Berkeley office some 25 years ago. "Do the little children in your schools write? How do you arrange for its beginnings?"

My visitor spoke only Italian. So, through his translator, the late Loris Malaguzzi, the founder of the well-known Reggio Emilia preprimary system in Italy, talked about a *we*, to echo the line from the poet Marge Piercy. Writing began, he said, when children put little gifts in one another's mailboxes—a small piece of candy, perhaps, or a bit of ribbon. That small gift was a shared pleasure and a mediator of a relationship. To use current academic language, within this recurrent social practice—this activity frame—the children could move into offering one another, not small treats, but pictures or written notes that might contain only their names and maybe a little heart—a literal giving of the self to the other.

This story of writing's beginning, tied to the humble mailbox, captures the reciprocity that is the foundation for any symbolic medium, including language (Tomasello, 2009). Whether oral or written, language is a tool for coordinating attention within a shared place. From infancy on, we learn to participate in the social activities—the shared times and spaces—that comprise our lives. We come to anticipate others' actions in those goal-directed activities and to act accordingly ourselves. Our world thus becomes meaningful. In Nelson's (2007) words, "the lifelong adventure of gathering meaning from experience is in the service of two overriding motivations—to make sense and to make relationships" (pp. 14–15).

In Mrs. Kay's and Mrs. Bee's rooms, children were indeed in search of relationships and meaning. Composing was a potential mediator of their unofficial relations and practices and, in this way, figured into the production of their own shared childhoods. The social dramas in this book, though, did not unfold in schools like Malaguzzi's: organized around children's desires to interact, to play, and to examine their world. Mrs. Bee and Mrs. Kay were under enormous pressure to teach "the basics." In their rooms, written language officially began, not in relationships, but in the progress of individual children who were diligent, independent, and, we hope, standing tall against linear measures of progress. The writing of this book was fueled by concerns, not only about conceptions of "the basics," but also about the individualistic ideology that informs our ways of understanding and monitoring children's composing.

Bare-Bones Basics: Writing Out (Silencing) Childhoods

Educators have long critiqued traditional basics instruction for its decontextualized nature, that is, for the absence of a compelling social practice within which those basics matter (Goodman & Martens, 2007; Street, 2000). The basics are thus undergirded by a hierarchical and homogeneous view of language, in which it is a set of neutral rules; whatever the situation, those whose speech and writing follow the rules are proper, a cut above those who do not.

Instruction focused on the basics, and efforts to cultivate "proper" children, are most visible in schools serving low-income children (Hirsh-Pasek, Golinkoff, Berk, & Singer, 2009). Uniformity of lessons, and of the pacing of those lessons, is underscored. Such instruction is fueled, at least in part, by a desire to make sure that "the *all* children" have a firm foundation—the basics (Dyson, 2003b).

But the instruction it yields is too often a bare-bones education, *a pedagogy of poverty* (Haberman, 1991) that writes out of consideration the particularities of children's lives. And yet children themselves are not uniform; the nature and extent of their literacy experiences are shaped by cultural, linguistic, and socioeconomic factors, along with personal interests and situational dynamics (Barton & Hamilton, 1998; Genishi & Dyson, 2009; Heath, 1983; Levinson, 2007). It is those experiences and interests that couch their understandings of the ABC's and their basic baggage.

In addition to discussions of bare-bones basics, recent critiques have called attention to the multimodal nature of fast-changing literacy practices, particularly those mediated by digital technologies. The traditional basics minimize this multimodality and, I would add, the semantics of written graphics themselves (e.g., variants in letter size and font, in spatial organization and capitalization [GET ONE FREE], in deviant spelling, absent punctuation, and disappeared spacing [thinkwebaddresses.org]). Such design elements of multimodal texts are on display in neighborhood signs, commercialized city blocks, and in popular literacy practices familiar to many young children (e.g., Dyson, 1997, 2003a, 2003b; Marsh, 2013; New London Group, 1996; Newkirk, 2002; Siegal, 2006).

These critiques of basics instruction figure into the dramas to come, as does an alternative conception of those basics—one that transforms them from static rules to communicative resources. Yet, most recently, these critiques have been harder to hear. Talk of what "successful" children should know—the listing of grade-by-grade, even term-by-term, "standards" to be met and test scores to be achieved—has drowned out talk of how children learn and, most relevant for this book, who they are, that is, their humanity. This humanity is realized in *we-ness*, so to speak, in children's relationships with others.

The "I" Without the "We": Isolated or Independent Selves?

In written language curricula, the dominant ideology of child selves is a particularly "unattractive" version of individualism, to borrow from the philosopher Kwame Appiah (2005, p. 15); in this ideology, individuality and sociability are competing goals. Thus, to learn to compose, one goes inside oneself, applies oneself, does one's work; one does not play around with one's seatmates. There may be structured times when children are to share their plans with one another or provide editorial critiques to a partner. But, often, the ultimate goal is for the individual to quite literally produce texts, and thereby selves, in which "you [the author] matter most" (Appiah, 2005, p. 15).

In conventional basics instruction (e.g., Moats, 2004), the successful child moves to the head of the class by quickly mastering the rules of writing conventions and, thereby, learning the best means for self-expression. So, for example, "you and I" always beat "me and you," no matter who, when, or where "me" and "you" (and perhaps "a dog named Boo") might be (a little nod to an old '70s song).

In mandated writing-process or workshop approaches for early schooling (e.g., Calkins & Mermelstein, 2003), young children learn to express themselves, not only by learning to edit for those rules, but by going inward: Children are to "think," selecting a potential text from their repertoire of "real" experiences. There should be no copying from a media story or from a peer. As Mrs. Bee told her children, copying is "illegal. You have to have your own real story . . . about you." Indeed, critiques have long questioned the individualistic ideology seemingly embedded in *progressive* and *process* writing pedagogy at all school levels (Smith & Stock, 2003; for related critiques, see Boldt, 2009; Cooper, 2009; Newkirk, 2009).

Is this emphasis on the individual in the interest of independence? Or is it a troubling view of independence and, indeed, of language?

Writing Out (In) Childhoods: Textual Seesaws

As the mailbox metaphor reminds us, language is based in reciprocal relations. We are social creatures. Our very "individuality presupposes sociability" (Appiah, 2005, p. 20). To use the words of Vygotsky (1978), our minds take shape "in society." Bakhtin (1981, 1986) puts those minds, those selves, in motion. He envisions us as individuals moving among social spaces; we author complex selves by responding to others in those spaces. Each utterance we produce—the very way we arrange our words, whether oral or written—is grounded in a situated relationship. We even copy or appropriate words we have heard others use in similar situations, and we adapt those words as we read the ongoing social situation.

Thus we all, children and adults, accumulate experiences and become unique but flexible communicators in our worlds. This is a situated and relational view of language, not a hierarchical or neutral one. We do not become ourselves by crafting "proper" language in isolation from the world, but by responding to others as active participants in the world as we know it.

So, to use Malaguzzi's story, a child puts a piece of candy, a paper with a drawn heart and a name, or a bit of ribbon in another's mail box, and that other responds in turn (copies, as it were) with a sweet, a paper with a drawn heart and a name, or maybe a bit of ribbon. Inside an activity called *mailbox*, the children's actions complement one another's, their reciprocity allowing each an identity as *friend*. One can imagine that, if two children began to enact such a relation, others might copy them, adding new variations. And so a practice might solidify and spread, becoming part of how children compose—literally write out—a local childhood culture.

To further illustrate, using an example from Mrs. Bee's room, imagine kindergartner LaTrell, who is sitting by his peers Ernest and Charles during writing time. LaTrell has just heard Ernest announce that he has drawn three kids who are coming to his birthday sleepover. LaTrell looks intently at Ernest, who is fixing to write, not his name, but Charles's:

ERNEST: Hey Charles, how you spell your name . . .
CHARLES: C, H
ERNEST: (to Charles) How you write a H?
LATRELL: (piping up) H is like this. It's up— (moving his finger straight up and then finishing the letter in the air) I'm gonna have a birthday party.

Mrs. Bee sits down to give Ernest some help, telling LaTrell to get to work. Ernest tells Mrs. Bee that he is trying to write "Charles come over to my sleepover."

LATRELL: Put my name in there [in your text]!

LaTrell wants his name in Ernest's mailbox, so to speak, but he can't put it there himself. He has to get Ernest to put it there. On his paper, LaTrell writes Ernest (a word easily visible on Ernest's paper). And then he says to Ernest:

LaTRELL: I'm gonna have a birthday party. On March 4. [It's now December.] And somebody can come over . . . Ernest, on March 4, you want to come over to my birthday, on March 4?

Mrs. Bee has Ernest's attention, and she makes it clear LaTrell should mind his own business (not realizing that Ernest's paper is his business). In any case, LaTrell looks elsewhere.

LaTRELL: Charles, when you have your birthday party can I come over?
CHARLES: Yeah.
LaTRELL: Thanks.

LaTrell then erases Ernest's name, although Charles later adds that name to his own paper.

In just such a modest way, familiar cultural practices, akin to mailbox ones, could open up dialogic spaces—textual playgrounds, as it were. Children expected others to join in the common game and act appropriately, just as LaTrell expected that, if he included Ernest in his birthday party plans—and on his paper—Ernest, as his friend, should put *LaTrell* in his text and, thereby, in his plans. A textual seesaw results—I made my move, now you make yours.

The children's social efforts to construct reciprocal roles entailed sociolinguistic skills seldom considered "basic" to learning to write. Indeed the children's actions recalled the skills discussed by the media scholar Henry Jenkins. He argues that the burgeoning involvement of youth in popular culture has shifted "the focus of literacy from one of individual expression to community involvement" (Jenkins, 2009, p. xiii; see also, for examples, Fisher, 2003; Kirkland & Jackson, 2009). Participation in literacy practices is thus supported by "social skills developed through collaboration and networking" in playful, artistic contexts (Jenkins, 2009, p. xiii).

This book, informed by teachers' and children's experiences in underresourced schools in neighborhoods undergoing economic hard times, might seem an odd place to connect to practices of adolescents with access to digital technologies and much more control of their use of time and space. Indeed, Jenkins himself views "participatory cultures" as dependent on children having already acquired traditional skills (i.e., "the basics").

But this book suggests quite the opposite. In the schools entered herein are found children of the 21st century—playful, aware of the symbol-strewn landscape around them, and, most definitely, into one another and one another's business, so to speak. In their composing could be found material from their shared experiences, among them, birthday parties, chase games, playground handclaps, after-school sports programs, popular singers, movie characters, and familiar video games (i.e., known about if not actually owned).

That material could re-animate certain social voices associated with familiar events; its display could recall well-known objects and places that themselves were marked with letters, images, and other graphics. From children's early responses to the content of one another's multimodal productions came choreographed—deliberately coordinated—texts that played roles in unofficial social dramas. Those dramas shaped childhood participatory cultures and, moreover, led to my own extending and re-imagining of "the basics."

But I am getting way ahead in the story I have to tell. Let me slow down now and, with you on board, take a drive, first, to Mrs. Kay's school and, then, to Mrs. Bee's. I want to familiarize you with the spaces shaped by historical forces and societal ideologies, and with the lively children for whom these spaces are home places.

NEIGHBORHOOD DRIVES:
PLACES FOR CHILDHOODS PAST AND PRESENT

"No one lives in the world in general," writes Clifford Geertz. "Everybody, even the exiled, the drifting, the diasporic, or the perpetually moving, lives in some confined and limited stretch of it—the world around here'" (1996, p. 262). Geographic stretches, though, are deceptive (Feld & Basso, 1996; Massey, 2005). The roads and buildings, the borders between cities and suburbs, the informal labels associating neighborhoods with racial groups or social class distinctions—all seem literally set in concrete, asphalt, and corralled grass and trees. But geographic manifestations are human constructions, realizations of relations of power and of kinship. They bear the mark of restrictive covenants and property values, of migration and immigration, of economic histories tied to industrial innovation, wartime opportunities, and economic downturns.

This book is not an historical account of these neighborhoods; still, for our purposes here, the physicality of neighborhoods matters. It echoes with the voices of those who lived before, including those who brought their hopes and dreams for their children to cities-in-formation and whose lived experiences continue to shape children's lives.

Moreover, it is helpful to know the resources neighborhoods yield, the human relationships played out in a landscape spread with memories, routines, pleasures, worries, and, in fact, symbols that will take graphic shape in the pages to come. In these material circumstances, children live out the specifics of their lives; they are not the great un-named "at risk" or walking test-score statistics. The schools' "basic" conventions will have to find a sensible place amid the symbolic displays and communicative practices of children's everyday worlds.

The neighborhoods of our brief drives are in Midwestern cities, smaller than their referent big city, Chicago, but with economic, social, and racial histories that reverberate with cities across the country (Noguera, 2003). So, slide in the front seat with me and put on your seat belt. We are ready for our drives to introduce the neighborhoods, the schools, and the featured teachers and kids.

Driving to Mrs. Kay's School

Thank heavens that it is not the dead of winter, when you would not want to be in a car with me. I have been known to recite the rosary as I inch ahead, grieving for the lost California sun and watching out for little walking pillow cases—otherwise known as bundled up children on their way to school.

But it is spring in the upper Midwest! The roads are clear, the trees are forest green, and children once again take human shape, their limbs moving blithely through the air. We are on our way from a nearby suburb, a college town, to Mrs. Kay's city school. We travel past handsome homes and peaceful bike paths—and then, quite suddenly, the view out the window changes.

As we enter the city, the world seems to breathe in for a minute, taking the greenery with it; in its wake are small businesses here and there and abandoned lots. Look, over there, across from the convenience store. It's the vendor—a thin, middle-aged African American man who sets up his grill by the road for three of the year's four seasons; he cooks barbecue for anybody who cares to stop (and I have never seen him alone).

The greenery is coming back now with enthusiasm. Off to the left is a park, whose rejuvenation a neighborhood committee has been planning. It has served as a gathering place for drug dealers more than for families. Now, though, there is to be a space for local gardeners, a walking trail, and groomed places to play. These efforts speak of the economic hard times that have visited the city (particularly the stretch of it we are in right now), and of the resilience of people imagining, and working toward, possibilities.

We take a turn into a residential area near Mrs. Kay's school. We are deep in the city now. No loitering mailboxes on curbs; they all hang out on their houses. Those modest homes are of varied upkeep; seemingly every few blocks, one is, on closer inspection, a church proclaiming GOD'S WORD.

Although the state is known for its de facto segregated housing, this neighborhood is integrated (in part because the city area where African Americans primarily lived was disrupted by a highway). In the 1920s, African Americans came up on trains from the South, escaping the cotton fields and finding mainly service jobs; Mexican Americans came up on the road in the 1930s, at first for seasonal farm labor and later for work in the sugar beet industry. Even now, immigrants from the Middle East are settling in the neighborhood. The city's once flourishing auto industry has attracted many; the industry dates from 1897, although it employed few people of color until World War II.

During the 1960s and 1970s, this one-time solid blue-collar neighborhood began showing signs of stress, as more economically able residents moved out to the suburbs. The hard times persisted and deepened. Hence, that park and look, the spot where day laborers gather across the street from the school ("Labor . . . Safety is Priority. . . ."), and, kitty corner to that spot, the small convenience store ("Food Market"), whose windows are periodically boarded up. Here too, though, there are signs of rejuvenation. The Neighborhood Center, located next to the labor pick-up location, has posters announcing the upcoming Farmer's Market, community meetings, and English classes, held at the school itself.

The neighborhood's economic precariousness and its racial history are evident in the present lives of Mrs. Kay's young students. Eighty-five percent of the children in the school qualify for the federal lunch program. Moreover, as Chapter 2 will illustrate, the children talk openly of money troubles, and Mrs. Kay herself does not ignore those troubles. Indeed, she watches out for her children, making sure they have had breakfast and are warmly clothed in the harsh northern winter. Still, the resilient spirit of the neighborhood is evident in the children's lives as well, especially in their imaginations and their capacity for play—for enacting alternative worlds.

But I am once again going too fast. I'm going to park here, beside the school, so you can get a good look at it. As you can see, it is quite old—built almost a century ago; its basement windows are boarded up, its brick walls faded—even its graffiti is not fresh. The schools-of-choice program has not helped provide the district with funds for renovation, given the middle-class flight from the city's schools. The city is majority White, but the district is majority children of color, as is Mrs. Kay's school (46% of the children identify as African American, 32% as White, 20% as Latino, 1% as Native American, and 1% as Asian/Pacific Islander; the stated ethnicities of Mrs. Kay's children are given in Appendix B, Table B.1).

Still, the school has a fantastic playground, which soon will fill with lively children. Right next to the school is a concrete slab and then a black-top area, perfect for clapping games, cheers, and jump rope. Mrs. Kay herself will jump on occasion, and she can be relied on to swing the rope and chant the rhymes. Behind the blacktop is a wood chip area with a playground structure complete with climbing bars, open towers, and two slides—just right for sitting under and planning plots and enacting scenes. (Mrs. Kay's children like to sit under a tower and play bad children in the principal's office or mean stepmothers, among other games.)

Beyond the structure is a wide expanse of green grass that ends with a fence surrounded on the outside with pine trees that litter the ground with cones—irresistible projectiles; these will figure in The Pine Cone Wars to be reported in Chapter 7. The grass invites all kinds of chase games, some involving gender play, like "girl attack." To the side of the green expanse is a place for kickball and, next to that, another blacktop area with a basketball court. The side of the building itself can be used for varied ball-throwing games.

Such a playground, if children get to use it, is a place where imagination can literally run free. This is not so true of the official literacy curriculum. The school is under pressure to make "adequate yearly progress" and, to this end, has sought federal and state-distributed funds, including for a literacy program targeted to low-income children. Mrs. Kay's children must take a standardized test on "the basics" at the end of the year. Moreover, Mrs. Kay, a 20-year veteran of this school, has to prepare her children for the paced district curriculum, and thus she feels obligated to use each textbook in each subject. She feels that this new text-driven curriculum limits her own imagination and her love of literature-based projects, which have been squeezed from her day.

Still, whatever the curricular demands, Mrs. Kay does not deny her children opportunities to run, jump, throw, and imagine on that inviting playground when the weather allows. (If it does not, the children still have an activity time mid-afternoon, when they are free to build with manipulatives, race marbles down chutes, construct with paper, scissors, and glue, play card games or work puzzles, read books or play school, or invent some play scenario all on their own.) There is Mrs. Kay now, coming out of the building with her class for a mid-morning break—the short White woman with the thick blonde hair, curved just below her ears. Yes, the one with the big smile, 50-something, wearing a blue jean jumper and, around her neck, a whistle for calling her children in from this big ol' playground when the time comes.

I want to point out a few children for you, especially Tionna and Eze-kial. I feature them in the pages to come in part because they are different in sensibilities and approaches to writing; in addition, although they are both companionable, they have overlapping but distinctive groups of friends. Through them, we will meet the children who attend Mrs. Kay's class throughout the year (bearing in mind that the mobility rate at this school is relatively high: 40%).

See the little girls doing the hand clap game on the concrete? Can't you hear them? "Mailman, Mailman, do your duty," they chant, "I have a date, with an African booty." (Children's folk games can be risqué play [Sutton-Smith, Mechling, Johnson, & McMahon, 1995].) Tionna is the smallest girl, the one clapping the air and giggling with her two bigger girlfriends, who are clapping with one another. She often wears that mischievous smile—she knows she is funny (she has told me) and, Lord knows, she is cute. A speaker of African American Language (AAL), she has a head full of tiny braids secured with colorful baubles; she is wearing a Tweety Bird t-shirt in her favorite color, pink, and blue jeans. She and her playmates, Mandisa and Janette, go from rhyme to rhyme—they know lots. The fourth member of this close group of friends, all African American, is Lyron; on the playground, though, Lyron usually prefers chase games, while Tionna and the others tend to rhyme and jump rope. (In truth, when Lyron has tried to join them, they have firmly proclaimed their rhymes as girl stuff. Mrs. Kay will have none of that, though; when she is around, any boys wanting a turn to jump get one.)

Tionna, as you will see (and hear), is verbally playful and socially attuned—she can even adopt my observer stance and field note style (a rather humbling experience). Ezekial, on the other hand, is more visually alert. That's him over there, with Joshua. Ezekial plays with everyone, but he has struck up a particularly close relationship with Joshua. They are taking turns throwing a ball against the school wall and then running to catch it. Ezekial is the shorter, sturdier of the two boys; he has the close-cropped hair and that seemingly persistent smile. (It strikes me as so sweet, I have to smile right back.) Like most of the children on this spring day, Ezekial is wearing blue jeans and a t-shirt that stretches down to his knees. (I suspect those shirts are hand-me-downs from his teenage brothers.) Notice how quick Ezekial is—in running races, he can beat children with much longer legs.

Ezekial names himself as "Mexican;" like most of his peers, his English is the local vernacular, with its sometimes stigmatized features (e.g., "ain't," double negatives). He does not speak Spanish, or so he has told his Spanish-speaking, Mexican-American student teacher, Ms. Hache. (His mother and grandmother do, he has said.) Ezekial identifies strongly as both a basketball fan (even though, as his peers tell him, he is probably going to be too short to play well) and a churchgoer, who often relays biblical events. My favorite memory of him is when, during a lesson on the Pilgrims and their ocean travels, Ezekial mentioned Moses, who had parted the Red Sea and would have been very helpful to those tired-out Pilgrims.

Ezekial's pathway into literacy has been different than Tionna's, in part because he is so visually attentive. Remember those neighborhood signs we passed, with their propensity to vary their graphic dimensions with their message, aiming to grab our attention? Such signs were fuel for Ezekial's own deductions about written language, sometimes clashing with "basic" rules, sometimes leading to conciliatory settlements. Both Ezekial and Tionna were social beings who valued "fiend sip," to use Ezekial's spelling. In their pathways into school writing, those relationships mattered, as did playful practices. Through their participation, Tionna will underscore for us the playful possibilities of social voices, while Ezekial will highlight the multimodality of texts, including the visual flexibility of written graphics.

There goes Mrs. Kay's whistle. The children are lining up on the concrete slab, soon to enter the hallways of that old, beloved building. We will enter later. But now, we need to visit the other neighborhood, whose children will soon enough join with Mrs. Kay's in the book's discursive work of refashioning the basics. So back in the car we go, and, with a little textual magic, we cross state borders, several hundred miles (and a couple of years), and end up close to Mrs. Bee's school neighborhood.

Driving to Mrs. Bee's School

We are starting once again on a university campus, this time in a small metropolitan area in the midst of the rural Midwest. We are headed to Mrs. Bee's school. I was initially interested in this school because, on the surface, its demographics and policies seemed similar to Mrs. Kay's school. It too serves primarily a low-income population (83% of the children are so categorized); and it also serves mainly children of color, although its surrounding city is majority White. The children are classified as African American (43%), Hispanic (42%), White (9%), and Asian (6%). Moreover, Mrs. Bee's school also closely follows a mandated and paced curriculum, with the institutional intention of closing district racial achievement gaps and making mandated yearly progress on standardized tests.

But Mrs. Bee's school, and its surrounding neighborhood, differs in its particularities from Mrs. Kay's. I'll tell you about that as we make our way to the school.

The route to the school contains no idyllic, pastoral scenes. We move up a long, traffic-clogged street through campus; I lean out over the steering wheel, looking, not for small bodies on the loose, but for larger ones playing race-with-traffic-lights on this late morning. Finally we're out of Student Alley, turning onto a main thoroughfare crowded with small businesses. We move past food marts, a used-car lot, and varied small restaurants. Look! There's the Mexican place where Mrs. Bee likes to get takeout for lunch! It will not be long now.

We turn off the main road and cross the railroad tracks. Immediately the scenery changes. We are entering a residential area that, in some ways, is like that near Mrs. Kay's school. Trees line the roads; small bungalows and tired looking apartment complexes are interspersed with churches, most also small with a homelike façade. Throughout the neighborhood mailboxes are curbside in style but located close to front doors.

There are *many* home day cares, like Lily's (a sign tacked to a fence post); see the small play structures and plastic pedal cars in the yard? Mrs. Bee's children often refer to their day cares, although some children take a van after school to the local Boys & Girls Club (praised as really "fun" by LaTrell, whom we will soon meet). If it were later in the day, we would see people sitting out on lawn chairs, visiting in the early evening.

As we drive through the neighborhood, notice the well-groomed bus stops, with their newly provided glass sheltered benches (an Extreme Makeover, the sign says). Look to your right and you can see a small strip mall with a Hair Design salon, a radio station (urban contemporary), and a laundromat. The children often refer to commercial establishments outside their neighborhood, though; among the most referenced are Walmart, the local mall, a movie theater (where Tinker Bell and Hannah Montana have recently made cinematic appearances), and Brian's (a restaurant chain with an All You Can Eat buffet—popular for Thanksgiving, or so the children say).

You should know that we are in a historically Black section of the city. In the 19th century, African Americans began coming north to the state, working on farms or on the burgeoning railroad. In time, Black families moved to the north end of the city-in-formation, at least in part because they sought secondary schooling for their children. Nearby a Black business district developed, as White businesses moved out. The activism of the neighborhood itself (given little attention by the larger city) led in the 1930s to the building of a community center offering recreation, meeting space, a library, and a public park well-used by Mrs. Bee's children. I have been known to make my own way to the park during the summer, where I chat with children now familiar to me from my time in Mrs. Bee's school.

As articulated in a local media project, some long-time community residents feel the neighborhood has changed. In the 1970s and 1980s, housing opened up throughout the city and more affluent folks moved out. Conversely, new residents moved in, some from closing Chicago housing projects. Mexican immigrants settled in a nearby trailer park, and small numbers of Asian immigrants also found their way into the neighborhood. Thus, for those older residents, the neighborhood feels less cohesive—they no longer know everyone.

Nevertheless, this year, Mrs. Bee's class is composed almost entirely of two extended African American families—everybody is somebody's cousin. (The children in the class are listed in Appendix B, Table B.2.) The Mexican-heritage children are placed primarily in separate bilingual classrooms (the school houses the district's only such program). For the most part, the children play with their linguistically-compatible classmates (with the exception of LaTrell's cousin Charles, who, as a 1st-grader, will tell me that he wishes he was "Spanish," reasonably if inaccurately linking ethnicity and language; his wish is linked to his desire to speak like his across-the-hallway friends).

The challenge of promoting interaction among the school's dominant populations is not front-page news in the local newspaper. The problem of keeping White parents committed to the public schools (and decreasing their movement to private schools) *is*, along with the more particular problem of attracting them to Mrs. Bee's school.

As in Mrs. Kay's class, neither Mrs. Bee nor her children are ignorant of racial divisions and economic stresses. At lunch, I have heard children talk about parents losing jobs or having trouble arriving at work on time. As you will hear in Chapter 2, Mrs. Bee herself talks to them about money struggles. Through word and deed, she lets them know that they can have fun for free by playing with words and movement. Indeed, the children respond with great enthusiasm to those unpredictable times when she does hand claps and singing games with them.

Those singing games, though, are seldom heard on the playground of Mrs. Bee's school, that playground being an underused resource. The school is not far from here, so soon we can give it a closer look.

There, you can see it already, the long, flat building, whose main hallway stretches out across half the width of a city block. A side door opens out onto the playground that starts narrow and then expands as it stretches back the full length of the block. The playground (which is also a community park) has shade trees, swings, and a play structure that includes slides and towers. There is a basketball court, a space for kickball, and a baseball field. But there is limited blacktop space for street games like jump rope and hand claps. Still, on weekends and after school, the park is a regular destination of children wanting to play (and, in Mrs. Bee's room, those sidewalk games did make an appearance—on textual sidewalks, as will be seen).

Mrs. Bee's children have 10–15 minutes of recess after lunch, weather and adults' judgment of their cafeteria "behavior" permitting. Recently, they have been using that time to play Queen of New York City. (No one, by the way, has ever been to New York City, although a Midwest band has just released a song so named.) Led by the royalty—lately that's been Coretta as Queen and Cici as Princess, the girls chase the boys; and the boys, led by Jamal or Lamont, run and then chase back. Alicia, though, whom we will soon meet, continues to gravitate to the swings; she flies through the air, seemingly without a care.

Mrs. Bee's children are at lunch now. We can't depend on their having recess, so let's park and take a quick trip inside the building so you can see Mrs. Bee and the children who, along with Tionna and Ezekial, will feature prominently in the pages to come. We hurry up the steps, ring the buzzer so the secretary can let us in, and, then, right in front of us is the gym/lunch room.

Breathe in. Smell it? Today is the children's favorite lunch—a pancake wrapped around a sausage, with carrots on the side. The children do not care so much about the carrots or the sausage, but when the pancake smell drifts all the way down the hall to the kindergarten, they sniff and smile at other, "Pancakes!"

There's Mrs. Bee. Yes, that's her—the statuesque, middle-aged Black woman, her hair in a smooth page boy, reading glasses perched on her head, sensible, stylish slip-ons on her feet. She is attending to each child, helping this little one ease the Styrofoam plate onto her tray, that one to get a better grip on the tray, scurrying one child along the line, asking another to tell her what the trouble is.

Mrs. Bee projects a comforting authority, calling each child by name, whether or not they are in her class. She has never before taught in what she describes as an inner city school, having spent years teaching in rural preschools. These parents are so young, she has told me; they work two jobs to make ends meet, and even then, it's so hard. She had expected kindergarten, like her preschools, to involve children learning through play. But she was wrong. At the beginning of the year, she felt enormous pressure to get her children reading and writing conventionally and to keep up with the pace of the expected lessons. She would go home so tense she could not sleep.

Right now, though, the immediate goal is to get the kindergartners through the lunch room line. Once through, they sit on the first of the long benches that stretch across the lunch room in parallel lines. There they are, putting their tray on the table and maneuvering their bodies onto the bench with the skill of lunch-room old timers.

See the stylish little girl with the upswept hair and a little pouf of a bun? Yes, the one with the pink hoodie tied around her waist. That's Alicia; she is climbing in next to Cici and across from Denise. This is Alicia's second time around in kindergarten—I met her last year, when I started observing in Mrs. Bee's room in January. Unlike in Mrs. Kay's school, in Mrs. Bee's kindergarten retention is not common. Still, Alicia was retained. She had not been to preschool, which was not in her favor, and she kept slipping outside the group activity of the moment. This year she does not get up in the middle of a lesson to use the restroom or inspect something that seems to merit a closer look.

Still, like last year, Alicia displays her orientation to friends—classmates who respond collegially—as she has no love for competitive play. In her first year of kindergarten, she would write quickly with wavy lines, all the while describing her affection for, or irritation with, friends at her table. Her first written word, other than "Alicia," was "Willo" (her best friend even now, although Willo has gone on to 1st grade). As you will see, her attunement to others has helped her find a way into composing. Valued activities in city spaces have sometimes been transformed into textual places for friends. Indeed, one of my favorite drawings of hers is of an imagined car ride, her classmates squeezed into her automobile.

Right now though, Alicia has a problem. Her friend Denise has brought a bologna sandwich for lunch, and she is looking with longing at Alicia's lunch (a desire I cannot understand). As Alicia keeps eating, Denise's face goes from longing to intense irritation. Alicia tells her she is going to give her some; she just wants a few bites first. After taking them, she is true to her word. She pushes the tray between her and Denise, and using their forks, the two girls work from opposite ends of the desired delicacy, peacefully eating away.

Further down the table, there's someone else I want to point out. There he is—LaTrell—as usual sitting up very straight. Yes, that one, the slim little boy in the long black tee. He is sitting by Ernest and Kevon, though usually Charles, his regular companion and a cousin, is nearby. LaTrell is unraveling the pancake from the sausage, dipping it in the syrup, and stuffing it in his mouth.

As we move closer to the table (I try never to interrupt a conversation), we can hear the boys discuss the possible shapes of pancakes—they can be "round," "rectangles," and this rolled-up "hotdog"-shape. The discursive push toward representing the world accurately is one trait of the humble but critical LaTrell. He has never bought Mrs. Bee's assertion (based on her writing program guidebook) that kindergartners are like picture book authors or artists. He feels that you have to be *"really* good" to be so designated. At this time of the year, LaTrell himself is trying to be a good student, sometimes erasing and then erasing once again his pictures, his words, or both. Like the older Ezekial, he is particularly visually attentive. Well before he firmly grasped the alphabetic principal (i.e., the connection between sounds and letters), his drawings displayed symbols originally found on the front of the local Boys & Girls Club, on a screen of Cartoon Network, on scoreboards for basketball games, and on his own house.

Initially LaTrell was less concerned with "truth" in content. He (like his cousin Charles) narrated drawings in which actions unfolded fluidly, influenced by his interaction with paper and peers. They took place at his home or the neighborhood park, but they were not "true" beyond his text. They could feature, for example, monstrous birds and bug-eating monsters, or snowmen who took over his front yard, to the chagrin of his broom-wielding mama. Now, LaTrell is more attuned to curricular values; he aims for accuracy (although, as you will see, his cousin Charles does not).

Like the older Tionna and Ezekial, Alicia and LaTrell are firmly anchored in classroom relationships. For them too, written texts can be metaphoric mailboxes, places to offer the gift of inclusion or to carry out the reciprocal actions of play. Perhaps because they are less experienced in school, or because Mrs. Bee herself is so sensitive to new curricular demands, they will underscore most starkly the ideological conflicts between composing time competencies in official and unofficial child worlds.

Mrs. Bee's children are getting up to take their trays back. As it happens, there will be no recess today—they are headed back to the classroom to put their heads on their tables and have a little nap. We should move on too.

Part I

BASIC LESSONS AND BASIC TENSIONS

The child's interpretation of the world is strongly pragmatic; she seeks knowledge in relation to her own interests . . . and constructs new meanings there from. But the child is also always having knowledge thrust upon her in the guise of teaching. The relation between the child's . . . and the teacher's [perspective on what is relevant] is a classic conundrum. (Nelson, 2007, pp. 14–15)

"Oh man:::n."

That had been Tionna's response when she had not gotten to read her journal entry during yesterday's writing time, which, in Mrs. Kay's room, typically ends with a quick reading of their day's text by as many children as possible. When writing time begins on this day, Tionna seeks out an audience for her entry.

"'Today is my cousin's birthday,'" she reads.

"*Yesterday* was his birthday!" objects Lyron.

"I *know*," Tionna replies. "I'm reading what I wrote yesterday." She continues reading her text:

His mom and dad decidite that me and his sister Miah can come to Chuck E. cheese. Because he likes me and Miah to play whit him. We play SupPrduper man in the summer time he brings his warter gun the girls run and if you get skerted you havt to be a boy and you havt to put some purple stuff in your moth.

Tionna stops reading. The student teacher Ms. Hache is on her way to her table with the date stamp. If she is to share her yesterday's writing today, she needs to interrupt the official routine of putting the day's date on a fresh, clean page. Tionna quickly tries to scratch the old date off. When that doesn't work, she starts to rip that date off ever so carefully. But Ms. Hache arrives, turns to the next page, and STAMP! Too late for the ripping tack.

Tionna's experience in the above event illustrates the theoretical understandings that undergird the book's next three chapters, which focus on the official school world (see Appendix A for an explanation of the transcription conventions used throughout this book). The chapters feature that classic conundrum Nelson described above; that conundrum is caused by differences in what teachers and children judge as meaningful and relevant as they enact writing curricula centered on "the basics."

Implicit in Tionna's reaction to the approaching Ms. Hache is her sense of the norms of the daily writing time, that is, her sense of official expectations for how a child *should* participate in the recurrent activities—the practices—of the official school world. From a sociocultural point of view, it is such practices that make learning possible, as they organize human actions and interactions toward valued goals (Miller, 1996; Rogoff, 2003; Vygotsky, 1978).

Children, as newcomers to practices, observe their enactment, listen to stories about their workings, play with their roles and actions, and join in as best they can. In these ways, they come to anticipate how the practices work. In literacy practices, children not only enter into locally valued ways of using written language but also of relating to, and being with, others through that medium (Bakhtin, 1986).

Given this view of practices, it is impossible to reduce writing or writing development to a set of textual features or conventional rules to be mastered (i.e., the proverbial basics—capitalization, punctuation, spelling, usage). Any official school activity is a situated enactment of a *practice*; that is, it's a social happening, an event (Street, 2000). Children are attuned to patterns in those happenings—to who does what with whom, when and how, using what kind of tools, adopting what kind of mood, articulating what kind of voice, for what sort of end.

In Mrs. Kay's view, she stressed the basics during writing time. For example, she daily modeled the writing process, explicitly referring to the use of capital letters and punctuation marks and to the incorrectness of the incorrigible subject "me and [somebody else]." But her direct instruction was embedded—and embodied—in social actions and interactions. For instance, she always turned to a fresh page on her large chart tablet to model her text; the blank top section of the page was for quick sketching, the lined bottom for the all-important writing. For most of the school year, her daily writing fit on that one chart page. Moreover, the day's writing was relative to the present. Mrs. Kay talked and wrote about what she would be doing, or did, yesterday, today, or maybe this weekend.

Tionna had not mastered the basics. Capitalization and punctuation often seemed to elude her (but note the period in "Chuck E. Cheese," the name of a valued entertainment establishment). And she never abandoned the "me and somebody else" construction. Like that "Chuck E. Cheese," her conversational writing, like her conversational storytelling, bespoke the times and spaces and the linguistic practices that located her in larger cultural worlds (Baynham & Prinsloo, 2009). Those voice-filled worlds did not necessarily echo on the list of written language basics, except as sources of errors to be fixed, problems to be overcome.

Still, Tionna was socially attuned to practice norms. She had learned that the date was a key feature of official writing practices and, also, a key regulator of time and space: Each day brings a new date and a new page. She strove to regularize her text—to make visible valued features (Hanks, 1996). Tionna, though, was not simply an apprentice waiting to slip into the slots of school writing practices. She *did* want to read that old text as if it were new—she was a performer who made her peers laugh. After the student teacher left, she substituted "yesterday was" for "today is," and then made some adjustments and extensions so that "yesterday's" text indeed continued on to the next page and, therefore, qualified as "today's" writing. She added, for example, that that purple stuff was from "lunchoble" (a packaged food), and that if you do not eat the dreaded purple stuff, her cousin will "swot you softthe lee with the boom." That is, he doesn't swat hard with the broom, just softly, not meaning to actually hurt anybody and ruin the play.

Tionna's writing actions were made possible *and* problematic by the social organization of writing time and by "the basics." Like Tionna, all children enter school—the official space for the public's children—with their experiential and linguistic resources, their need for social relationships, and their particular dispositions and preferences (Clay, 1998; Comber & Kamler, 2005; Dyson, 1989, 2003a, 2003b; Genishi & Dyson, 2009). There is no simple transfer of knowledge from teacher to child, nor any guarantee that what is relevant and meaningful to the teacher in any activity will be what is relevant and meaningful to children.

In the chapters to come, Tionna will take a place in the company of her 1st-grade classmates, and in the textual company of Mrs. Bee's kindergarten children; as she does so, her individuality will become clearer as will the common nature of the kinds of tensions and puzzling miscommunications—the conundrums—that children and their teachers face. These are brought to the fore by curricula oriented to the conventional basics and directed to children who live in a fluid world of diverse communicative resources. In such curricular circumstances, children themselves may call their teachers' and our attention to their social and semiotic attunement and, thereby, to basic matters that are deeper and broader than A-B-C.

With these notions of practices and conundrums in mind, we are ready to enter Mrs. Kay's and Mrs. Bee's rooms, where teachers and children await.

CHAPTER 2

Welcome to Writing Workshop

"Wake up, sleepy heads," sings Mrs. Bee.
　　"Wake up, sleepy heads," sing her children right back.
　　Then all together they sing, "You need to go to bed at night."
　　Another call-and-response of "Wake up, sleepy heads" follows, before
the final line is sung out: "You need to be awake and bright."

Mrs. Bee had written that song for her kindergartners. She, like Mrs. Kay,
used music to bring her children together in a communal activity. Indeed,
each teacher worked to build a responsive community of responsible children who attuned themselves to one another and to the world around
them. During writing time, though, a different ideology of child selves
emerged. This was not one of community-responsive children but of the
hardy child who forges ahead (following directions of course).

　　Listen, for example, to Mrs. Bee in October of the school year; she is
following her curricular guidebook and stressing the importance of working independently:

MRS. BEE: You have to begin to carry on independently. What does
　　independently mean?
ODETTE: Work by yourself.
MRS. BEE: Work by yourself.

Mrs. Bee explains that the children should get their supplies "by yourself,"
sound out spellings "by yourself," and choose a topic "by yourself." LaTrell
repeats her words with conviction.

LATRELL: Do it by yourself!
MRS. BEE: You need to decide on a topic [now]. What's a topic?
CHILDREN: WORKING BY YOURSELF!

　　Mrs. Bee's children listened to the conversation, attuning themselves
to the proper response. Whatever a topic is, many seemed to conclude,
it surely has to do with this lesson, the topic of which is: "WORKING
BY YOURSELF!" Soon, these socially attuned children would gather

around tables, sitting side-by-side. Supplies would be negotiated—even argued about, guidance would be sought for "making the words," and talk about topics would weave the children's composing into a social network of ideas.

In this chapter, I serve as guide to Mrs. Bee's and Mrs. Kay's teaching situations, introducing the regular rhythms of writing time in each classroom. The teachers' writing programs were not identical, nor were their teaching circumstances and styles. Still, each emphasized "the basics," as defined by local mandates (influenced by federal policies, testing regimens, and mandated texts). These basics had to do with learning the conventions for getting the text right; and they were practiced through the production of texts that were to be kept quite literally real. No fooling around with superheroes on the page (even though writing could seem a brave, even super heroic act).

Each teacher's program also was undergirded by common ideologies of child selves and written language; among them, this notion of rugged individualism, as it were—of children boldly going forth to plant their mark on the blank page. This ideology contains within it notions of learning as an individual enterprise; and it implies too that a text is a one-sided effort, not a conversational turn or a note in a metaphoric mailbox written in response to and in anticipation of another's turn (Bakhtin, 1981).

This official emphasis was in some tension, not only with the children's ways of approaching writing, but also with each teacher's efforts to support her children as mindful, thoughtful participants in the classroom and in the larger world. Indeed, it was in some tension too with the teachers' own ways of modeling writing, which were often performative and multimodal and, as such, were highly engaging to their children—although it was the sense of story and of human connection that seemed to engage them, not "the basics."

Before I detail the specifics of each classroom's writing routines, and the official emphasis on the basics, I provide a discordant backdrop. This backdrop is not about hardy individuals but responsive children and the official emphasis on responsible, and sometimes playful, participation.

THE CLASSROOM AS COMMUNITY: WORKING (AND PLAYING) TOGETHER

Each morning, the children in Mrs. Kay's and Mrs. Bee's classrooms left their homes and made their way to their respective schools. They walked or ran, were driven in family cars or school buses, and traveled down some of the same streets we traveled through in Chapter 1. Once they arrived, they were Mrs. Kay's child or Mrs. Bee's. As the school year unfolded, as experiences accumulated, the children in each class became a *we*. Whatever their prior relationships with one another, school children in the same class were kinfolk of a sort.

Despite the many differences between the teachers' classrooms, their practices displayed qualities that furthered children's sense of we. Among these qualities were an enveloping discourse of story and song, an expectation of inclusiveness, and explicitness about the pleasures and challenges of living in their particular "stretch" of the world (Geertz, 1996, p. 262).

The Storied Classroom

Mrs. Kay's 1st-graders have just made their way to the school basement, where a book fair is going on. As they walk amidst the tables piled with books, Tionna spies an old friend—the book *If You Take a Mouse to School* (Numeroff, 2002).

"Oh! We got this book!" she says, grabbing the book and holding it up to show her teacher.

"Yeah, we do, don't we?" responds Mrs. Kay.

Now Ezekial holds up *Take Me Out of the Bathtub and Other Silly Dilly Songs* (Katz & Carrow, 2001).

"We just sang a song out of there today, didn't we?" says Mrs. Kay.

And right then and there, Ezekial bursts into the title song. Mrs. Kay does not shush him. She joins in with him, and the other children follow after her, bringing a silly scene to voice in the middle of the book fair.

As just illustrated, Mrs. Kay, like Mrs. Bee, used music to slip her children into an imagined role in a pretend scene, thereby adding official school material to their unofficial repertoire of verbal plays, commercial jingles, and popular songs. Both teachers also used conversational, often-performative stories to envelope children in a narrative world.

Such storytelling was, in fact, a common feature of writing time. As will be elaborated upon in a section to come, the teachers modeled the writing process, and in so doing, they told "real" stories in a performative way. The stories—and more particularly their styles—often gripped their children's attention, their curiosity, and their desires to respond with a story themselves; sometimes, when their own composing began, they abandoned the real and imagined themselves into their teacher's story world, as happened the day Mrs. Kay told of an upcoming trip involving a hotel stay. Lo and behold, child after child had just stayed in a hotel or had trip plans like Mrs. Kay's. Tionna, in fact, wrote that she had stayed with her cousin in a hotel just the night before! (Neither teacher approved this borrowing of experiences [if they detected it], see Chapter 4.)

Actually, the modeling process was *supposed* to be a time when children paid quiet attention to the teacher composer. Indeed, when both teachers trained their student teachers, they emphasized that children were to listen quietly, but children did not listen quietly to them. They listened responsively.

"I have to tell you about this," Mrs. Kay might say, before beginning her drawing and writing. Imagine her sitting in front of her 1st-graders on a teacher-sized wooden chair, a large tablet opened on the easel beside her. Her children are sitting side-by-side in zig-zaggy rows on the classroom rug. Mrs. Kay begins her story:

"I have to tell you about my neighbor down the street. It's the 1, 2, 3—the third house down from me. And he has the coolest house on the block."

"He does?" responds Brad.

"Yeah. As a matter of fact, . . . his house was on the news—

"What happened?" asks Jason.

"—just because he does such awesome things for Halloween. He makes his whole yard into just Halloween Heaven. [She turns to the pad and begins to draw.] He puts a graveyard in his yard!"

"Cool" sounds the response.

"And he had a big—I'm just trying to make this look all hairy. . . . He had a big gorilla."

"Gorilla!" the children turn to one another echoing their teacher.

"And you know what?"

"What?"

"It was a gorilla suit but" (lowering her voice to a whisper) "somebody was really in it. It was really cool. And he had these mummies, and all these jack-o-lanterns all around. And then in his garage—I'm gonna put a little arrow 'cause it was inside. He had a coffin on a table."

"What is a coffin?" asks Brad.

"A coffin is where they put a dead body"—

"My neighbor had a dead body!" says Janette, all excited.

"What happened?" asks Jon.

Soon Mrs. Kay finished "modeling" her story production, and the children took over. Their oral tales were, for the most part, about trick-or-treating. ("Be sure to say 'Thank you,'" said Mrs. Kay. "People appreciate that.")

Mrs. Bee could be even more performative, sometimes standing up from her seat and dramatizing her actions. She also slid more often into a motherly or even preacherly stance, pointing out any story lessons, or dispelling any potential misperceptions, about appropriate behavior. While Mrs. Kay's stories centered on her daily life as a suburban adult, Mrs. Bee often went back to her own rural childhood.

One day during modeling time, Mrs. Bee told her kindergartners how her grandfather taught her to ride a bike. The children, sitting on their classroom rug in their own zig-zaggy lines, expressed sympathy about her spills from her bike ("O::!"); and they responded with their own stories. As we listen in, Charles and LaTrell are sharing their learning-to-ride-a-bike narratives, just before Mrs. Bee begins a related tale:

"When my mommy teach me how to ride a bike," says Charles, "she pushed me all the way until my bike ran away from me."

"That's how you teach somebody how to ride a bike," responds Mrs. Bee nodding. "You have to walk them through it."

"My mama teach me how to ride with training wheels," explains LaTrell.

"We didn't have training wheels back in my day," says Mrs. Bee, before launching into a story of how her grandfather also taught her "to drive a car—"

"OO::!" say the children, impressed.

"Only he didn't push the car; he was in the car with me. And you'll never know, you'll never know how old I was [when] I was driving . . . delivering dinners for my church."

"Was you 5?" asks Cici.

"Close," responds Mrs. Bee. "I was 8."

The children gasp.

"But back in those days, back in those days, where I lived, there were dirt roads, and there were no streets like this. And there were not many cars. Everybody didn't have a car. So we'd sit on my grandfather's lap and steer."

"Was there a police over there?" inquires Coretta quite logically, given the visibility of the police on her city streets.

"No," responds Mrs. Bee. And then she is quite clear. "Do not get in your parents' car and try to drive. You could get hurt or killed. It's a dangerous thing to do."

This back-and-forth storytelling, this inviting "you know what?" or "you'll never guess" marked both teachers' styles. There was nothing monologic about their storytelling, nothing that said a story was an individual production, not a social turn in a relational space. Mrs. Bee used childhood experiences—learning to ride a bike—to connect with her children; embedded in those experiences were references to church and to economically tight times, both sociocultural touchstones common in her children's talk. Mrs. Kay drew on her economically comfortable adult life, but she used popular culture—the Halloween holiday—to find common ground with her children. Sometimes both teachers explicitly voiced what the sampled stories at least suggested—their valuing of community-mindedness.

The Inclusive Classroom

"You all have brains," said Mrs. Bee to her children one day. She expected all her kindergartners to use those brains and to recognize one another's accomplishments; when Mrs. Bee praised a child as making a "so smart" comment, the others clapped for that child, with no evident directive from Mrs. Bee. (They sometimes clapped for her after she read a story they particularly liked.) Neither Mrs. Bee nor Mrs. Kay tolerated any intellectual put-downs of one child by another. ("That is *rude*," Mrs. Kay would say in a quiet but firm voice, with eyes that fixed the offending child in the spotlight. "You wouldn't know either if someone hadn't taught you" Mrs. Bee might say, putting both the offended and the insulting child in the same boat.)

All these children with brains intact were to be included in classroom and school happenings, unless respect for family beliefs dictated otherwise. Ezekial's family, for example, viewed Halloween as "celebrating to the devil," as he explained after the 1st-graders shared Halloween stories. This was unsettling to some children—"When I'm trick-or-treating, some families are celebrating the devil?!" Mrs. Kay explained that Halloween was, for many of them, good fun. But people have different beliefs about God and about what a good person does or does not do; and that is just the way it is.

On special occasions, like birthdays or Valentine's Day, children might bring items from home to share, but this was allowed only if items were brought for everyone. Consider Valentine's Day in Mrs. Kay's room. Children did not *have* to bring valentines, but, if they did, they had to bring enough for everyone. Lyron was not going to do that, he reported, because his dad said that he could only give valentines to girls. ("But I have a valentine for you," said Brad tearfully to Lyron.) This family belief, so to speak, affected classroom fairness, and Mrs. Kay responded firmly. Lyron just didn't know the classroom rule for bringing valentines. She reiterated that rule. "You've got it now, right [Lyron]?" And he did.

Or, consider the time Jamal brought Mrs. Bee's class crispy cereal treats whose main ingredient, other than cereal, was marshmallows. Jamal had to enact a series of steps to ensure that no child would be left out. He counted the number of children in the class and then the number of treats he had brought. Next, each treat went on a paper towel and was delivered by Jamal to each child, who said, "Thank you." (I had never seen, nor ever again saw, the children as quiet as that day Jamal brought those treats. "This is *good*," Alicia had said with feeling, taking tiny, tiny bites, making the treat last.)

We are to be mindful of our classroom kin. Our actions as social beings have consequences for others as well as ourselves. This is (or should be) true of composing too. We as writers are entering into relations with others and must consider the social consequences of our authorial choices. (I am certainly worrying about *you*, dear readers, as I write these words.)

As the examples suggest, inclusive intentions can be complicated by societal divisions, among them, those of religion, gender, socioeconomic circumstance, and race. A final quality that marked an official communal ethos was openness about the societal forces that shape everyday life.

The Situated Classroom

On the way to that book fair, with the familiar book friends, Mrs. Kay overhears Ezekial, Tionna, and Lyron commiserating about their financial state. The book fair has books for sale, but "I don't have no money," says Ezekial, and Tionna and Lyron each voice a "Me either" in response.

Mrs. Kay stops the zigzagging line of children. "Sometimes," she says, "you're just going to have to remember that Mom and Dad . . . might tell you, 'I don't have the money right now,' and you're just gonna have to say, 'That's ok.'" Anyway, she goes on to explain, "everyone can enjoy the books." Then the zigzagging line of children continues up the hall, down the cement stair case, and to the basement room where they have a good time at the book fair.

This straightforward acknowledgment of socioeconomic circumstance characterized both classrooms. Both teachers were knowledgeable about family news, their joys and struggles (e.g., births, deaths, trips, jobs), and both welcomed parents with a warm hello when they stopped by for whatever reason (e.g., picking up a child for a dental appointment or bringing a birthday treat [cf. Noguera, 2003]). This sensitivity to local matters may have furthered or, at the very least, made space for children's own sensitivity.

Mrs. Kay's 1st-graders were particularly vocal about economic matters. Not only were they older than Mrs. Bee's children, but they were located in an area where people and their troubles were readily visible (recall, for example, the gathering point for day workers across the street from the school). Moreover, their school displayed its institutional concern for children's needs beyond strictly academic ones. For example, the school collected winter gear for children who were not dressed warmly enough, and Mrs. Kay herself would provide a coat if one could not be found that fit a child.

Children, without fanfare, also attended to these matters. When Jon noticed Jason's wet feet after recess one day, he pointed out to his teacher that the upper parts of Jason's boots had separated from the insoles. When Brittany, worried about waiting for the bus in the rain, would not budge out the classroom door after school, Tionna silently retrieved her umbrella from her locker and handed it to Brittany (who was not a regular playmate of hers). Tionna was going to the after-school program, she had no immediate need for that umbrella.

On another day, the children's commercial social studies text was aiming to lead them toward identifying an abandoned building with a large parking lot as a potential site for an urban garden. But one child after another objected to this idea. Rather than gardeners, the city needed builders who would "make houses for people that don't have 'em," to quote Brittany.

"For *free*," emphasized Jon.

Mrs. Bee too did not hide from children's awareness of economic troubles. She sometimes used it to emphasize her kindergartners' responsibility to do their part for their families. Once, when a child had misbehaved in the lunch room and narrowly escaped suspension, Mrs. Bee talked about her own children's school behavior. When they were little, she told the class, they could not behave in ways that might get them suspended. If they did, she would have had to stay home from work and lose a day's pay—the money for the family's food and rent. On another occasion, when Mrs. Bee read her class the children's book *A Chair for My Mother* (Williams, 1984), Mrs. Bee discussed with them the low pay waitresses receive and their dependence on customers leaving tips, as well as the fun of saving change (like the character's tips) in a special container.

Relations among people of different racial identities were, on occasion, officially discussed (e.g., in Mrs. Kay's room, the Civil Rights Movement; in Mrs. Bee's, the election of the first Black president). Children in both classrooms used racial markers easily (e.g., references to a Black child, a Mexican or, in Mrs. Bee's room, a Spanish child). In her more diverse classroom, Mrs. Kay explicitly shifted seating assignments to promote community and to avoid children staying within gendered and ethnicity-related patterns in friendship. Rarely did either teacher address their students with the gender-marked "boys and girls"; their classroom kin were a collective "you," part of an inclusive "we," or, in Mrs. Kay's room, a group of "friends."

In Sum: A Discourse of Inclusive Stories amid Hard Times

So Mrs. Bee and Mrs. Kay acted on visions of how people live together. They taught particular children in particular circumstances that were shaped by societal forces that reached back through time to migration, discrimination, industrial changes, and market forces. The children's voices, in varied American Englishes, bespoke the rhythms and melodies of their families and neighborhoods. Their references to training wheels, parks, lack of money, and police presence articulated the material conditions in which they fashioned their childhoods. The children were 5-, 6-, and 7-year-olds going to school, where they were told to follow the Golden Rule—to always remember, in Mrs. Kay's words, "Would you like somebody to do that to you?" Empathy and imagination were on display as they found their ways into others' stories (including their teachers').

These were not classroom utopias, but qualities of kinship were furthered. In the writing program, however, contradictory ideologies of human relations were on display. Implicated in these relations were *remote actors*—institutional sponsors (Brandt, 2001)—of teachers' and children's literacy lives (Brandt & Clinton, 2002; Luke & Greishaber, 2004; Reder & Davila, 2005, p. 174).

THE BASICS AND THE
OFFICIAL WRITING LIVES OF YOUNG CHILDREN

Mrs. Bee and Mrs. Kay, both conscientious teachers, carried out literacy programs in response to their children and, also, to the material presence of those institutional sponsors: federal policies, state standards, district pacing guides and grade level benchmarks, assessment regimes and commercial teacher guides. These were the material means through which society's institutions figured into the daily workings of their classrooms (Brandt & Clinton, 2002). They focused teachers' attention on "the basics," the methods through which children should be taught, and the tools through which each child would be evaluated.

Writing basics were similarly conceived in both Mrs. Kay's and Mrs. Bee's classrooms. Their states' curricular frameworks put forth goals for written communication that were broadly applicable (e.g., for early elementary) and general in vision (i.e., promoting a mastery of conventions and a breadth of genres). More influential were documents that linked state grade-level standards to district pacing guides and, ultimately, assessment requirements. The nature of assessments (i.e., what, how, and when benchmarked skills were tested) was a steady presence, keeping Mrs. Bee up at night with worry and Mrs. Kay longing for her closeted language arts units (i.e., those not organized by a required text). The teachers' reactions to their test-regulated curricula were similar to those of teachers all over the country (Au, 2007).

As discussed in Chapter 1, the basics were to provide children with a firm foundation in the skills; these included knowing letters and their sounds and the rules by which those letters are laid out on a page (but not necessarily in birthday cards, city signs, graffiti on school walls, or even school picture books). Capitalization, punctuation, grammatical usage—these will be the basics highlighted in Mrs. Kay's 1st grade, our starting point for remote actors and local enactments (and my own starting point when I began following the trail of "the basics").

1st-Grade Basics

Mrs. Kay's school was in the process of applying (successfully) for federal support, and as required by the state's federal grant (entitled Reading First grant), all primary-grade children (K–3) took a standardized achievement test (Iowa Test of Basic Skills [ITBS]). Her writing program was influenced by provided teacher-support materials and by the looming ITBS.

In the federal grant program, writing was of secondary importance to reading. Indeed, writing was a means for monitoring and furthering children's awareness of the sound units of language and their grasp of phonics lessons. From this viewpoint, writing begins in earnest when spellings become orthographically sensible, that is, when children can stretch out their pronunciation of words and listen for probable sound/letter connections.

In the 1st grade, those stretched out encodings were to be organized in coherent personal narratives or information pieces of 3 to 4 sentences. Those sentences should evidence appropriate conventions, that is, those of capitalization, punctuation, and grammatical usage. Kindergartners were to have mastered grammar basics such as orally using the correct form of irregular verbs like *go, have,* and *do*; making verbs agree with their nouns; and selecting the right pronouns in compounds (e.g., "Somebody and I are going somewhere" [but "Me and somebody" are going nowhere]). First graders, then, should write all these forms with properly placed capital letters and periods.

These expectations were consistent across the teacher handbook provided by the federal grant, the state grade content standards, and the district expectations sent home in a booklet with each child. The ITBS did not assess actual child writing, but it did test conventions through a multiple choice format. Indeed, tested conventions extended beyond capital letters and periods to include commas in lists and breaking apart effusive sentences that are linked with *and* after *and* (like many that I myself write; pardon me).

As I familiarized myself with these basics, I also came to know Junie B. Jones, a regular visitor to Mrs. Kay's class. Junie B. is the star of a book series for the 5- to 8-year-old crowd (and a favorite of Tionna's). Oddly enough Junie B., who regularly makes the *New York Times* list of bestsellers for children, speaks in ways that mark her as a charming child—and as a student who fails to master the basics. Portrayed as White and middle class, her talk displays common developmental features beloved by greeting card companies and corporate advertisers. For example, Junie B. "runned home" when upset by "mean Jim" on the bus, but "me and her [my 'bestest' friend Grace]" eventually retaliated (Park, 1993, p. 30). Nobody worries about the linguistic features of a middle class child, but developmental features, not to mention sociolinguistic and dialectical ones, of the "at risk"—these are not charming at all. They are to be quickly obliterated by the "basics" (an unsuccessful mission, as the Chapter 3 will illustrate).

In Mrs. Kay's curriculum, basic skills, like the grammatical ones, were to be taught through modeling, direct instruction, and provision of structured practice, or so advised the literacy handbook. Mrs. Kay did use textbook exercises on grammatical usage, but she also used extended child writing and teacher-led editing conferences to reinforce taught skills. These latter methods were organized in the daily writing workshop, which took place schoolwide. The workshop, said Mrs. Kay, provided children with an opportunity, not only to write "their life stories," but to practice their skills.

The writing workshop followed the afternoon recess and was the last activity of the school day. As set by the district, and elaborated upon by the teachers at her school, Mrs. Kay's workshop unfolded according to a set routine. It began with the modeling practice, which took place on the large rug that spread out just beyond the classroom door. The modeling involved multimodal composing, even though it was deemed a "writing" activity: Mrs. Kay drew and told her "true story" about a planned or recent experience. Officially, drawing—a *quick* drawing or sketch—was the major strategy for planning such a story; in actuality, though, the drawing functioned to depict the spatial layout of key referenced entities (e.g., the layout of spooky items in the neighbor's yard).

Mrs. Kay's conversational style during drawing continued as she began to write her story. She called her children's attention to periods and capital letters, to spacing, and to arranging letters and words. Speaking a conversational English with a "standard" grammar, she monitored her encoding, saying aloud each word as she wrote it. She periodically reread her text for *fix-its*—for words left out and errors of convention. Although she used that inviting "And you know what?" before modeling this fix-it or that punctuation decision, the children did not respond—unless they were curious about a word, critical of her sense, or reminded of a story they had not yet shared. Following is an excerpt from the writing portion of the modeled event on the neighbor's Halloween decorations:

"'I, like'—I'm going to space again." And Mrs. Kay carefully puts her left pointer finger down after *like* and then goes on to write *to*.

"'Watch,'" she says and then notes, "I'm leaving a space between every word." And then comes that written word *watch* and, also, *my*.

"You know what?" she says, with great enthusiasm, but, alas, no "What?" back from the children. "I'm going to space again." Once again down goes the left pointer finger.

"And you know what?" she says again, to similar silence. "I already know that I can't fit *neighbor*'s on here so I'm gonna swoop back [to the line below] and start *neighbor*'s here."

"And you know what? I have to have that apostrophe *s*. . . . And now I'm gonna say, "'He really decorates it spoo::ky.'" When Mrs. Kay says "spooky" in a low quiet voice, the word drawn out, a little vibrato in her voice, the children say "spoo::ky!" in return and make eyes at one another. One day soon, Tionna, who loves words (and has told her friends so), will go back and find *spooky* on her teacher's chart tablet so she can write that delicious word in her own story.

The children were surely learning from Mrs. Kay's modeled composing, despite their silence during her actual writing and their quiet ongoing social games, like sub-rosa tag (touching one another's leg, back, or arm, all the while looking straight ahead) or slipping one's arms out of a t-shirt's sleeves so that those sleeves flail about (quite spookily—a favorite game of the boys). The rules of conventions, though, were not learned by rote, nor did they comprise the whole of what children were learning. From the modeling practice as a whole, they were learning about the ways writing was realized in text-mediated space and time (including that daily date stamp Tionna had dreaded), the kinds of experiences that became valued topics (like fun weekend plans), and the uses of multimodality during writing (including the relatively unsupervised space of drawing).

Children's interpretations of writing time possibilities and constraints became visible and audible as they went off to their worktables after the modeling activity. They drew, wrote, and talked, as Mrs. Kay circulated and chatted briefly with this child or that one, helping them plan, spell, or reread their writing. Then she sat at her worktable and called several children over, one-by-one, for an editing conference, another key practice. There were no classroom computers or other digital media available for composing (but there was a periodic trip to the computer lab, mainly for exploring and game playing).

At the end of the writing period, the children read their day's writing to the class *if* there was time. The clock, though, inevitably hurried toward the get-ready-to-go-home bell. In the winter especially, children needed time to retrieve their gear from hall lockers and, then, to transform themselves into those walking pillow cases noted in Chapter 1: They had to zip up jackets, pull on hats, wrap scarves around necks, and search pockets for mittens. Some children needed to hurry out to climb onto buses that did not wait for stragglers. Thus, the sharing practice was often quite rushed. If there was not enough time for all the children to share, their disappointment was audible (and this was especially the case for Tionna).

In Chapter 3 we will experience some of Mrs. Kay's and the children's conundrums as they wrestled with the basics. As that chapter proceeds, the children will be more visible, as their "basic" responses are played out. Their puzzles did not include the alphabetic nature of the writing system or the expectation that they would write complete sentences. These puzzles were to be solved in the kindergarten, and that was the case too in Mrs. Bee's school.

Kindergarten Basics

During the time I was visiting Mrs. Bee's room, I wandered into a local bookstore and met Miss Bindergarten, another kindergarten teacher. Unlike Mrs. Bee, Miss Bindergarten is a popular *fictional* teacher. One look, though, at Miss Bindergarten preparing her classroom for the first day of kindergarten is enough to distinguish her teaching life from Mrs. Bee's—and I am not referring to Miss Bindergarten's biological status as a dog (Slate, 2001). Miss Bindergarten readies the childsized book shelves awaiting picture books, the housekeeping center needing pots, pans, and "babies," and the multishaped construction blocks. (She is tempted, of course, to balance those blocks in a monument of her own.) Miss Bindergarten unfolds the paint easels and, with a little help from her pet parrot, organizes the paint. She puts up the alphabet chart, the dolphin mobile, and on and on until, a little swipe of her lipstick, and she is all ready for her kindergartners.

Miss Bindergarten was preparing her classroom for children who would learn through organizing their experiences in talk, drawing, and play, and (as her books attest) whose written language would be situated in all this activity. However popular Miss Bindergarten was with those parents who frequented the local bookstores and libraries, this traditional kindergarten was not the one portrayed in district documents, and not the one for which Mrs. Bee prepared. Her classroom schedule was a lot like Mrs. Kay's (although Mrs. Kay's 1st-graders had regular periods for play).

Mrs. Bee's room was filled with worktables and a meeting time rug—no housekeeping center, no big block area; its easels were for holding large books and lesson tablets. In a nod to digital times, her room had four computers sitting on tables that divided the worktable area near the classroom door from the rug area that spread out against the far wall. Those computers, though, were not functional and served only as platforms for the papers and books balanced on their tops.

To prepare her classroom for writing, Mrs. Bee studied the guidebooks for the commercial writing program, attended professional training for that program, and followed the advice of the coach sent by the program's main site to help her enact the program correctly. She also examined the district's guide for pacing her class through the program's lessons, its directions for quarterly assessments, and the kindergarten report card. She tacked the program's writing strategies on a wall, readied the writing folders as directed, and organized the trade books used in the program's lessons.

Initially there were no provided state learning standards specifically for kindergarten. The district kindergarten writing benchmarks were in fact tied to the commercial program; its organized set of lessons was readily susceptible to the district's lesson pacing guidelines. Still, the essence of Mrs. Bee's adopted program—its sense of children as individual writers, not as collective players, its emphasis on the *real* as opposed to the imagined, and its quick push to orthographic conventions—were not atypical aspects of early elementary writing classes. Indeed, they were similar to Mrs. Kay's class. The interest here is not in critiquing the commercial program but in critically examining enacted manifestations of common "basics" assumptions.

Among such assumptions were the district benchmarks for kindergarten conventions; these included connecting letters and sounds, to be practiced through inventing spellings during the daily writing activity (Read, 1975); these inventions were listed on the pacing guidelines for the second month of school. Initially, most kindergartners were grappling with their names, exploring letter shapes, and composing messages by drawing; they were not yet attuned to the alphabetic system. Thus the program induced that earlier noted pressure Mrs. Bee felt to meet expected benchmarks.

As the year unfolded, formatting conventions—placement of pictures, labels, and sentences; spacing between words—and beginning punctuation (i.e., periods) were delineated in the pacing guidelines. As writing readable words assumed importance, drawing was to be transformed from a communicative means to a way of remembering one's story. That is, as in Mrs. Kay's room, drawing was to be a quick sketch before writing.

Finally, also as in Mrs. Kay's room, the children were to write an organized or coherent "true" personal story (the basic text). This coherence was a matter of explicit instruction in Mrs. Bee's program. The children were to think before they put pencil to paper; and beginning the second month of school, they were to envision a three-page narrative. As should already be evident, the children had no difficulty telling stories, but discussing writing terminology and genre features outside an ongoing activity—that was difficult (cf. Clay, 1998). (Readers may recall the "DO IT BY YOURSELF!" response to Mrs. Bee's query about topics.)

State kindergarten standards became available 9 months into my research project. The writing benchmarks they detailed were not as stringent as those governing Mrs. Bee's kindergarten: Children should write their letters and begin to invent spellings by the end of the year. They could represent their stories not only in print but also orally and in drawing, play, and dictation (the latter two of which were not listed on district guidelines).

To meet the district standards, Mrs. Bee, like Mrs. Kay, enacted a series of practices during her late morning writing period. Guided by the lessons in the commercial program's handbooks, Mrs. Bee began with the whole class meeting on the rug. Usually, she had a particular teaching point (e.g., planning a coherent story, stretching words to hear their sounds, or using the *word wall*, a wall-sized evolving dictionary of commonly used words). She regularly modeled composing by dramatically telling her own story, making a quick sketch of its key objects and characters; then she would move from storytelling and drawing to the all-important writing.

Like Mrs. Kay, Mrs. Bee used a conversational English as she modeled writing a message in a "standard" grammar. She talked her children through the process of articulating a message, spelling a word, rereading what was written to remember what to write next, and then spelling again, all the while carefully arranging letters on her lined chart paper. Like Mrs. Kay's children, Mrs. Bee's were more alert to story sense than to form, as in the following interaction:

On this October day, Mrs. Bee is writing a list of what she likes, a potential strategy for choosing a topic. She has written *traveling*, discussed the word's meaning with the class, and is now making a list of where she likes to go. The children respond conversationally to every named place, but Mrs. Bee keeps her focus on the list (the function of which is of questionable clarity to the children):

MRS. BEE: I like to go to the circus.

Mrs. Bee writes *circus*, as varied children report "I been there!" and "I saw . . ."

MRS. BEE: I like to go to Six Flags [an amusement park].

Mrs. Bee writes *Six Flags*, as once again children report their desires (e.g., "Oh, we going there, Ms. Bee!")

MRS. BEE: I like to go to Tennessee.

Mrs. Bee writes *Tennessee*, as a voice rings out "Oh! I never been there!"
    Then Mrs. Bee writes *things that I like*, and there is great enthusiasm at the writing of *ice cream*. Mrs. Bee selects that word for her sentence writing, *I like ice cream*.

MRS. BEE: So I made my list. . . . You guys have had trouble . . . sketching
    quickly. Now I said "I like ice cream," so I'm gonna sketch it real quick.
    (She does so.)
        Then I'm going to write. Mmm. I gotta think. "I" (writes *I* and then
    writes *l*.) What am I writing?
CHILDREN: ICE CREAM! (with great confidence and joy)
MRS. BEE: No, "ice cream" doesn't start with an L.

The modeling has shifted into a new phase, from generating potential topics to writing a sentence by stretching sounds and choosing letters. The children are now relatively quiet, but a few voices offer a corrected response—Mrs. Bee is not writing *ice cream* but *like*!

MRS. BEE: What other sound do you hear? Let's stretch it. /l/ /i::/
ALICIA: I!
MRS. BEE: I! Good job, Alicia.

And so Mrs. Bee and the children proceed to spell *I lik ics krem*.

    At the conclusion of Mrs. Bee's lesson, the children were sometimes directed to tell a partner what they were planning to write. Then they went off to their work tables, where they opened their writing folders, re-trieved a sheet of paper, and began to make their marks. As curves, lines, and shapes filled their pages, children described evolving scenes (as Alicia did with her never-ending birthday party pictures) or narrated evolving stories (as LaTrell did about drawn monsters, bugs, and other creatures). Thus, although Mrs. Bee had no regular sharing time, the children did share. As in Mrs. Kay's room, peer talk filled the social space around the children's composing in pictures and words.

Mrs. Bee circulated as the children composed on their papers, often settling on a tiny kindergarten chair to help this child or that one (usually with encoding). As the clock hurried on toward lunch, Mrs. Bee would reiterate the expectation that children think for themselves, then quick sketch, and, finally, make the words as best they could. Her children, though, would not decipher the conventions of the written system only from listening to Mrs. Bee, nor would they readily abandon drawing or think in terms of school genres (like those three-page personal experience narratives).

Most strikingly, they initially showed no awareness that official school composing might necessitate reconfiguring their relationships with others. Indeed, on the day Mrs. Bee wrote her own text about ice cream and the children voiced their approval, she expressed some frustration as the children began to represent *their* liking of ice cream. "Don't you like something else other than ice cream?" she asked. The children, though, were continuing their appreciation of that cold treat, seemingly oblivious to the complexities of "doing it yourself." After all, in Mrs. Bee's room, as in Mrs. Kay's, the governing ideology beyond writing time was that we are responsive in our communications. We are human kin—and, like Mrs. Bee, most of us quite like ice cream!

WIDE-AWAKE CHILDREN AND BLINDS-SHUT BASICS

For school districts, test regimes, commercial programs, pacing guides, and benchmarks are means for making offered curricula uniform across school sites with differing demographics (Salvio & Boldt, 2009). They are not, of course, a means for making children's experiences uniform.

In their respective districts, Mrs. Kay and Mrs. Bee responded as complex, caring human beings to their teaching situations. They interacted with their children in ways that promoted community, a sense of participation in a collective that acknowledged human diversity. And they also acted to ensure, as best they could, that their children, stereotyped as "at risk," met uniform benchmarks for basic skills.

However, the teachers' offered curricula were transformed as they were enacted with their children—cultural beings, wide-awake to the world around them and to one another. Hence, the children posed some problems for "basics" curricula, with their uniform march to a mastery of valued skills, indeed, with their very textual uniforms sized to particular idealized child selves who stick to the literal truth and want to be writers, not players.

The resulting social dramas are already peeking through this chapter on official basics and expected lessons. In Chapter 3 those dramas become more audible and visible as I consider the conundrums that evolved as teachers' and children's perspectives diverged. The discursive site of these conundrums are identified fix-its, or basic errors in how proper texts should look and sound. Tionna is waiting for us even now in Chapter 3, so that she may introduce the nature of these basic conflicts.

Looking Good and Sounding "Right"
Fix-Its

Tionna has agreed to check my writing, more specifically, my transcription of a playground rhyme for my field notebook. I read slowly and deliberately, matching voice and print, just like the children do when they read to their teacher, Mrs. Kay.

"Mai:l man, Mai:l man/ Do your duty."

"No," says Tionna firmly. "It's '*do* ya,'" and she recites the rhyme in the proper spirit. Aiming for accuracy, I automatically adjust voice and print from "do your" to "do ya," which meets with her approval. (Both of us, I hasten to add, can read *your.*)

As the above exchange makes clear, Tionna thought I had a *fix-it* (the local word for textual "errors"). Based on her oral experience, she did not think that my text sounded right.

The question "Does that sound right?" is common in writing classrooms, including those of Mrs. Kay and Mrs. Bee. Usually, though, that key question is linked to a homogeneous and hierarchical view of language: Those whose speech and writing follow the rules sound right. Their speech and writing are "proper" and ranked above those whose language does *not* follow the rules. Tionna, however, seemed guided by a different language ideology—a situated or relational one. She had a sense of how a voice should sound in a particular situation, given the relational contingencies of the moment (Duranti, 2009; Hymes, 1972). She was, after all, talking to me, her diligent observer, not to Mrs. Kay, her instructive teacher.

Tionna used her experience as a player in the clapping game to participate with me in a new practice, that of composing accurate records of children's words and deeds. In fact, in clapping games, Tionna and her friends regularly corrected one another if they violated expected wording, rhythm, or movement; they implicitly knew that the success of a game depended on the rhythmic articulation of sounds as well as bodies. So, given her experience as player and evaluator, she let me know quite firmly that the correct wording was "do ya," not "do your." In this way, she recontextualized her handclapping prowess for the activity of writing field notes.

Tionna illustrates how children's experiences as communicators and symbolizers provide the landscape against which they make sense of new practices and find niches for new tools, like written language. Driven by the desire for meaning and for relationships (Nelson, 2007), they orchestrate what they deem relevant resources for the activity at hand; among those resources may be thematic content (e.g., the words of a clapping game), social role (e.g., a player, an evaluator), technological (including orthographic) conventions, and symbolic tools, like talk, drawing, and play. Indeed, Vygotsky (1978) noted that gesture, play, and drawing are earlier developed forms of writing, that is, of giving material shape to voiced intentions. Through these means, children enact their desires or their fears, as they construct real or pretend worlds (see also Dyson, 1989, 2003a; Matthews, 1999; Stetsenko, 1995).

In addition to Tionna's handclapping, other illustrative childhood practices, rich with resources, include Ezekial's social talk with his peers about basketball games (with their epic heroes; their material manifestations in scoreboards and print-marked uniforms; their summary litanies of facts about players and teams; and their narrative replays in varied media, from fact-based TV newscasts to fictionalized films and video games). Also included are LaTrell's dramatic narratives while drawing, often with threatening creatures, like cartoon-inspired monsters, and potential victims. All these practices were rich with resources that could support social and symbolic pathways into school literacy.

Still, this very diversity of resources could problematize the textual expectations and uniform progress of the basics curricula. For example, Tionna's sociolinguistic and aesthetic sense, evident in correcting "your" to "ya," and the language flexibility that entailed were inaudible in the official world, in which one was to speak and write "right." Similarly, children's exploration of the flexibility of print's visual features was officially invisible. Written texts might have street names in ALL CAPS, just as they were on the street signs visible from classroom windows. Drawings could have graphic bubbles filled with talk or, perhaps, uniformed sports figures adorned with capital letters and numbers. Many a small boy drew a scoreboard with its particular arrangements of letters and numbers; Ezekial's in particular were informed by sports media broadcasts (which led to his use of *VS* as a word). Finally, the dialogic process of drawing, fueled through interaction with peers and paper, could grind against the linear expectations of the writing workshop.

The children, with their diverse resources and experiences, quite gamely entered into the making of sense and of story; they aimed to connect with their teachers and with one another. As responsible teachers, Mrs. Bee and Mrs. Kay were alert to the benchmarked skills evident in children's efforts—to complete sentences and "correct" usage, coherent true texts and sensible spellings, and properly placed punctuation and capitalization. Hence what could result were moments of disconnection, most often evident in discourse about fix-its (the range of which are displayed in Figure 3.1).

Before I begin sampling those moments, I reiterate that the interest here is in problematizing the taken-for-granted basics, including those introduced by mandated curricula. Mrs. Bee and Mrs. Kay were skillful, dedicated teachers, and the children clearly benefitted from their responsive attention. Their willingness to allow us to reflect on common "basics" as articulated in their local circumstances—their classrooms—is a professional gift. Now I turn to official fix-it concerns in the kindergarten and the 1st grade.

Figure 3.1. Hierarchical Conception of Writing Fix-Its

I. Grammatical: Making It Sound Better
  A. *Adjusting Usage.* Example: fixing personal pronouns in compounds, indefinite articles, verb agreement.
  B. *Adjusting Sentence Structure.* Example: fixing incomplete sentences; fixing repetitive coordinating conjunctions for grammatically equivalent elements, as in items in a list or run-on sentences.
II. Content: Being Productive
  A. *Writing More/Drawing Less.* "Just a quick sketch, you can write more."
  B. *Adding Details.* In order to "write more," add details like who, what, where, and when.
  C. *Organizing Text.* Stay "focused" on a topic; in a narrative, detail what happened first, second, third (related to formatting concern IIIB).
III. Graphological Conventions: Following the Rules
  A. *Using Upper and Lower Case Letters and Punctuation Marks Correctly.*
  B. *Formatting Pages Correctly.* Example: fixing the arrangement of print from top to bottom, left to right, with adequate room for letters and space between words; arranging a coherent personal narrative across three pages.
  C. *Attempting to Encode Words (Spelling) Correctly or Reasonably.* Related to "listening to how you say it."

Source: Adapted from Dyson, 2006, p. 18.

KINDERGARTEN FIX-ITs:
WHERE DO WRITTEN STORIES COME FROM?

During the opening weeks of school, Mrs. Bee's kindergartners mainly drew during composing time. Sometimes they filled the one or two lines that stretched across the bottom of their papers with the alphabet or with seemingly random letters or letterlike forms.

In her reading lessons, Mrs. Bee emphasized alphabet names and sounds and the matching of voice and print (e.g., pointing to each word in a brief text as it was read). In the daily composing time, Mrs. Bee modeled drawing and then writing her own text. By week 5, the children were to be stretching out their own words and writing them, or at least so dictated her curricular guide and district pacing scheme. That is, children were to slowly speak a word they planned to write, listen for the sounds of the word's letters, and identify at the very least the word's first letter.

Moreover, the children's written words should yield a coherent and sustained if brief text. The children were not to wander from one topic to the next. As described in Chapter 2, the children were to think about their experiences, choose a topic—ideally something real that happened or happens—quickly sketch that experience, and then represent it in writing by spelling as best they could.

Undergirding that expected process was an assumption about where stories come from. Officially, stories came from thinking about things that happened. Unofficially, though, stories tended to come about as children *made* things happen, as creatures appeared and plots were transformed in the midst of symbolic activity and social talk. These differing approaches to story undergirded some of the official fix-its in Mrs. Bee's class.

Content Fix-Its

Each day as children composed, Mrs. Bee circulated and responded to the problems children seemed to be having. She aimed to help them fix it. Sometimes, when many children had a common fix-it, she would bring it to the attention of the class as a whole. She would ask the children to stop and listen as she explicitly discussed the problem. As the year progressed, four fix-its became dominant concerns—three about content (considered in this section) and another about encoding.

One content fix-it arose when drawing lost its curricular place of honor to spelling. The children continued to spend their time drawing. Thus, children needed to draw less (quickly sketch) and write more (Figure 3.1, IIA).

Another content fix-it accompanied a curricular move from one-page compositions to three-page ones. During weeks 5–8, a major writing benchmark involved staying on topic across pages (i.e., stretching the day's true story across three pages, yielding a picture and words for each of the three pages about a single happening). The children, though, continued to treat each page as a new opportunity to compose. Hence there was a new fix-it, this one about children's need to stay on topic (Figure 3.1, IIC).

A third content fix-it was related to another curricular move, this one to stressing children's plans for their story writing. Planning was not so easy to do, hence the resulting need to fix one's plans. Explaining this fixing requires a little pedagogical history, as it is a content fix-it (Figure 3.1, IIB, adding details), with links to grammar (Fix-it IB, adjusting sentences so that they are complete).

Following her guidebook, Mrs. Bee had initially helped her children write labels next to drawn objects on the top open space of a page. To be real authors, though, children needed to write a story on the lines stretched out on the bottoms of their papers.

For months, every day Mrs. Bee asked her children what they were going to write that day, and they responded, not with a story, but with an object they planned to draw (e.g., "a car"). In response, Mrs. Bee sometimes used another key term from the curricular guidebook: *details*. She explained that the children had to say more than a "label"; they had to say "a label with details" (Figure 3.1, IIB). In effect, by saying more, children would use "complete sentences" (Fix-it IA), that is, sentences that "made sense." (Confused?)

In the examples below, all three content fix-its frame our view of La-Trell and his peers.

The problem of writing "a plane": Tension between talking drawing and talking writing. It is the fourth week of school. In the following interaction, Mrs. Bee is working to fix how her children are responding to questions about what they are planning to write. She wants them to use complete sentences, or as articulated in this example, provide "details" (Figure 3.1, IIB):

MRS. BEE: 1, 2, 3. Eyes on me. . . . When I come to you and ask you what you're going to write about, don't just say, "I'm just gonna write a car." What about a car? Did you go some place? Did you ride in the car? Did you drive a car? I hope you didn't. Did somebody drive you in the car?
CHILDREN: (with enthusiasm) YES!

Still, the problem continues as she asks Antone what he is going to write:

ANTONE: A plane.

[Mrs. Bee restates the need to say something about the plane. Antone tries again:]

ANTONE: Flies in the air.

. . .

MRS. BEE: Who flies it in the air? (Antone is quiet.) Are you talking about a
    toy plane or a real plane?
ANTONE: A toy plane.
MRS. BEE: OK. . . . And who's gonna fly it in the air?
ANTONE: I'm gonna play with it. . . .
MRS. BEE: OK! You can't just write "a plane" . . . You have to be able to tell
    about it. "Well, I decided that I'm gonna be a jet plane pilot. And I'm
    gonna fly a plane, from the ground."
ANTONE: You is? (Impressed, apparently assuming Mrs. Bee is having a
    conversation, not modeling language.)

The sense of Mrs. Bee's concerns here eluded many children, including LaTrell and his regular tablemates, among them Ernest, Jamal,
Charles, and Cici. The source of their disconnection seemed to be children's use of the familiar symbolic tool of drawing to gain a participatory
foothold in school writing (Dyson, 1982; Matthews, 1999; Stetsenko, 1995;
Vygotsky, 1978). Following her curricular guide, Mrs. Bee's intention was
to help children more fully represent an experience on paper. The children, however, were stating their intention to draw an entity (e.g., "I'm
writing [drawing] a plane"), not to write a word needing details (e.g., "I'm
writing *plane*").

Indeed, after the lesson, Ernest and LaTrell each "wrote a tornado."
LaTrell described himself as "playing" with his, as it spun around his
paper.

***The problem of snakes and cookies: Tension between children's
narrative play and prescribed narrative writing.*** As professional writers
sometimes do, children did not so much think before they composed as
think "at the point of utterance" as voice and marker interacted with page
and peer (Britton, 1982, p. 139). Consider, for example, how LaTrell's attacking bird story came about.

The task that October day (in the 7th week of school) was to work on
a three-page book; the children were to quickly sketch three pages that
ideally would detail an event in their lives. The previous day children had

decided on a topic, which Mrs. Bee had written on the top of their first page. LaTrell was sitting by Jamal, who was to compose about "waiting for the bus"; Jamal, though, was drawing snakes and cookies (because snakes like cookies, he had explained to the curious me). Jamal's snakes inspired much snake-making at the table, including by LaTrell (whose topic was "transformers"). LaTrell's snakes acquired some bulk and evolved eventually into bug-eating monsters:

JAMAL: I made a snake. And I can make more snakes.
ELLA: What is that?
JAMAL: A snake.
LATRELL: A snake is like this (making his own snake).
JAMAL: I can make a snake like this.
ELLA: . . . That's my snake (indicating her snake). That's a *big* snake.

LaTrell gives his "snakes" some width, so that they become "ghosts." Then he extends an aesthetic and symbolic interest that has been evident for weeks— the possibilities of jagged and curved lines as extensions of enclosed spaces; he makes such lines around his ghosts and soon names them "dinosaurs," equipped, as they are now, with spiky body armor. Next LaTrell locates his jagged lines, not only outside an elongated circle, but inside. And thus:

LATRELL: He got sharp teeth! He got sharp hair [like the cool "man with bling" he will later draw]!
MRS BEE: (to the class as a whole) No more sketching [Figure 3.1, IIA], not until you've done your first and second page.

LaTrell continues drawing, now sometimes referring to his "dinosaurs" as "monsters." One small potential monster does not have jagged teeth and becomes the first of several drawn bugs—dragon flies, more precisely. One ends up in the mouth of the biggest monster!

LATRELL: They ate it [the bug].
JAMAL: Why don't you make another one?
LATRELL: I'm gonna make a bird. (draws) I made a bird! I'm gonna make a bottle, so I can spray. I'm gonna spray some water on that [bird]. 'Cause that bird's trying to get that [bug]. [Mrs. Bee has arrived at the table and is talking with Jamal. So I ask LaTrell, "Why are you spraying it?"] 'Cause I'm trying to let that one [bug] get away. 'Cause that is, that is a *big* one [bird]. . . . I made a big tail.

In the meantime, Jamal has been explaining to Mrs. Bee about snakes and cookies (with sprinkles). Mrs. Bee is concerned because he is not following through on his chosen topic.

MRS. BEE: (to the class) 1, 2, 3. [Eyes on me.] . . . I came by and wrote the
title you said . . . But you have to write about what you said. If you wrote
a story about you walking to the bus stop, everything you say has to be
about walking to the bus stop. What could happen on the way to the bus
stop?

ERNEST: Stand by the bus stop, and when the bus comes, you get on it. (a
sensible response)

LaTRELL: You can sit by your friends too. (in a cheery voice)

And then LaTrell returns to his monsters, birds, and bugs.

As just illustrated, Mrs. Bee had added to her fix-it concerns the expectation that children would plan 3-page depictions of an event (as per
her curricular guide). The children, though, did not seem to realize that
the task had changed from composing freely, one page per day. Still, they
aimed to please Mrs. Bee. They responded to her conversationally ("You
can sit by your friends too"), or during whole class discussions, slipped
into a recitation mode; they would repeat whatever the last child said if it
had met with Mrs. Bee's approval. Listen as Mrs. Bee talks with the children 5 weeks later (during the 12th week of school) about this continuing
"problem" of sustaining a topic over three pages; she is going to provide
them with the topic of Thanksgiving:

Mrs. Bee has summoned the children's attention. If the first page of their
book is about Thanksgiving, she asks, "can the second be about Christmas?"
With seeming great confidence (and volume) her children say "NO!" Mrs. Bee
continues:

MRS. BEE: Why not?

AVEY: It *can* be about Christmas.

MRS. BEE: It can be?

AVEY: It can, because Christmas is coming.

MRS. BEE: . . . (smiling) She has a point. But when writing a three-page
story—that book right there, "When It's My Birthday," I think that book is
all about (pause)

CHILDREN: CHRISTMAS!

Mrs. Bee regroups. She explains that, given the title, she would expect the
whole book to be about somebody's birthday. Making an analogy, she then
asks:

MRS. BEE: So when it's Thanksgiving, it's gonna be all about (pause)

CHILDREN: BIRTH-DAYS. (in a loud, monotone chorus)

And so it continues, until Mrs. Bee asks the children what they are going to do on Thanksgiving. Well, they are going to play in the park, go to Brian's or another restaurant, eat corn, pizza, and maybe turkey! LaTrell himself is anticipating turkey, and he spends the work period trying hard to make a drawn turkey fit on his drawn dinner table.

Content fix-its or curricular fix-its? Against the list of benchmarked skills, the children's difficulties might seem straightforward. And yet, the children, as speakers, did narrate stories (using complete sentences), predict happenings in tales Mrs. Bee told and read, and stayed on topic when they understood the shared conversation (e.g., Thanksgiving Day plans). These aspects of language use were not a problem—but isolating them or, to borrow from Wenger (1998, p. 249), "extracting" them from ongoing practice seemed a problem. The children's fix-its were at least in part a construction of the curricular context, one which highlighted their relative inexperience, not only with written language, but with talk about that language (McDermott & Varenne, 2010).

To escape momentarily Mrs. Bee's paced benchmarks, if we viewed the children's efforts within a different frame, we could reinterpret the goings on. Within that frame, a sociocultural one, the children were participating in a new story-making practice by leaning on familiar social and symbolic tools. Daily composing was initially a playing on paper and, even a kind of mailbox, a way of reaching out to others. So LaTrell and Ernest drew tornadoes together, and Jamal and LaTrell noted the plight of his threatened bugs.

Through my old eyes, the children were beginning in ways that recalled the writing beginnings of many other children observed over the years (e.g., Rachel in Dyson, 1983; Joshua and Jake in Dyson, 1989; Lamar in Dyson, 1993, the list goes on). Their efforts to make a world, and to tell stories about imagined scenes, were potential "leverage points" for adding to their communicative repertoire (Wenger, 1998, p. 249).

For example, as I imagine possibilities, I envision their drawing-mediated play providing contexts within which children could (and did) begin to explore written language in varied ways—to write numbers on houses, letters on street signs, signs on buildings, and character talk in dialogue bubbles. Writing could be considered, not a substitute for drawing, but an aspect of their multimodal story-making. I imagine that children telling their stories to peers in a daily formal sharing time might help them organize their efforts—anticipating an audience is a fundamental aspect of communication of any sort (Bakhtin, 1981). In preparation for such sharing, a teacher might sometimes take dictations, which itself presents opportunities to talk about a child's talk and to collaborate in the composing and the encoding (Cooper, 2009; Dyson, 1989; Nicolopoulou, McDowell, & Brockmetyer, 2006). The resulting stories might be literally played out by peers in a teacher-mediated authors' theater (Paley, 1981, 2004).

The curriculum, though, not only influenced how Mrs. Bee viewed her children but also how she viewed her own teaching resources. In her rural schools, she had taken dictation from children's storytelling. She had emphasized children's imaginative play and provided opportunities for incorporating letters and print in that play. But Mrs. Bee's repertoire during composing time was now constrained: no dictation for collaborative story construction, no emphasis on child imagination, less exploratory play with letters and names, and, indeed, little play. Mrs. Bee was diligent and did her best to make sure that her teaching followed the guidelines and her students met curricular benchmarks.

Yet the children could not be kept from social talk and imaginative play. As I will illustrate in the chapters in Part II of this book, Mrs. Bee's children sang and recited rhymes—and disagreed about how those rhymes should go (easily engaging in that talk about language that so eluded them in class discussions). They played collaboratively and even began to use written language to mediate relationships (e.g., readers may recall from Chapter 1 that LaTrell himself wanted his name in Charles's birthday text). Moreover, the children invented their own version of written games; within the first weeks of school, Jamal initiated a game involving writing down the names of naughty children: "Ms. Bee says, 'Your name is on this card? You going to the office.'" This game led to much guessing of first letters of names, seeking out of others' names, and, of course, much surreptitious giggling. This was pretty impressive for children just learning the alphabet and, indeed, the letters of their own names (like Jamal himself).

Now, though, I need to stabilize my wandering spotlight on the official world. There is another category of fix-its that needs to take center stage in Mrs. Bee's room, one related to the need to "make the words."

Encoding Fix-Its

Fundamental to the writing curricular guide was the phenomenon known as "invented spelling" (Read, 1975). That is, children were to stretch out the pronunciation of their planned words, listen to the sounds, and apply what they were learning about sound/symbol connections. The children were not to just scribble, Mrs. Bee said; they were not to play with the letters, trying out letter shapes and combinations (cf. Clay, 1975, 1998).

Doing such things, or doing no letter writing at all, led to the common fix-it, attempting an orthographically reasonable spelling (Figure 3.1, IIIC). Children were to take control and independently write at least the first letter they heard in the word they were writing.

The children *were* beginning to associate letters with sounds. However, the link between those associations and the production of meaning was not clear (Bialystok, 1991; Ferreiro & Teberosky, 1982; Tolchinsky, 2003). This whole business of putting speech, not an image, on paper was tenuous.

The problem of knowing the words: Tension between being independent and seeking help. As is common when learners are faced with a new task (Rogoff, 2003), children sought help with encoding. To encode, they had to grapple not only with the abstract relationships among *sentence, word, sound,* and *letter,* but also with the choreography of pencil, voice, and body twists and turns (to check out the alphabet chart or the word wall).

Following her curricular guide, Mrs. Bee urged independence, although she did provide guidance to children whose pages were devoid of letters. In the following interaction from week 4, Mrs. Bee is explaining to LaTrell that he needs to try, and he is explaining that he needs help:

"Look what I did," says LaTrell to Mrs. Bee one September morning. He and Ernest have been making robots. Mrs. Bee asks LaTrell what he is going to write now.

"A robot," he responds. Mrs. Bee continues in a familiar way:

MRS. BEE: What about a robot?
LATRELL: He can walk. (Indeed, his drawn feet have just recently acquired
 the option of drawn shoes, as opposed to straight lines or lines with five
 fingerlike toes.)
MRS. BEE: Write that.
LATRELL: I don't know the words.
MRS. BEE: That's your job.
LATRELL: I need to hear your words.
MRS. BEE: Okay, LaTrell. What are you going to say, my dear?
LATRELL: I don't know words.
MRS. BEE: Yes you do. You talk words every day.

But LaTrell was most definitely helped by hearing Mrs. Bee's words. Her speech was a Vygotskian (1978) meditational tool, helping him manage a complex process. In the following excerpt (from the 6th week of school), Mrs. Bee helps LaTrell write a sentence. He had earlier followed

Alicia into drawing a family birthday party at the park (although his featured a Sponge Bob kite).

MRS. BEE: Tell me what your picture's about.
LATRELL: It's about my mom—my auntie and my mom at my party. . . . It's the park.
MRS. BEE: OK, but what do you want to say? You got to make it sound like an author writes.
LATRELL: R! It start with a r.

Mrs. Bee struggles for a minute with the giggles; LaTrell has reacted to the word "sound" in what, for him, seems a reasonable way. With great confidence, he declares that "park" starts with an R. The neighborhood park is an important part of his picture; moreover, he can hear the sound of R in its name!

Mrs. Bee recovers and tries again, working toward "making a word" in a complete sentence (Figure 3.1, IB):

MRS. BEE: Tell me about this picture. You said it's where?
LATRELL: At the park.
MRS. BEE: Look at me. Can you say, "This is the park?"
LATRELL: This is the park.
MRS. BEE: How do we write "this"? It's tricky. It's like "the." You have to write a T and a H.
LATRELL: (writes a T, and then pauses) How you write a H?
MRS. BEE: Turn around. See the house [on the alphabet wall chart]? Now write a lower case [h]. No, the little one. Turn around and look. The upper case is the big one. There's the little one; it's the lower case. I want you to write the little one. Good! Now listen, what do you hear? /This::/. What do you hear last?
LATRELL: I don't know.
MRS. BEE: Don't say, "I don't know." What letter makes that sound? /This::/. /This::/. What letter makes that sound? /This::/.
LATRELL: S.
MRS. BEE: S. Write that. [LaTrell does so.] Next, "is." /I:s/. /I:s/. What's the letter in "igloo?" That's the same sound.
LATRELL: Uh, V.
MRS. BEE: Turn around and find the igloo [on the alphabet chart].

And so they proceed, until time is up, and Mrs. Bee offers some encouragement.

MRS. BEE: Don't give up. . . . It'll get easier as we go along. It's gonna get better. We have to keep working on it.

Letters and sounds, lower case and upper, find the house, the igloo (an igloo?), turn around, turn back—writing was a physical and cognitive feat, all held together by Mrs. Bee's reference to a sentence that LaTrell himself may not have recalled.

Nevertheless, LaTrell could follow Mrs. Bee's efforts to link word and letters. Some children's notions of the relationship between speech, writing, and reading were more fluid (i.e., they did not consistently link written letters to each spoken word [Ferreiro & Teberosky, 1982]). For example, when I asked Ernest about his writing, he read, "My daddy is going fishing. Going fishing. Fishing." As he did so, he moved his finger back and forth over the words he had just made with Mrs. Bee's help (*I am going fishing*).

LaTrell, though, sought out specific letters for specific words, particularly drawn items' names. Moreover, he did take some control of writing a few weeks after the park event. He may not have met all the benchmarks, but he made a mark on his own passage into writing in the Boys and Girls Club event.

The trouble with BCL (the Boys and Girls Club): Tension between benchmarks. The BCL event displayed LaTrell's visual attentiveness, which had been on display throughout the fall in his drawings. Numbers, letters, and letterlike symbols were drawn on houses, on people's shirts, and even on balloons. His first effort to orchestrate his orthographic knowledge without Mrs. Bee involved the support of a familiar symbolic tool (drawing) and an everyday sign—the one on the local Boys and Girls Club building (see Figures 3.2 and Figure 3.3).

Mrs. Bee had mentioned the club during the morning rug time, when she was talking to the children about their experiences. A number of them rode in a van to the Boys and Girls Club after school. LaTrell, who had been sitting upright, barely moving, became quite animated, because in his view, the Boys and Girls Club was "fun!" Mrs. Bee had used Boys and Girls Club as an example of a sentence that was not done—not complete.

Figure 3.2. Sign on the Boys and Girls Club Building

Figure 3.3. LaTrell's Boys and Girls Club Building

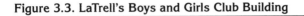

After the children had gone to their tables, LaTrell drew the club's building and then made letters on the building's door that, to you my readers, may look like text messaging (LOL) but, according to LaTrell, told people they could "push [the door]." Next at the top of the page, he drew the Boys and Girls Club symbol of joined hands on the building's sign and added the letters B for Boys and L for Club. Then he began drawing "a lot of girls and boys."

In the meantime, Mrs. Bee, sitting nearby, had been helping Ella write a sentence under her picture. Seemingly influenced by their activity, La-Trell then wrote CBL under *his* picture. I asked what he was writing.

"Boys and Girls Club," he said.

"Which word is 'boys?'" I inquired.

LaTrell pointed to the B. After a momentary distraction from the building's name to the name on the eraser (*Pink Pearl*) and brief but spirited peer talk about who was whose cousin, LaTrell began to erase his letters. Apparently my curiosity was the cause. *Boys* was the first word. So the letter B should be first. After adjusting the order of his letters, he read his text: B ["Boys"] C ["Girls"], and then, "/Cl::ub/. I think it's a L."

Done.

LaTrell had participated in a writing task in a new way, clearly evidencing insight into the alphabetic system, as he worked to represent an important (if regularly economically threatened) part of his everyday life: Boys and Girls Club. The content was reduced—no oral storytelling now. But the encoding effort was reasonable. Still, there was a benchmark looming over his monumental effort. Mrs. Bee saw it when she came by, that old fix-it complete sentences (Figure 3.1, IB).

"One, two, three," she said to the class, "Eyes on me." And she proceeded with that fix-it.

MRS. BEE: Remember we talked about sentences and if they made sense. I'm going to say one sentence and you tell me if it sounds right. "Boys and Girls Club."
CLASS: (in unison) Yes.
MRS. BEE: That sounds right to you?
CLASS: Yes.
MRS. BEE: Can you make it sound better?
ELLA: Boys and Girls Club (in a melodious, smooth voice)

That is not, alas, the meaning of "sound" in this instance. Mrs. Bee tries again. Finally, Alexia says "I go to the Boys and Girls Club." Mrs. Bee tells the class that Alexia made it sound better because she made a complete sentence. She then turns back to LaTrell, adopting an understanding voice.

MRS. BEE: I like the way you have it. But when we edit it—that means we're gonna fix it up—you gotta say, "I went to the Boys and Girls Club," or, "I like the Boys and Girls Club." . . . You have to make it sound right, make sense. . . . You are doing a really good job.
LATRELL: My mother said I'm doing real good.

Summary: Regulating Story Making to Pace, Guide—and Confuse

MRS. BEE: (writing on the chart pad for the class) This is a word, and this is a word. . . . I need finger spaces [between those words].
LATRELL: I can make a space man.

As noted in Chapter 1, Mrs. Bee followed the mandated curriculum, worried about its pace, and at the same time, wanted her children to be deemed academically successful. She saw her children's fix-its through that lens. She understandably worried about written productivity and grammatical, textual, and orthographic *sense*. The children, though, started composing in the only way they could, with what they knew; and based on that experiential knowledge and know-how, they responded to the sense of the activity on offer during composing time.

LaTrell, whose mother said "I'm doing real good," was my point person in the discursive rendering of Mrs. Bee's fix-it concerns. LaTrell embodied the eagerness widely evident in Mrs. Bee's room, as children took pleasure in taming lines and curves ("I can make a space man"), in attending to print and its use in their environment ("Your name is on this card?"), and in playing out stories on two-dimensional playgrounds.

The children's actions were consistent with dominant themes in their classroom community but inconsistent with the concerns of writing time. The curriculum was not about participating in a community of others, playfully imagining a world, or investigating the diverse sounds and images of print in their lives. There was no curricular time or space for individual children to untangle in their own childtimes the distinction between outer world *space* and word *space*, the metalinguistic feat of translating cookie-loving snakes and bug-devouring monsters into deliberately encoded stories, or the multiple meanings of *sound* in the academic discourse of writing ("Boys and Girls Club," sang Ella) (Genishi & Dyson, 2009; Greenfield & Little, 1979).

Rather, the children were to march down a benchmarked path to individual success with an academic subject called *writing*, steeped in new ways of talking. The written result of that writing was to *sound* right, both orthographically and syntactically. Children did not necessarily notice when official expectations changed, when they were to turn a developmental corner or stay within a newly constrained lane. The children did make progress down the path, supported by the responsive Mrs. Bee. Still, as I will demonstrate, progress could come at a cost, as imagination, social attunement, and multimodal flexibility could all be lost to the official world.

One evident truth on display in the kindergarten room was that, whatever the signs in their environment (including the name of their SCHOOL [note the capital letters]), the rules were clear, and as Mrs. Kay's more experienced students will suggest, the world seemed to violate those rules with abandon. With this thought in mind, I heed Tionna's voice even now calling for my attention. She and her classmates are eager to illustrate the fix-it concerns in Mrs. Kay's room.

1ST-GRADE FIX-ITs: WHOSE VOICE IS THAT?

Throughout the year, Mrs. Kay, like Mrs. Bee, attended to her children's productivity; she did not want them to spend the period drawing. Beyond that concern, Mrs. Kay's fix-its were informed by her curricular guides and the looming achievement test noted in Chapter 2. Mrs. Kay's children were more experienced than Mrs. Bee's. They did not struggle with the idea of writing words. Moreover, there was no demand that their three complete sentences (the minimum textual requirement) be spread over three pages. (The children *did* come to produce multipage texts, particularly after they broke the perceived rule of one page/one day discussed in the introduction to Part I.)

Still, Mrs. Kay's children too could find the designated "basics" elusive. In 1st grade those basics were relatively less focused on letters and sounds and more focused on graphological conventions, like punctuation (Figure 3.1, IIIA), and as suggested in this chapter's opening, school grammar (Fix-it IA, B). These fix-it types were linked, as both could be tied to *voice*—to a socially situated and intention-driven "speaking personality" (Holquist, 1981, p. 434). The children's voices indexed a societal, situational, and developmental diversity not acknowledged in the curriculum.

Grammatical and Graphological Fix-Its

Each day, when Mrs. Kay modeled composing, she used an inviting, conversational voice (see Chapter 2). Like any good student, Tionna attempted to "regularize" her writing, that is, to appropriate the expected voice of writing time—a conversational voice (Hanks, 1996). As Mrs. Kay urged, Tionna reread her text to check if it sounded right. But sounding right, as it happened, proved difficult and raised a key question undergirding the usual basics: Whose voice belongs on a page? On the one hand, children's chief resource for learning to write is their speech; as LaTrell and his peers illustrated, a major task is to objectify that speech on paper. On the other hand, children's speech, with its developmental, sociocultural, and situational features, can also be framed as a major grammatical problem.

In addition to grammar, properly punctuated writing was, for Mrs. Kay, as for many teachers, also a matter of listening to one's voice. For example, periods belong at the end of those sensible complete sentences so prominent in the kindergarten curriculum; a writer can supposedly hear the end of a sentence, because one's voice goes down. This is not, as it happens, a reliable guide in contemporary times, when "basic" punctuation rules are based more on syntax than sound (Crystal, 1997; Hall & Robinson, 1996).

In this section, I illustrate the fix-its that resulted when the "basic" skills of the 1st-grade curriculum were responded to by young children whose voices bespoke the developmental features and sociocultural diversity of American Englishes.

The problem with and, and, and: The disconnect between developing language and meeting benchmarks. The following *and* and *and* conference took place in early December. It is atypical only in that it was based on an assigned topic: If you had an alligator purse (like the lady in a traditional childhood verse), what would you put in it? In editing Tionna's product, Mrs. Kay discussed many fix-its, but she focused on the use of *and*. As she guided the conference, Mrs. Kay gathered Tionna into her expansive *we*, a we who shared a common sense of "better" language. That we, though, was disrupted by differences rooted in linguistic resources, classroom authority, and institutional alignment with the English variant of powerful adults.

At the top of a worksheet, Mrs. Kay had provided the starter line:

If I had an alligator purse I would put in

Tionna responded with her list:

sum makeup and a barbie house, and sum isrem [ice cream] and pazza [pizza] and sum bred sticks and a pop a apple and pizza . . . and bug spray

Mrs. Kay has just discussed the distinction between *sum* and *some* when the exchange below occurs:

MRS. KAY: Good job on [spelling] *make up*. You know what? You can use a comma right here [after *make up*]. Then you don't need that *and* right here. We can take the *and* out [crosses the word out] because that comma takes the place of *and* [Figure 3.1, IB, IIIA].

And so they continue, Tionna following Mrs. Kay's lead, putting commas for *and*s, until they come to that apple.

MRS. KAY: Would we say "a apple"? Does that sound right, "a pop, a apple?"
TIONNA: "Pop *and* a apple." (confidently)

"Pop and a apple" does sound right to Tionna. The use of the indefinite article *a* here is potentially a feature of her use of African American Language (Lindfors, 1987), though such use was common among all her classmates of diverse backgrounds (refer to Appendix B, Table B.1). Mrs. Kay explains:

Mrs. Kay: We're taking that *and* out. [Plus,] [w]e don't want to use that *a*. There's another word that would make it sound better . . . *an* [Figure 3.1, IA,B; IIIA].

Tionna continues to read.

Tionna: "and bug spray."
Mrs. Kay: "and bug spray." 'Kay. So now that we're at the end, we're gonna use that word *and*. . . . All right. Thank you.

Given the state grade level expectations, the teachers' guidebooks, and the hierarchical conception of language undergirding them, Mrs. Kay asked Tionna to do varied fix-its in order to sound better; the grammatical fix-it involving the repetitive *and* was linked to the punctuation fix-it involving commas in a list. Tionna, though, did not hear what Mrs. Kay heard. In her independent efforts, Tionna relied on what sounded right to her.

The only child who seemed to appropriate Mrs. Kay's modeling and editing of *ands* was Ezekial. But his products were misleading; he was not listening for what sounded better; he was quite literally using commas as an abbreviation for *ands*. In the vignette below, Tionna and her peer Manny help Ezekial to listen to his language, and when he does so, the commas have to be edited away.

At a school book fair on a December day, Ezekial's mother had bought him an NBA (National Basketball Association) poster displaying many of his favorite players. It had been carefully rolled up, so that Ezekial could take it home after school, but he had unrolled it repeatedly throughout the afternoon to look at it and to show it to other boys. During writing time, he sat by his current tablemates Tionna, Manny, and Brad, and wrote about his "best players":

Allne Iversin is my best player, Tras Mgote, Kobe Brite, Jasin Kid.

The following interaction began when Ezekial held his paper up (rather than his poster) for Manny, sitting across from him. "See what I wrote?" he asked, grinning.

Manny gets up and walks over to Ezekial's seat to see what he wrote. He looks intently at Ezekial's page, but he does not begin to read. Ezekial helps:

Ezekial: "Allen Iverson" (reading)
Manny: "Allen Iverson is my best" (pauses)
Ezekial: "player"
Manny: "player" (pauses again)

EZEKIAL: "and"
MANNY: "and"
EZEKIAL: "Tracy McGrady"

But Manny is not ready to go on.

MANNY: Where's *and*?
EZEKIAL: That's my thing for *and*. (pointing to the comma)
MANNY: You're supposed to put *and* there.
EZEKIAL: Read it! I put that. (pointing to the comma)

Tionna has now left her seat on the other side of the table and joined Ezekial and Manny. She takes charge and tells Ezekial to "Read it!" and he does.

EZEKIAL: "Allen Iverson is my best player and Tracy McGrady—that's my thing for *and*. . . . (Ezekial is once again pointing to the comma, which should be read "and.")
MANNY: It's supposed to be *and* there.
TIONNA: A-N-D right there.
MANNY: Put the [editing insert] caret [^] there.
TIONNA: Yeah, put the caret there, or you could write it up there [above the line].

But Ezekial erases his first comma and all the names after it. He rewrites, this time fully writing what he is saying. His completed text looks like this:

Allne Iversin
is my best player and
Tras Mgate and
Kobe Brite and
Jasin Kid.

Ezekial was trying to write "what sounded right" on paper. He was unusually attentive to visual symbols, and he had shown interest in the comma. He had quite literally assumed that a comma could stand for *and* (a view held by Janette and Brittany as well). It was an efficient graphic option, like other short ways of writing words that he knew (e.g., A.I. for Allen Iverson). However, Manny and Tionna felt he was missing a word that perhaps he could not spell (Figure 3.1, IB, IIIC)—their ear was different from Mrs. Kay's.

Indeed, repetitive *and*s were widespread in the class. Like many young children, they often strung sentences together with *and*s in their personal narratives, be they oral or written (Berman, 1996; Loban, 1976). Such constructions were not susceptible to easy correction. Similarly resistant were variants of "Me and so-and-so and somebody else" in the subject position. In a construction like "Me and Janette will live with [Lyron] when we grow up," "Me and Janette" might be seen as: a representation of joint agency; a developmental phenomenon of English-speaking children's syntax; a feature of many "nonstandard" vernaculars; an informal register of the ever-changing "standard" English; or as in school, "improper" English (Adger, Wolfram, & Christian, 2007). (The celebrated Junie B. Jones, of course, does not say that "my friend and I" are going to do whatever; instead, she anticipates that "me and that Grace" are going to have quite the good time [e.g., Park, 1993].)

Unlike repetitive *and*s and compound subjects with *me*'s, some fix-its were not widespread but related to very particular cultural and linguistic resources. Such a fix-it is illustrated below, as Tionna and Mrs. Kay work on her "big present" text.

The problem with i's: The conundrum of listening to a "nonstandard" social voice. On that December day when Ezekial was proclaiming his interest in the NBA (and grappling with his *and*s), Manny, Brad, and Tionna were all heavily into Christmas. They critiqued one another's singing of Christmas songs (e.g., is it open sled or open sleigh that is such fun to ride?), commented on the adequacy of drawings of Santa Claus, and alternately claimed to have the biggest tree and, at least in Tionna's case, the biggest present.

Tionna wrote about this present, and as the interaction below begins, she is listening to her own voice as she writes that "it's big."("It's" is pronounced "i's" in African American Language due to phonological rules [Smitherman, personal communication, June 6, 2004]).

Tionna's Writing	Tionna's Talk
	"and it" (planning)
and	"and, and"
is	"it's" (pronounced /i's/)
	"and it's" (rereading, again saying /i's/)
	"big" (planning)
big	"big"

Mrs. Kay has been circulating among the children at Tionna's table and stops to read Tionna's page. She then asks Tionna to read it herself. Tionna does so, at first reading "it is big," but self-correcting to "i's big."

MRS. KAY: Does that make sense, "I got it from my mommy and is big"?
(Mrs. Kay is not saying what Tionna said. Tionna said /i's/; Mrs. Kay is saying /iz/.)

Tionna does not respond, and so Mrs. Kay returns to Tionna's text, pointing to the *and*.

MRS. KAY: "a::nd" (hopeful pause)

Tionna still does not respond.

MRS. KAY: What word could you be missing?
TIONNA: "the"
MRS. KAY: "it"

Tionna rereads and then adds an editorial caret and writes *it*; the text now appears: *and it is big.*

TIONNA: I add a caret! (as she and Matt have just advised Ezekial to do)
MRS. KAY: Good for you!

Using her speech as a major resource, Tionna presented a fix-it problem to Mrs. Kay. The grammatical problem of a missing word (and thus faulty sentence structure [Figure 3.1, IB]) was not, though, the problem Tionna was having; her problem was spelling a contraction (Fix-it IIIC). In fact, the very next day, Tionna again spelled the contraction *it's* as *is*.

This is just one of many examples of how children were urged to listen to and rely on how language sounded, a reliance that made the developmental and sociocultural complexities of language an integral aspect of learning to write (Dyson & Smitherman, 2009). It illustrates as well the homogeneous and hierarchical ideology that undergirded official benchmarks and the testing of school grammar.

Such an ideology governed in Mrs. Bee's district too, although grammatical usage was overshadowed in the kindergarten by encoding and content concerns. However, on those occasions when Mrs. Bee did so intervene, she had an alternate stance—an insider's one. For example, the absence of the copula *be*, especially before an adjective (as in "She pretty"), was an AAL grammatical option regularly heard among the children; Alicia sometimes *wrote* that construction. One day in the fall, when she had written *the kac* [cake], she had this interaction with Mrs. Bee:

MRS. BEE: The cake what?
ALICIA: The cake big.
MRS. BEE: "The cake big?" Is that a complete sentence?

ALICIA: (silence)

MRS. BEE: Sometimes we talk like that, but it should be, look at me, "The cake *is* big."

Mrs. Bee was not talking about a situational choice, but a textual requirement. Still, Mrs. Bee did indeed share a "we" with Alicia. She was saying that you and me, as African Americans, sometimes talk like that; but, when we write, we use *is*. Alicia did not abandon this construction, just as Tionna and her peers did not permanently abandon "me and you" or a string of "ands" for that matter. But "is" was not an unfamiliar grammatical option, and, as Alicia's reading experience accumulated and her peers made use of the construction, for the most part, she did too.

The issues raised by societal differences and curricular homogeneity from the very beginning of schooling are ones we will return to (especially in Chapters 8 and 9). For now, "me and you" will turn to a final category of fix-its featured in Mrs. Kay's room, one that speaks to the contradictions between the semiotics of flexible graphics in the children's physical and media environment and the straightforward capitalization rules of school.

Lower-Case, Upper-Case Fix-Its

Written graphics are designed for more than the encoding of words and the organizing of grammatical information (e.g., complete sentences). There are matters of rhetoric and aesthetics, especially in multimodal texts (Kress, 2010). Indeed, children's everyday landscapes are filled with the multimodal and rhetorical flexibility of everyday symbols.

Mrs. Bee's LaTrell, for example, knew that CN (for Cartoon Network) belonged in the lower right hand corner of a drawn screen, that numbers could flow vertically on a house, that a building could shout out its name in big letters to passers-by, while doors might more humbly address all comers with a visually less overbearing *push*.

Mrs. Kay's children displayed all manner of graphological symbols from environmental scenes and textual displays. Those symbols came from scoreboards and sports fields, from store signs, game consoles (e.g., PS2 for PlayStation 2), and toy packages (e.g., Spider-Man). Moreover, many children evidenced an understanding that written graphics themselves could be designed to capture the sound of the human voice (e.g., capital letters indicating volume, as in *WOW*). This knowledge of graphic symbols was evident in children's drawings, but sometimes it was found in written texts themselves.

Ezekial, for example, capitalized every letter of STREET NAMES in his texts, just as they were in the actual street signs. Like characters

sometimes did in classroom library books, those in Ezekial's pictures
could shout out words in CAPITAL LETTERS. When he himself wanted
to shout out *in his text* about playing soccer with his peer Jason, he added
periods:

C.O.O.L. P.L.A.I.N.G.

"Why did you put all the periods?" I asked.
"Because I want all of 'em capitalized," he explained (i.e., he was following the rule that a capital letter comes after a period).
These sort of graphic appropriations were subject to fix-its. Punctuation and capitalization were common fix-its, since like most young children, Mrs. Kay's found syntax-based English conventions difficult (Hall,
1996). Ezekial was unusual in his relatively accurate use of periods, but
he also tended to write simple declarative sentences, unlike the complex
ones Tionna displayed, as in her text on playing *SuPrduper man* (see the
introduction to Part I).
Still, Ezekial and the children generally appropriated conventions
based on the use and features of the human voice (e.g., volume, elonga-
tions), and most often, these were found in their pictures. Indeed, 12 of
Mrs. Kay's 16 children included in the project used dialogue bubbles,
which were always round, unlike the boxes that surrounded labels (like
Doler Soer [Dollar Store]). Sometimes children repeated letters to indicate
elongated sounds as when Ezekial drew a coach yelling out a *boo* with 33
o's. (That was a pretty irritated coach.)
There were no 1st-grade fix-its centered on pictures (other than spend-
ing too much time on them). When the children stood up to share their
writing, they read the words without reference to the pictures. Indeed,
dialogue conventions were officially listed as a 3rd-grade skill. Drawing
was thus a space of symbolic freedom where space, voice, and graphics
could merge.

Voice as Potential Resource and Potential Fix-It

Like Mrs. Bee, Mrs. Kay worked to help her children master curricular benchmarks for 1st grade, which themselves were tied to the testing
linked to federal funding, and indeed, to the survival of the school itself.
The conventions, labeled "1st-grade goals," included periods that were
to appear when one's voice went down, commas which substituted for
too many *and*s, and *me*'s that were never to go first and, anyway, were
not as good as *I*'s. And then there was that "i's," which loses its "it" and
becomes "is."

It was all a tad confusing, at least as suggested by the children's silent responses to Mrs. Kay's queries about what would sound better. So much to remember and who knows why? Certainly not Tionna, who tended to follow her own ear. As we will see, that ear for language was alert, not to syntax, but to the situated voices of the people around her. Those voices included family members, community workers, media figures, and her own fun-loving teacher, Mrs. Kay.

And then there was the contradictory world of children's textual landscape. Their everyday world displayed a graphic flexibility that challenged an unyielding set of rules, as dramatized by Ezekial, who one day wrote that he was *100ed sad* on a snow day because he missed his best friend Joshua, who drew the coach that *booo* . . . ed at his disappointing soccer team, and who thought it was so *.C.O.O.L* that he would be playing soccer with Jason. Such enthusiastic exploration was tiring enough to make one need to *zzz* (another graphic move in a dialogue bubble).

Like Mrs. Bee's mandated, paced benchmarks of basics, Mrs. Kay's lead us to wonder about the consequences of actually learning what the curriculum is teaching. Do we want children to learn that vernacular resources have no place in school? What about those used by renowned authors for the young (e.g., Lucille Clifton, Eloise Greenfield, Gary Soto)? Are we not interested in how texts are designed? Do we want our children to close their eyes and ears to the world around them? They won't, of course; but they may take that attentiveness to the unofficial realm, along with the strength of their imagination and the social attunement of their collegiality (Paris & Kirkland, 2011).

THE BASICS IN A SYMBOL-MEDIATED, VOICE-FILLED WORLD

The kindergartners are doing the calendar. Mrs. Bee says they are done now with September. What, she asks her children, is the new month?

ODETTE: Octember.
MRS. BEE: When's your birthday, Odette?
ODETTE: October.

In this small exchange, Mrs. Bee illustrates a fundamental pedagogical principle: Start with what the children know. In written language instruction, the same principle applies. Children start with what they know. In Mrs. Bee's and Mrs. Kay's classrooms, these resources included story-making practices of play, social talk, and drawing; familiar voices from home, community, and school; and the sorts of symbol use they observed in the spaces of their everyday lives. The children's developmental challenge was to find a niche in their communicative repertoire for written language.

The paced basics, though, could march undeterred through the stuff of children's lives. In that way, children's products could be removed from their intentional sense-making. Each child's product could become a mere "sclerotic deposit . . . linguistically observable and fixable" (Bakhtin, 1981, pp. 289, 292).

The ideological underpinnings of this programmatic march were found in that "unattractive" version of individualism introduced in Chapter 1 (Appiah, 2005, p. 15). Children were not only to learn to write but to be independent and honest truth-tellers. The ethics of the writing program brings its own disconnections from children's lives, the topic to which I now turn. Nobody illustrates these disconnections better than Alicia. She has been quiet throughout this chapter, but she is anxious to add her voice to the mix. She is present in the final chapter of Part I.

CHAPTER 4

The Ethics of Writing

On Truth and Ownership

Imagine a classroom set up for young children's writing time. The chairs are all tucked underneath three long tables, all neatly awaiting their intended occupants. On the table in front of each chair is a paper. The children will be expected to slip into their designated spaces and concentrate on the paper in front of them. As each finishes, his or her paper will take its place in a folder, as part of the hoped-for progression of child writing and of mastered benchmarked skills. Perhaps children who are finished will get a moment in the spotlight to read their text to their peers.

Now imagine Tionna, LaTrell, Ezekial, or Alicia slipping into their spaces—and into one another's spaces as well. For them all, individual spaces could be socially linked to form new places for imagination and play. This social (and disruptive) dynamic was evident in the preceding chapter, as children's interactions peeked out from the sides of the fix-it episodes. Indeed, even in the earliest weeks of the kindergarten, children's composing evidenced a social attunement that transformed a potential audience of peers into participants in an ongoing interaction. (Recall, for example, the proliferating snakes and the play with tornadoes, which linked separate spaces into shared places.)

The social dynamics in both Mrs. Bee's and Mrs. Kay's classrooms posed new kinds of conundrums, given the curricular guidelines. These puzzling miscommunications were more about ethical violations than fix-it errors: They had to do with children's learning to become school writers in ways deemed honest and good. Such a writer speaks her or his own "truth"; he or she does not copy someone else's truth.

This notion of the honest writer who owns her or his text is grounded in an ideology of individualism, to which I return in this chapter. I emphasize its two interrelated dimensions: the concern with an individual's "real experiences"; and the emphasis on individual ownership of ideas, topics, and texts. Finally, with Alicia's help, I underscore the central official practice of both classrooms, the one embodying this ideology most clearly: the authentic "life story."

"A REAL STORY ABOUT YOU"
(THE YOU THAT IS NOT SPIDER-MAN)

It is text-sharing time in Mrs. Kay's room, and Brad goes to the front of the rug, turns toward the children all sitting cross-legged before him, and begins:

BRAD: Today we did the Pledge of Allegiance of the United States of America to the Republic George Washington DC [on the intercom].
JOSHUA: That was a good one. . . .
MRS. K.: It *was*. He told about something that he just did this morning, didn't he?

"A real story about you" was seldom an official issue of contention in Mrs. Kay's room. The children's stories generally seemed quite real. Mrs. Kay's children *were* more experienced in school than Mrs. Bee's. Still, as will be evident in the chapters to come, the 1st-graders did not necessarily write the literal truth; rather, they had ways to pretend play through seemingly true writing. And "true" writing was important to both Mrs. Kay and Mrs. Bee.

As readers may recall, in September Mrs. Kay reacted with displeasure when children seemed to borrow her textual claim to a hotel stay, just as Mrs. Bee did when her children borrowed her experiences. Listen to Mrs. Bee's comments in November:

A lot of you copied my story [about snow skiing]. That is not good. That's illegal. You can't copy my story. . . . You have to have your own story, your own thoughts, your own idea. . . . I know there are many things that you guys like to do and have already done.

The evident concern here is with copying and ownership. Undergirding that concern, though, is one about being true to one's own experiences, to the real things "you guys like to do and have already done." The children are not to appropriate the experiences of others.

However, this notion of being truthful, and of its apparent link to valuing one's real life, is highly problematic. In part, this is because cross-culturally, a major aspect of children's *real* life is *pretend play*, although its substance and perceived value varies (Lancy, 2007; Montgomery, 2009). In that play, children may imagine themselves into others' experiences—appropriating, improvising on, even mocking them. As at least suggested in Chapter 3, not only may children play through composing, but once they are in the play *frame* (Bateson, 1956), their intentions and feelings are quite real. LaTrell, for example, was determined to save that poor little bug trying to get away from the great big bird.

In addition, a good "story" worthy of telling may dramatize an experiential germ of a story and thus transform it to become engaging, if not literally true. In my observations, performative storytelling (involving, for example, vocal rhythm, image-creating metaphors, or exaggerated plot action) was not confined to any one categorized group of children. Nevertheless, a performative telling of a "true story"—which is definitely not true—is one aspect of the African American storytelling heritage. In such an event, the teller's tale may emphasize an encounter with social or physical adversity (Heath, 1983; Smitherman, 1986).

First-graders (especially Tionna) often told exaggerated (and amusing) stories, as did kindergartners LaTrell, Charles, and Alicia. The kindergartners in particular drew and told narratives about confronting sharks in the local lake and the city pool, tornadoes swooping up all in their path, even snowmen invading a yard!

Finally, the emphasis on truth was problematized by the enacted curricula themselves. In Mrs. Bee's commercial program, a teacher was to use children's fiction (e.g., a textual talking raccoon) to guide young children's crafting of their literal truths (e.g., including narrative details). And, in both classrooms, certain popular and child-oriented fictions were promoted as "true," just as they are generally in the society. These fictions featured a small fairy and a big jolly man.

The True Stories of the Tooth Fairy and Santa Claus

LaTrell and Charles are sharing their recent woes as they sit awaiting the pencil can. Charles had had a stomach ache, and LaTrell had lost a tooth.

LaTrell: I put my tooth under my pillow. And then: um: when I was watching TV. Then I went to sleep and um—
Charles: Because when I put my tooth under my pillow and I went to sleep, and somebody put something under my pillow and turn my TV off. It was my mom! . . .
LaTrell: Tooth fairy is real! He give you money, a green dollar.

Certain fictions are deemed part of the charm of childhood and its magical aura. Among these fictions in American society are the tooth fairy and Santa Claus (Clark, 1995). Neither Mrs. Kay nor Mrs. Bee ever expressed any doubt to their children about the existence of Santa Claus and the Tooth Fairy. They were real beings who could exist on a child's page without any adult displeasure.

In fact, one day during writing time, when Brad, Ezekial, Manny, and Tionna were discussing (or, more accurately, arguing about) the "realness" of Santa, Mrs. Kay intervened on the side of the believers:

MRS. KAY: How could your mom and dad buy all those presents? How could they?
TIONNA: Santa Claus help them!
MANNY: I was thinking that.

Mrs. Kay's comments reflected her awareness of the children's financial constraints, and she used those constraints as an argument for why there must be a Santa. On the basis of extensive interviews with children and parents, Clark (1995) suggests that Santa Claus, like the Tooth Fairy, may be a symbol of childlike wonder for adults themselves. Those figures are clearly commercialized (especially that big man with the bag of toys), but adults may socialize children into the reciprocity associated with these beings. The Tooth Fairy, after all, gets the tooth (to do what with, I wonder), and Santa may receive an offering of a snack. Children may also be encouraged to emulate Santa by giving to others. (At Mrs. Kay's school, there was a holiday store where, for pennies, children could pick out child-made gifts for family members, like bookmarks or Christmas decorations.)

I mention these "real" stories of childhood because they illustrate the ideological precariousness of "truth" in even official composing time. Children were to compose real stories about their unique experiences—but neither Mrs. Bee nor Mrs. Kay ruled out of bounds shared stories about societal fictions (even though their realness was under some dispute by the children themselves). Indeed, if Mrs. Bee or Mrs. Kay had banned such figures, they might have been viewed as overstepping their roles as teachers and interfering with family pleasures. This was not the case with other popular beings, including the generation-spanning Spider-Man, found in comics, movies, Saturday morning kid shows, video games, toy stores, on t-shirts, backpacks, and even in fast food places.

The "Untrue" Stories of Spider-Man and Other Fake Phenomena

It is writing time in the kindergarten, the 7th week of school. Lamont is just beginning to draw.

MRS. BEE: Lamont, what are you writing about?
LAMONT: SpongeBob (almost whispering)
MRS. BEE: I can't hear you!

LAMONT: SpongeBob.
MRS. BEE: This has got to be something real, honey.

A dismissal of children's composing about popular culture is not unusual; media-based offerings in particular are viewed as part of the commoditization of childhood (unlike Santa?) and as vulgar, violent, or a just plain silly waste of time (Marsh, 2013).

Still, in Mrs. Bee's and Mrs. Kay's rooms the main concern with popular culture was curricular—references to its products were not consistent with the emphasis on children's real experiences. In Mrs. Bee's room, such experiences were to be laid out in a what-happened-first-second-and-third sequence on three sheets of paper, each with a picture, each with written words. No unruly, to-be-continued worlds of impossible doings were allowed. In both classes, children could write about getting a Spider-Man toy or game for a birthday present; they could write about their wish for such a toy from Santa or report about going to see the superhero in a movie. In other words, given the ideology of real authentic writing, the commoditization of childhood pleasures was just fine. These small children could not, however, take Spider-Man seriously during composing time; that is, they could not appropriate the superhero's awesome power and fly through the air on paper.

This was not, I hasten to add, the choice of Mrs. Kay or Mrs. Bee, who had their own popular pleasures. It was a matter of curricular guidelines. Mrs. Bee explained the situation to her children:

MRS. BEE: I don't want you dreaming up something about Superman,
    Batman, and all those folk. Because they're not really real. . . . You can't
    say anything about Spider-Man 'cause you don't know who that is.
CHILDREN: I do! I do! (voices ring out)
MRS. BEE: No you don't.
CHILDREN: M:: m. ("Yes I do," the children are saying, quite assertively.)
MRS. BEE: Do you know the *real* Spider-Man?
CHILDREN: Yes. (emphatically)
MRS. BEE: No, you don't. Spider-Man is not a real person. He's just a
    character.

After Mrs. Bee finished, the children at LaTrell's table talked among themselves about Spider-Man. They all agreed that Spider-Man *is* "fake." They noted that he was in a movie—a being on a screen (not, for them, in a comic). Still, being fake does not make a superhero unappealing as a figure of play or related media less desirable for family fun, nor does it mean that children cannot blend the fantastic and the real (cf., Applebee,

1978; Dyson, 2003a; Paley, 1986). "Want me to tell you where Spider-Man work at?" Cici asked her tablemates near the end of the discussion. "My mama said Pizza Hut." (Her mama might more likely have said Burger King, where Spider-Man toys were on offer.)

Negotiating the Real

By the winter months, most of Mrs. Bee's children softly "ooo'ed" when a child declared their intention to write a superhero, although fake characters continued to appear now and again (Jamal had a soft spot for SpongeBob, Charles liked cop shows with good guys and bad ones, and the first time around kindergarten, Alicia was fond of Dora the Explorer, and the second time she was into Tinker Bell, whose movie had just appeared).

Still only Charles regularly crawled into stories from varied human and media sources, acting them out using talk, drawing, and writing. One story about surviving a tornado, which destroyed his house, was *true*, he told me one day. "Remember they said on the news [last night] that they had a tornado?" I did remember; it was in South Florida. In contrast, LaTrell's writing eventually settled on riding his bike, eating cereal, and playing in the park. He was becoming a "good" writer (except for those folks sneaking about on the back of his papers, like the basketball people with Halloween faces and birdlike feet and the *bling* man with grills on his teeth).

The 1st-graders, as already noted, tended to display socially and semiotically attuned negotiations between the real and the unreal. Lyron's drawing (see Figure 4.1) is a vivid preview of coming attractions in Part II of this book: The accompanying writing reports that he and his friends played war during recess, which was true; the drawing captures the true playground adventure. (Do not worry, gentle readers; there were no "real" fighter jets on the playground. Lyron had merely slipped and fallen—he was not being pummeled by those jets.)

Moreover, in both Mrs. Kay's and Mrs. Bee's rooms, it was not so easy to tell what was fictional and what was not. Modest social happenings, often involving peers, could be completely invented. For example, Tionna and Lyron included one another in modest tales about going to a grocery store together (and both appropriated Mrs. Kay's very appealing drawing of a shopping cart). But these close friends had not actually taken a trip together to the store, nor had they even been to one another's houses, as Lyron explained. Of course, their similar texts could look like one had copied the other, and copying was not what a good writer did.

Figure 4.1. Lyron's Playground Adventure

YOUR OWN STORY (THE ONE THAT IS NOT COPIED)

MANDISA: Tionna! You want to write about you-know-what?

Mandisa was asking Tionna whether, once again, they—the two of them—should write about their temporary crush on Jon (which upset their long-time friend and play boyfriend, Lyron, but more on that relationship later). Tionna did not want to write about Jon again, even though (to quote just briefly her text), "his heir is the stilly [style] he has a cute smile . . . his teeth all ways stay clean his breth never steks [stinks]." (What more could a girl want?) Tionna had, in fact, already written this text twice. She had copied herself (!) because she did not get an opportunity to read the first piece to the class.

Two children coordinating their separate texts, a child copying her own text—what does such behavior say about children learning to express themselves as individuals?

Ideological Conflicts, or Being Out of One's Own Space

Tionna and Mandisa dramatize ideological problems for the writing classroom. There is a disconnect between Mandisa's inquiry of Tionna at the start of the writing period and the overriding ideology of individualism. All children are to turn their attention to that paper in front of them, to think, and then to express the true self, the singular *voice*. If papers end up with the same ideas, then a logical conclusion is that they have been copied, and this is not acceptable. Indeed it is "illegal," to quote Mrs. Bee. One day, in frustration, she said to the kindergartners:

> The reason I don't want you guys . . . to talk to each other because you guys are using the same ideas. I want you to use your own ideas. Don't tell anybody what you're doing. And keep your eyes on your own paper.

Of course the children kept talking and sharing ideas. On occasion a child certainly could copy because that child needed help. More commonly, though, children engaged in social activities that resulted in related texts. In other words, like Mandisa's and Tionna's coordinated composing, their writing actions were mediating a relationship. Moreover, those actions tended to be tied to children's desires for companionship and for play—for appropriating the voices and images around them, trying them on, imagining possibilities, and exerting some control over a sometimes confusing and precarious world.

Indeed, in the theoretical perspective guiding my project, writing is never an individual production (Bakhtin, 1981). Rather, it is always socially organized in cultural time and space, and it is also always a response to a landscape of others' voices. In fact, learning the ways in which literacy practices mediate participation in varied communities is an aspect of the situated "basics" toward which I am building. Certainly community participation mattered to Tionna, who copied herself in order to get to read "today's writing" to her class during sharing time. (Readers may recall her extension of her text on Super Duper play, also in service of an opportunity to read [see Part I's introduction]).

Ironically, learning to be legal could work against the very individuality the curriculum aimed to foster. The children in both classes shared varied experiences, and in Mrs. Bee's room, they were members of a tightly knit neighborhood. Her children could orally narrate particular and highly *tellable* tales (i.e., stories viewed as engaging and relevant by other children [Ochs & Capps, 2001, p. 34]). However, their inexperience as writers—and their emerging understanding of curricular demands for realness—could reduce elaborate stories to simple statements of liking this or that and going here or there. This was especially so for LaTrell, who tried hard to be "good." The more he understood about what good writers did, the less individual his texts became. So, by midwinter, LaTrell, the little boy who imagined monsters and saved bugs, was just another child swinging at the park in his writings.

From Legal Texts to Competitive Ones: "I Got It First!"

Neither Mrs. Kay's nor Mrs. Bee's children interpreted copying as a simple matter of individual dishonesty. Indeed, initially, Mrs. Bee's admonition against sharing ideas did not even seem salient to her new school entrants, the kindergartners. Their composing time activity tended to be deeply embedded in interaction with paper *and* peers. Below is a partial summary of a long, complex event involving Alicia and LaTrell in November of the school year:

LaTrell is drawing snowmen invading his yard, and Alicia is making relatives attending birthday parties at the park. Soon LaTrell begins to draw his own relatives among the invading snowmen. When Alicia adds a baby brother, LaTrell does too. When LaTrell has his brother bit by a dog, Alicia brings up her own dog. When LaTrell adds a sun, so does Alicia (although LaTrell's spells doom for the snowmen). In this dialogic way, LaTrell's yard full of imposing snowmen and Alicia's park full of celebrating relatives take shape together.

When Ernest, sitting nearby, decides that he will make a snowman too, the more experienced Alicia sees trouble ahead:

ALICIA: Ooo::. He copied offa you.
LATRELL: So?

With his "so?," LaTrell suggested that he saw no significance in Ernest's action. In fact Alicia herself was copying LaTrell, and he was copying her. They were both contributing to and appropriating from the conversational gathering of ideas (referred to years ago by Jimmy Britton [1970, p. 29] as a "sea of talk"). This was a common dynamic among the children "independently" doing their work.

Given her structured curricular guides (which she was to copycat, so to speak) and her inexperienced writers, Mrs. Bee made more explicit efforts to prevent her children from copying than did Mrs. Kay. Moreover, she spent her time circulating among the children at their tables, unlike Mrs. Kay, who spent much of her time conferencing with a child at a separate table. Mrs. Bee, then, was more likely to see a child's text as it sat amid others. When her children did begin to appropriate the admonition against copying, they used it as if it were interchangeable with the phrase "I got it first." That is, copying was a matter of who first claimed ownership of some entity (like snowmen), just as they claimed rights to any valued object that was not private property (e.g., a ball on the playground).

One day in May, the kindergartners were to write their plans for the summer. The children at LaTrell's table had very similar plans. LaTrell began writing, and orally monitoring, the sentence "I go to the park." Cici started writing too and, in similar fashion, began a sentence about playing at the park.

"Me too, y'all!" said Precious joyfully. "I like to play at the park!"

In the background, Mrs. Bee can be heard telling children at another table not to copy off of anybody's paper.

"And Precious," said LaTrell now. "You can't write that 'cause I said that."

"I said 'I like to play at the park with my friends,'" noted Cici in a matter-of-fact voice.

"Actually," piped up Ernest, "I was going to write 'I am going to the park.'"

And so they all wrote about going to the park. No one copied anyone, although they did help one another with spelling. They all just happened to be planning to spend their summer playing at the park.

WRITING A LIFE STORY (OR WRITING IN A SOCIAL LIFE?)

The children in this book were responding to a variant of a particular kind of writing curriculum, one founded on individualism. In this curriculum, children learn basic skills and apply them in their writing, especially the writing of one's life story. In this foundational genre, children draw from the substance of their lives and craft experience on paper—planning, focusing, editing, and (in Mrs. Kay's class) daily sharing.

Such a curriculum seems so sensible—children should learn to write in ways one imagines real writers write (or at least real writers of children's books). But, as evident throughout, this was not the way many "real" children found their way as composers. Certainly children could draw in literally "true" ways on their experiences. However, they assumed elbow room, imaginative space, and authorial relationships that the official worlds did not. Alicia, for example, was much more interested in using writing in her life than in writing her life. Her first year in kindergarten provides vivid illustrations of this elbow room.

When I began observing, in January of that first year, Alicia's writing seemed to consist of quick wavy lines or seemingly random letters, but the situation was more socially and discursively complex than that. Alicia sometimes expressed her feelings about her friends as she made wavy lines on her paper. Moreover, Alicia would ask her friends to write their names on her paper (and their phone numbers if a birthday party was at hand). She would work the letters of their names into her own writing.

Consider, for example, the following event from February of her first year. Mrs. Bee had written a dictated title on each child's paper, and the task was to think about that title and then write a sentence or two. Alicia's title was "Flower," but she seemed preoccupied with her friends Regina and Willo, who were sitting a few chairs down the work table from her:

Alicia is writing today with angled wavy lines. In response to my query, she tells me that she is making "a whole world of flowers" (a lovely thought). Soon, though, the talk accompanying her wavy lines indicates a different agenda.

"Regina's in bad trouble," says Alicia, as her pencil moves up and down across the page. "Willo looks nice and pretty," she continues, as her pencil keeps up its wavy progression.

Alicia looks up and glances at Regina, who gives her a warm smile from down the table. Alicia returns to her writing.

"Me and Regina, me and Willo is friends," she continues, orally reciting the words.

"I'm her friend!" says Regina cheerfully, still looking Alicia's way from the other end of the table.

Alicia takes an eraser and rubs out the earlier made wavy lines. When I ask her why, she explains "Because Regina will be mad."

It seems safe to assume that Regina would not be able to read Alicia's writing; nor was there a sharing time when Alicia would be called upon to formally read her work. Still, the event illustrates Alicia's orientation to her peers and, given that orientation, to a relevant message. It also illustrates how disconnected Alicia was from the individualistic ideology of the curriculum. She was not an individual looking inward, finding her "own" ideas; she was an individual looking outward, finding herself, and her writing, in relation to others. Her social attunement was not a valued resource in the curriculum, but it was a resource nevertheless.

A second vignette, from a few months later, in May, displays Alicia acting within the familiar context of peer play as she makes a more focused composing, and encoding, effort.

Sitting across from Willo, Alicia announced her intention to draw her family. "I'm your sister," declared Willo.

No problem. "I can put you in with my mama and my dada," said Alicia, and she added an extra figure to her hand-holding line of schematic people, all with hearts on their heads. "We're playing sisters, on paper," said Willo joyfully when I asked about the picture.

After this representation of her family, Alicia quickly wrote letters on each of four lines, ending each line with Willo's first and last name. (Alicia had had lessons on the spelling of that name from Willo herself, who did not like her name misspelled and so had taught Alicia using a magnetic letter board.)

When Mrs. Bee came by, Alicia read her piece, which, officially, was to be a letter to her mom for Mother's Day:

Mom, you is me and Willo mommy.
I see Willo in my dreams.
Her is my best sister.

"Hey," said Willo. "There's no two 'Willo,' " and she read her name repeatedly, pointing to each of the four lines where it was displayed.

Willo was thus offering a basic lesson on voice/print match, a concept assumed by the curriculum. You should have read *Willo* more than twice, she was telling her friend, because there are more *Willo*'s in your text.

Alicia had followed directions to a point, clearly writing a piece for her mother or, perhaps, bringing her mother into the play. But she had also responded to her friend Willo. Their conversation was steeped in the pleasure of play and that play provided a context in which Alicia grappled with accurate letters and complex relations between what is written and what is read.

Alicia most certainly benefitted from her work with Mrs. Bee; as Alicia's alphabetic sense grew, her teacher sensitively helped her write brief "true" sentences, much as she helped LaTrell (see Genishi & Dyson, 2009, for a fuller discussion of Mrs. Bee and Alicia). Alicia's actions, though, suggested that her relationships with friends, enacted through expressive messages and pretend play, provided the social energy for her interest in making meaning through graphic symbols. Measured in letters and sounds, orthographically sensible spellings, and focused if brief statements about the self, Alicia had not measured up. The second time through kindergarten, Alicia's writing, like Alicia herself, was more conventional, more attuned to official expectations. Still, Alicia's writing remained an avenue of social participation. She, and the rest of the "basics" kids, will be threaded throughout the chapters to come as they use writing to participate in and construct their lives together.

A CHANGE IN ANGLE OF VISION

Mrs. Bee's and Mrs. Kay's children slid into their seats at their designated tables. Their teachers worked hard to instruct them in the conventional basics. In so doing, they enacted curricula that worked to socialize children into new relationships with one another and, indeed, with their own imaginations (Schieffelin, 1999). The children were to mine their own minds in search of experiential resources for personal truths. The properly progressing child would craft those experiences into proper written language, laid out in the customary way of their primary classrooms—drawings on the top of the page, perhaps accompanied with labels, and topic-focused written sentences on the lined bottom.

But the children had their own agency, fueled not only by their desire to do good for their teachers and their moms, but also by their desire for companionship with peers. This social orientation is key to understanding why, despite the prevailing individualistic ideology, children kept talking to each other. It is key as well to understanding why writing life stories was often more accurately described as writing a shared life.

It is to this shared life that I now turn in the chapters in Part II. In so doing, the official world expectations will be present, but they will fade to the background. To the foreground will come the prevailing ideology of unofficial worlds, which gave rise to its own set of writing ethics and to its own expectations for proper child behavior (and the need for new kinds of skills to meet them). Let's move forward now to the grand social dramas in Part II, to the intricacies of child play on textual playgrounds.

Part II

WRITING "BASICS" IN CHILDHOOD SPACES

> *Play is an arena of choice . . . where life options are limited; play can therefore illuminate how children create autonomous and indigenous arrangements in settings . . . over which they may have relatively little control. (Kirshenblatt-Gilmblett, cited in Dargan & Zeitlin, 1990, p. 28)*

Lyron is the best boy in the
class he is cute to me and Janette
we will both live with him
when we grow up me and Janette
like him he side [said] oh pless [please] he
is verry cute to me and Janette.

In the official world of Mrs. Kay's classroom, Tionna's text had fix-its that needed attention. There was, for example, that pervasive grammatical bugaboo, "me and you" (in this case, "me and Janette"), and then the usual absence of sentence capitalization and punctuation (except for that period marking the end). The student teacher, Ms. Hache, helped Tionna fix her text as follows (results of editing indicated with bold type):

Lyron is the best boy in the
class. **He** is cute to me and Janette.
We will both live with him
                              Janette and I
when we grow up. **[crossed out** *me and Janette* ^**]**
like him. **He said "Oh please."** He
is verry cute to me and Janette.

In the unofficial world, though, there was a drama unfolding. That drama had to do with an ongoing gender game of who likes whom, one that intersected in certain ways with racial identity and, also, with age; the children viewed themselves as "too little" for the real thing (note the reference to "when we grow up," to "11 or 12," or so said Tionna). Despite the anomaly of Tionna's textual declaration of her peer Jon's admirable qualities (see Chapter 4), Lyron was her usual "boyfriend," whom she shared with her friends Janette and Mandisa (both African American, like Lyron—the only African American boy in the class).

However, in her piece, Tionna had mentioned only herself, Janette, and Lyron. No Mandisa! During composing, Lyron had told Tionna to put Mandisa in the text, but Tionna had said she would do that "next time." Months later, when I asked Tionna to read the teacher-edited text, she struggled with the official editing of her grammar. However, she was aghast at the unofficial error—the absence of Mandisa in her text.

It is the last day of my project. School is ending. I tell Tionna that I would love to hear her reading her journals one last time. I turn to her text about Lyron, and Tionna begins.

TIONNA: (reading) "Lyron is the best boy in the class. He is cute to me and Janette. We will both live with him when we grow up. Me, Janette, and I, and Janette—Me, Janette, and I" (pause)
DYSON: I think that's where she [the teacher] was doing that editing.
TIONNA: (sigh) "We will both live with him Janette and I when we grow up. Me, Janette and I and Janette!". . . Supposed to be Mandisa in there too. "And I did—did [inserted] like him. He said, 'Oh please!' (in a tone of exasperation, sounding like Lyron) He is very cute to me and Janette." Where's Mandisa? I ain't put her name in there just once.

Tionna could not make any sense out of the editing of "me and Janette," but she simply could not believe that she left Mandisa out of her text! She had violated some expectation in the peer world that mattered to her.

Part II of this book centers on unofficial peer relations and on the children's expectations for one another's textual actions, given particular practices and, more broadly, particular social relations. Official worlds, and their concerns with conventional basics, by no means disappear; indeed, the official worlds provided key resources for unofficial action, among them graphic materials, social companions, and, of course, guidance on written language itself. But unofficial worlds provided familiar social relations, shared experiential knowledge (like media figures and local pleasures), and common practices (like dramatic play) that could make writing "relevant to [a child's] life" (Vygotsky, 1978, p. 118).

The children's textual productions thus became hybrids, simultaneously belonging to multiple worlds (Bakhtin, 1981). Unfolding texts were subject to fix-its in the official world *and* in the unofficial one. The unofficial fix-its—particularly the children's efforts to monitor appropriate social roles and actions—suggested new kinds of skills, ones necessary for developing, maintaining, and participating in a complex peer world (cf. Jenkins, 2009). As Bauman (1982) noted over 30 years ago, when we look beyond the social roles and participation structures of school, we find children displaying linguistic and sociolinguistic flexibility as they organize and enact social roles in play (see also Goodwin & Goodwin, 2006).

Children's unofficial or peer cultures have been documented by ethnographers working in preschools and elementary schools (e.g., Corsaro, 1985, 2003; Dyson, 2003a; Thorne, 1993, 2005). These cultures are dynamic, interactive, and played out in recurrent activities undergirded by shared values (Corsaro, 2011). During composing time in Mrs. Bee's and Mrs. Kay's classes, children's interest in one another's activity helps situate their writing within, and contributes to, peer cultures. Unofficial worlds align with the ideology of responsiveness so evident in these classrooms beyond writing time. In this dialogic ideology of child selves, children articulate their *selves* as they respond to other selves with whom they construct their lives (Bakhtin, 1990).

In the chapters to follow, then, children imbue official time and space for writing with social and cultural meanings. Writing workshop thus becomes, at least sometimes, a place for the choreography of children and of textual actions, organized by practices on no one's list of expected lessons. In such a place, there is a need, not only to be an officially "good" writer, but also an unofficially good companion who, to quote Tionna, knows how to "play fun games." Of course, the resulting peer worlds are not idyllic—nor are the children, for that matter. (They are, after all, *our* children.) Their actions can entail local manifestations of the power dynamics of societal constructs like gender and race.

In Chapter 5, I take another look at texts and consider a new typology of fix-its, one grounded in a relational, rather than a hierarchical, view of language. As Tionna and Lyron have suggested, these fix-its are situated within the social expectations, practices, and histories of peer relations. In Chapter 5 I also introduce five participation modes—or *indigenous arrangements*—of the children's play, which form the organizing framework for Chapters 6–8.

Listen, dear readers, can you hear Mrs. Bee's and Mrs. Kay's children calling one another to task over some textual violation, a basic slight, as it were? Let's move on so you can get a sense of what all the ado is about.

Shifting Expectations and Differing Ethics
Entering Childhood Cultures

I am in Mrs. Bee's kindergarten on this May day, sitting by Jamal. Coretta comes over, wanting to read me her story, and I am quite agreeable. On the first page is a picture of a car in front of a big building with double doors, and, on the second, three girls standing in front of that building. These are stick-figure girls with chin-length curved lines on either side of their heads (marking them as Coretta's just-a-quick-sketch girls, with no elaborate hair dos or high-heeled shoes). Coretta's written text is about liking to go to the mall and about her plan to bring her friends along with her on a mall trip.

"What about me?" says the observant Jamal. "I'm your friend." Moreover, he continues, *he* is the one driving the car to the mall. "For real."

Coretta, who is standing, leans over, puts her paper on the table, and, in full view of Jamal, begins drawing another stick figure, one with no hair hanging down, just a line across the top of the head. (In truth, Jamal has dreadlocks.)

"You're gonna add him," I say, quite interested in the turn of events.

"I *have* to," says Coretta softly.

"I *have* to," said Coretta, but, in the official world, she did not have to. Mrs. Bee was not telling Coretta to fix her piece. This fix-it arose from a situated encounter between two children who identified as friends. "I *have* to," said Coretta, but she did not have to. She could have responded by positioning herself as a girl; that is, she could have said, "Only us girls are going to the mall," but she did not. She could have responded as a good student; that is, she could have said, "You make your story how you want it; this is my story," but she did not. She made a choice as an individual—an individual who defined herself in relation to others in a particular kind of textual circumstance. In this circumstance, as Jamal rightly surmised, Coretta was playing with her friends—she was pretending to go to the mall, and he wanted to play too. He would be the driver (perhaps the *male* driver, taking *the girls* to the mall, but that is just a perhaps).

Like Tionna (in the introduction to Part II), who did not respond positively to Lyron's request to add Mandisa, Jamal and Coretta bring us deep within the children's worlds, in which a different ideology of selves prevailed and, thereby, a different notion of the good writer. The good writer that Coretta was trying to be, and Tionna could not believe she failed to be, has responsibilities tied to human relations and human identities. That is, the good writer is an individual whose symbol-making decisions are negotiated against a social horizon.

This notion of the good writer has links to the philosopher Appiah's analysis of ethics as tied to "thick relations . . . to our identities" (2005, p. 233). We feel a sense of obligation, and of purpose, through our membership in particular communities, be they large ethnic ones, or smaller ones among family or friends. Similarly, this take on the ethical writer also has links to the language philosopher Bakhtin's dialogic stance. As Clark and Holquist (1984) explain, Bakhtin connected ethics to responsiveness; ethics are not

> abstract principles but [rather] the pattern of the actual deeds I perform in the event that is my life. My self is that which through such performance answers other selves and the world from the unique place and time I occupy in existence. (p. 64)

Through language use, the self enters into relationships with others and, in the process, negotiates a particular social situation and, at the same time, a sense of how she or he belongs in the world—that is, a complex, multifaceted identity. Am I a friend? Jamal asks Coretta. If so, I should get to play on your paper too.

The angle of vision, then, is now firmly on the dialogic, not the separate, self; and it locates texts in relationships, not in hierarchies of correctness. From this angle, children's writing entails new kinds of basic knowledge and skill—the social ability, for example, to attune to others and to an ongoing activity, to adopt a relevant role, to contribute relevant material, and to coordinate with another. Being relevant entails knowledge of locally valued cultural material, be it media pleasures, traditional folklore, or indigenous (peer-constructed) games. Textual decisions are not just about the crafting of an experience but also about the negotiating of identity, role, and activity.

This analytic angle allows me to hone in on children constructing writing as part of their construction of childhood relations and practices.

The dynamics of Mrs. Kay's and Mrs. Bee's children's social and textual work were most visible and audible when a child felt another's textual action needed correction. Thus, in the children's worlds, new kinds of fix-its appeared. In the following sections I introduce these fix-its and the child-organized social frameworks through which their relations, and their texts, took shape.

RELATIONAL FIX-ITs:
"PUT MY NAME IN THERE!"

The fix-its introduced by the children were not isomorphic with those officially introduced. In official, hierarchical fix-its, the textual problem was evident on the page—a word was missing, a capital letter was awry, a sentence was incomplete. In situated (or relational) fix-its, child evaluators looked, not just at the page, but at the social world beyond the page (see Figure 5.1).

Relational fix-it episodes are illustrated in the chapters to come. I provide here samples of the two dominant categories of situated fix-its (i.e., samples of Figure 5.1, I. Textual Choices and II. Content Adjustments).

Situated Textual Choices:
The Discursive Problem of Male Friendship

Tionna, Lyron, Jamal, and Coretta have already introduced the problematic nature of articulating friendship. Their examples, however, all entailed "liking" between boys and girls or among girls themselves. Liking among boys was a more tenuous textual venture. One's wording mattered. In both the kindergarten and the 1st grade, boys had "frns [friends]," to use LaTrell's spelling, but a declaration of liking could be viewed as in need of fixing, as in the following episode:

One March day, 1st-grader Brad writes about his current table-mate and sometime play companion, Lyron: *He is so cool I like him.*

Lyron seems pleased when Brad reads him his piece. (Later, during sharing time, Lyron will tell his classmates to "Listen!" when Brad goes to the front of the class to read.) Still, Lyron has a fix-it for Brad:

LYRON: Brad, you should say, I like him *for a friend.* Otherwise they'll [the class will] think you like him [me] as a boyfriend.
TIONNA: No we won't. (dismissively)
JON: You're just friends.

Figure 5.1. Situated Conception of Writing Fix-Its

I.   Textual Choices: Making It Sound Better[1] Given . . .
     A. *Ideological Ramifications.* "Say it like this, or people will think"; example: the implications of boys declaring that they "like" other boys.
     B. *Practice Expectations.* Either "That doesn't go there" or "Say this"; example: "The End" does not belong at the end of a "playing-at-somebody's-house" text.
     C. *Aesthetic Judgments.* "Does this [e.g., joke, song] sound good?"
     D. *Utterance Performance.* "That's not how it goes"; example: a known song, a line from a fictional or actual character.
II. Content Adjustments: Being Appropriate Given . . .[2]
     A. *Social Expectations for Inclusion.* Example, "You said I was coming [so why didn't you write my name?]"
     B. *Reciprocal Obligations.* "You better write about this too"; example: in the text-mediated "playing-at-somebody's-house" game, in which children wrote plans for fictional get-togethers.
     C. *Prescribed Identity.* Example: "You [girls] don't even know about war," and thus shouldn't be writing about it.
     D. *Group Knowledge.* Example: being accurate in saying who likes whom when enacting girl friend/boy friend play.
     E. *Bureaucratic Negotiations.* Example: adjusting date of entry and/or adverbials ("yesterday" for "today") in order to be able to read an already written but not shared text as "today's writing" to the class.
III. Graphological Decisions: Making Better Graphic Choices Given . . .
     A. Aesthetic Aspirations[3]
        1. *Qualities of the Human Voice.* Example: "I want to make it sound happy" through use of the exclamation point.
        2. *Visual Qualities of the Page (and, Potentially, of Screen).* Example: "I made it look cool" through reformatting the page, writing two words per line.
     B. Time/Space Exigencies
        1. *Efficiency.* Example: "I can do it shorter" through using abbreviations, or to avoid erasing, through using "carrots" for insertions and slash lines for deletions.
        2. *Boundary Extensions.* Example: responding to the perceived formatting requirement of one (and only one) page per day by putting any additional text on the bottom of, or in a drawn box on, the next page, thereby saving the bulk of that page for the next day's writing.

---

1. The kindergartners initially wrote by drawing, and moreover, most children's texts were multimodal. For that reason, variants of Category I occurred that focused on graphic features and "making it look better," rather than just "sound better." This was particularly evident in Mrs. Bee's kindergarten.

2. Similarly, variants of Category II occurred that focused on graphic content beyond written language; this was again particularly evident in the kindergarten.

3. Ezekial also used editing symbols for aesthetic reasons—he used carets to make his lines of text zig zag, so to speak, but this did not involve fix-its.

Source: Adapted from Dyson, 2006, pp. 18–19.

Lyron suggested that Brad fix his wording and sentence structure for ideological reasons (Figure 5.1, IA). Lyron tended to judge strictly children's verbal and social behavior against his sense of gender appropriateness, judgments regularly countered by others. Readers may recall (from Chapter 2) that Lyron had planned to bring Valentines only for the girls until Mrs. Kay intervened. Nevertheless, Lyron's stance on the gendered and sexualized *like* was consistent with unofficial local conventions. A girl could write that she *liked* another girl with no apparent censure, but boys seemed confined to having a *friend* or liking a boy—usually many boys— *for a friend*.

This is but one example of a fix-it based on contextualized ideological ramifications. Gender ideologies were textually at play in both Mrs. Kay's and Mrs. Bee's classrooms. As the master early childhood educator Vivian Paley commented years ago, young children "think they have invented the differences between boys and girls and . . . must prove that it works" (1984, p. ix)—or that it doesn't. For Brad, the fix-it issue with Lyron led to Writing More and Adding Details (refer to Figure 3.1, IIA, B). That is, an unofficial and situated fix-it could provide a reason for officially valued *hierarchical* ones. (Brad did not, by the way, add "for a friend" to his text, as Lyron suggested. But he did add that Lyron had girl friends and named them; that addition met with Lyron's approval.)

Situated Content Adjustments: Beyond Inclusion to Reciprocity

For one child to name another in their text could be seen as a gift (or, at least potentially, as an insult [Lensmire, 1994]). Moreover, as Jamal and Coretta illustrated, inclusion could be expected, given peer relations, ongoing practice, and textual content (Figure 5.1, IIA). If Coretta's friends were going to the mall, why then, Jamal should be going too.

More socially sophisticated were reciprocal obligations (Figure 5.1, IIB) among writers. As discussed in Chapter 1, LaTrell wanted Ernest to put his name in the planned birthday sleepover text; to this end, he wrote Ernest's name on his own paper as he discussed *his* upcoming birthday. In so doing, LaTrell was attempting to transform the boys' individual texts into an opportunity for a mailbox exchange, so to speak—I make my move, now you respond with yours. Although LaTrell was not successful, it is such reciprocal relations, when copied by others, which may give rise to local childhood practices.

In part because kindergartners were new to writing and writing workshop, they did not necessarily understand the desires of a peer wanting textual admission. Early in the project year, Alicia, who had learned about reciprocal possibilities her first time through kindergarten, was quite frustrated with Jamal, as illustrated below:

It is the third week of kindergarten. Mrs. Bee has given a spirited lesson on the importance of independence and of each child thinking about their experiences and what they plan to write. When the lesson is over, the children go off to their tables. Jamal, Alicia, and others at their work table have been drawing and talking about mermaids. Jamal has made clear that, on his paper, he is "a mermaid, but I'm not a girl mermaid."

Alicia has made a row of mermaids, and one, she announces to the table, is Jamal! Indeed, there is a "J" underneath Jamal the Mermaid (see Figure 5.2).

Figure 5.2. Alicia's Mermaids

Alicia now tells Jamal that he needs to put her and her name in his picture (Figure 5.1, IIB). But Jamal does not. She tries to show him how to write her name on his paper. But Jamal grabs his paper away. Alicia complains loudly that he doesn't want her in his picture! But Jamal is not moved.

Moreover Jamal feels that Alicia has misrepresented his identity (a variant of Figure 5.1, IA, Ideological Ramifications, focused on how a product looks, not how it sounds). Alicia's mermaids have circle heads out of which emanate roughly rectangular bodies (most are longer than those of her usual people); mermaids or not, all have short arms and legs. In Jamal's view, the gender implication of the body shape is not appropriate:

JAMAL: Hey, you got me in a dress!
ALICIA: No I didn't, no I didn't, no I didn't, no I didn't.
JAMAL: I do have a dress on. That's me [the shorter "mermaid" alongside
    the elongated swimming ones in Figure 5.2; that mermaid has a more
    triangular than rectangular body]. And you gave me a dress.
ALICIA: I'm not—this is not a dress. . . . That's boys' pants. Boys have pants
    with ties. (Of course, one might wonder if boy mermaids have pants with
    ties!)
JAMAL: You gave me a dress though.

Jamal's own mermaids, like his people, were in the main composed of a single circle for body and head, with appendages (legs and arms). After talking with Alicia, he attempted to make a mermaid like hers, with a differentiated head and body. (He did not, however, give the mermaid a name, like "Alicia.") As for Alicia, after this encounter, she abruptly changed her way of making people. She drew stick figures (no more bodies like dresses), and when she needed to differentiate gender, she did so by drawing hair of differing lengths, just as Coretta did. (Examples of Alicia's new people are presented in Figure 5.3.)

Alicia's fix-it, grounded in a sense of reciprocal obligations, led Jamal to a fix-it comment of his own. The children's encounter revealed tensions in their sense of the ongoing social event and, moreover, in ideological positioning: the child declaring the self as a "*boy* mermaid" had differing sensitivities than the one who could adopt the usual gendered identity of "mermaid." This tension led to more deliberate use of "organized material [symbolic] expression," to borrow from Bakhtin's colleague Volosinov (1986, p. 84). Their multimodal products became more differentiated—more developed, as it were.

For kindergartner Alicia, as for 1st-grader Brad, more deliberate symbolic action resulted from a situated and relational encounter. In the

Figure 5.3. Alicia's People Riding in Car

chapters to come, the social dynamics in the children's worlds will sometimes lead to more sophisticated official texts (i.e., ones evidencing traditional literacy "basics"). At the least, they will situate writing within the
relational work and imaginative play of evolving childhood worlds.

ORGANIZING AND ENACTING RELATIONSHIPS:
"CAN I PLAY?"

If we are to probe deeply how children's writing is contextualized in childhood relationships and practices, I need to provide you, valued readers,
with a vocabulary for talking about these social formations. An interest

in understanding a child culture would seem to suggest that the focus should be on routine activities (Corsaro, 2011). That is, one would ask, what is it that children do together that constructs their very experience of childhood?

Since the concern here is unofficial writing basics, the focus would now logically turn to those recurrent activities oriented around producing and using text. There is a problem with this, though. Mrs. Kay's 1st-graders and, especially, Mrs. Bee's kindergartners, were just learning to write. Their practices could be quite nascent and unstable. For that reason, I offer another way of initially capturing what children do together—*participation modes*. These refer to identifiable ways that children in both classrooms organized their interactions with one another (cf. Goffman, 1981; Goodwin & Goodwin, 2006; Philips, 1972). As Hanks (2000, p. 171) explains, such social frameworks allow a text to have a "voice"; that is, texts have a "reconstructible framework of participants for, to, and through whom the text speaks."

Sometimes children's interactions *would* become identifiable practices with expected (fix-it generating) norms. In Mrs. Kay's 1st grade especially, what began as playful interactions between two or three children could spread throughout the class, becoming recognized practices driven by certain goals and comprised of certain anticipated if schematic textual actions (cf. Corsaro & Johannsen, 2007). In these instances, the practices were spread by children's desires for inclusion, especially in games of love, war, and get-togethers.

Chapters 6–8 are organized around participation modes. The modes will not be unfamiliar to readers. After all, children have been interacting throughout the pages of this book. For example, the modes include a *collegial interest* in one another's symbol-making. From the earliest weeks of kindergarten, children's talk revealed how cognizant they were of, and interested in, one another's doing. Recall, for example, from Chapter 3, how Jamal's drawing of snakes and cookies garnered much interest from other children—and a spontaneous proliferation of snakes! These collegial relations undergirded other ways in which children organized themselves vis-à-vis one another.

Among those other modes were children's efforts for deliberately *coordinated actions*. The simplest form of this mode was heard in Chapter 4, when Mandisa called out to Tionna, inviting her to share a familiar topic: "You want to write about you-know-what?" (And Tionna did know "you-know-what.") An ability to coordinate one's composing with another itself gives rise to new possibilities. Key among these possibilities are *complementary relations*, in which children not only share a topic but also separate their roles as social players and, thus, as composers. Birthday party play involved this mode of relating. If I as author invite you to a pretend party, then you as author should write that you are coming to my pretend party (in truth, this is the only kind of party we'll be having).

The reciprocity at the heart of complementary relations undergirded those fix-its about inclusion and reciprocal relations earlier discussed. In nascent form, these relations could involve only one child author and an aggrieved other; for example, Jamal felt he should be in Coretta's text about friends. The full-blown capacity to enact complementary relations as authors and social players undergirded the most complex dramatic narratives to come, those in which child relations took the form of *collaborative improvisation*. In improvisation not only were children's roles contingent on one another (e.g., party giver, invitee), so too were their very words, which evolved dialogically. In war play especially, the metaphor of a textual playground was literally played out. Indeed, when Tionna first decided to join in that play, she asked, "Can I play?"

Finally, there is one last major participation mode to be played out in the chapters ahead—*performance*. In this mode, a child performer played to an audience of others. In Mrs. Bee's kindergarten, children often had to seek out, or imagine, an audience. In Mrs. Kay's 1st grade, children could anticipate the official sharing-time event and plan for specific kinds of reactions; most often, they aimed to amuse. Using a traditional cultural perspective on performance, Tionna and others will be viewed as they exploit the aesthetic power of both voice and image in their texts to garner others' attention and appreciation for such practices as song-writing and storytelling (Bauman, 1992). Using a sociolinguistic perspective, they will also be seen manipulating symbolic material—including grammatical variation itself—in order to adopt different voices in their texts and, thereby, assume different relations in the world.

These were the major participation modes shaping, and shaped by, children's ongoing symbol making, but they were not the only modes that occurred. As readers may recall, in Mrs. Bee's kindergarten, children sometimes assumed competitive stances toward one another, since in their view, they needed to claim a topic first to avoid copying. Still, writing in and of itself was not a competition. Occasionally, a child might say to another "beat you" when finishing a day's writing, but that was a boast, not a call to compete. Most dramatically, competition could be a playful relation and, at heart, a collaborative enterprise. This was the case in 1st-graders' textual war play—one child's team aimed to defeat another's; the resultant collaborative improvisations were full of boasts as to who would beat whom.

Pedagogical relations also could occur, in which one child would help another. The seeking of help was much more common in Mrs. Bee's kindergarten than Mrs. Kay's 1st grade, particularly at the beginning of the year when children tended to seek help from anyone who seemed to know how to "make the words." Still, as the year progressed, LaTrell, Alicia, and most of their peers sought help from, and provided help to each other as part of a collegial mode. There was a mutual helping with no recognized authority (except for Alexia, unusual in Mrs. Bee's room, as she entered school with sound/symbol knowledge; Alexia positioned herself as someone who helped others but took no help herself).

In sum, through participation modes and practices, children positioned themselves within ongoing activity; they slipped into roles and aimed to be relevant, in sync, and included. They used their symbolic resources, and their social know-how, to participate in peer worlds that were linked to, but distinctive from, official worlds. I, as their adult friend, observed their efforts, attended to their textual actions and their textual fix-its, and in the process, re-imagined the "basics" of written communication.

A CAUTION ABOUT DEVELOPMENTAL ORDER

Mrs. Bee's and Mrs. Kay's classrooms were distinctive cases, but in both, children were actively participating in official and unofficial worlds. In the chapters to follow, the children from both rooms join together in my own textual play to illustrate the basics of writing in childhood worlds. The chapters are arranged in order of social and textual complexity. That is, the later-discussed modes (complementary relations and collaborative improvisations) included more deliberate, more extended textual interaction.

The most extended interactions appeared in Mrs. Kay's room. However, I make no claim for a set developmental order. Children in each room exploited local opportunities for composing. Mrs. Kay's children *were* more experienced students and more experienced writers than Mrs. Bee's. However, they also had more opportunities to play, and as will be seen, this allowed practices to migrate across classroom places and to be enacted through varied media, among them construction blocks, body movements, cut-and-paste craft, and written genres possible only outside the constraints of official writing time. Thus, practices could interconnect and, thereby, accrue rich layers of cultural meaning.

Notwithstanding these differences in classroom opportunities and constraints, I do make a major claim: By focusing the research angle on children's social interactions, it is possible to see how children's composing is organized by a desire for companionship. When children act on their interest in one another and on what others are doing, their social and textual attunement can give rise to participatory childhood cultures. In the process, children may learn something more basic than letters, sounds, and sight words (although they may find a reason to concentrate on those particulars); they may learn a sense of meditational agency, that is, a consciousness of how symbolic media are used to participate in and shape the social world.

With caution and claim explained, it is time, then, for the curtain to rise on childhood cultures in formation in Mrs. Bee and Mrs. Kay's rooms . . .

CHAPTER 6

Collegial Relations and Coordinated Actions
Textual Handclaps

Writing time has ended. Mrs. Bee is getting the lunch cards ready as the kindergartners sit at their tables. Soon two little girls begin a rhythmic clapping game that spreads throughout the room, encompassing girls and boys.

"Shame, shame, shame," it starts, as, on each beat, the partners sweep their praying hands against one another's. Then the rhythmic clapping begins:

> I don't want to go to Mexico
> No more more more
> There's a big fat policeman
> At my door door door

The lines that follow depend upon the version of the game being played, but, in all, that problematic policeman does damage, grabbing one by the collar or the hips, looking for a dollar or lips.

Mrs. Bee has her lunch cards together now. She shushes her children, gets them in line, and the coordinating twosomes now stretch themselves out in a wavy line and wind out the classroom door and down the hall.

Clapping games, like rhythmic plays and cheerleads, were heard in both Mrs. Kay's and Mrs. Bee's rooms, although not to the same degree nor in the same way. In Mrs. Kay's ethnically diverse classroom, African American girls were the dominant hand clappers and rhythmic players out on the blacktop. The little girls, like Tionna and her 1st-grade friends, watched the older girls in other classes and learned new plays from them. Mrs. Bee's children had neither blacktop nor extended recess time, but, still, a game or two could show up in down times in the classroom when children were waiting for the next event—like lunch!

As folk traditions, these games and plays are passed down through generations but localized to current conditions (Powell, 2012). They have not only crossed historical time and geographic location but also societal boundaries. In Mrs. Bee's room, boys did not resist the rhythmic beat of the "Shame" game; and, in Mrs. Kay's, the girls' racialized and gendered playground boundaries were crossed by diverse "others" who wanted in on the action (even by Lyron, who tended to monitor gender boundaries diligently). Such games highlight, not competition, but dramatic action and group participation. They are "a beautiful and democratic tradition, full of joy and the juices of life" (Jones & Hawes, 1972, p. xxi).

This sort of coordinated action, a common choreography of child cultures (Corsaro, 2011), could also be found in children's composing times. This chapter introduces these textual handclaps, including both deliberately coordinated actions for text-mediated affiliation and less organized collegial interest in others' productions. There will be some literal textual handclaps in Chapter 8, but for now, metaphoric ones are of interest—these ways in which children responded to and coordinated their textual actions with one other.

WRITTEN LANGUAGE AND THE
MEDIATION OF CHILDHOOD CULTURES

ALICIA: (to Ella, who is drawing and writing next to her) Here you [Ella]. Here Denise [another peer]. Here my auntie.

ELLA: Where's the bathing suit?

ALICIA: I don't have a bathing suit.

ELLA: So you're gonna be naked. . . . Don't make me naked. Put some clothes on me. . . . (to the kindergarten girls drawing and writing around her) Whoever got me in the[ir] picture will come to my birthday. It will be in the summer. It will be in Chicago.

ALICIA: O::!

The weather was unusually warm on this late February day, and Mrs. Bee had asked her children to write about a hoped-for summer pleasure. Alicia, Ella, and the other girls at their table all found themselves swimming in the water. To be included in someone else's drawn pool was valued—worth an invitation to a birthday party (even if the invitation itself *and* the party, were imagined). Thus, Alicia and her peers used composing as a meditational tool both to represent a desired summer scene—swimming in the local pool—and to negotiate their own relationships. Alicia said to Ella, "This you"; in so doing she transformed her lines and curves into Ella swimming with her in the pool—and, at the very same time, she brought Ella closer to her in the ongoing social world. Ella was pleased to be in Alicia's pool, so to speak, although she did not want to be naked in that pool! (An ideological fix-it, refer to Figure 5.1, IA.) In response, Ella offered Alicia—and anyone else who included her in their symbolic world—a place in her birthday party. Moreover, she then included Alicia in her picture and wrote "I am pw [playing with] alcha [Alicia]," thereby avoiding a potential fix-it of reciprocal obligations (Figure 5.1, IIB).

In such ways, children learn the cultural act of writing—of participating in the social and intellectual life around them through the "relevant" tool of written language (Vygotsky, 1978, p. 118). Children seem more likely to engage in such dialogic actions with their peers, rather than with their teachers, at least in part because they are closer in status, interests, and position in school. The fundamental relation undergirding their joint participation is a collegial one.

"Me Too": Collegial Relations

Children's talk during writing revealed how cognizant they were of, and interested in, one another's doing. This articulation of interest is referred to herein as *collegial*. Such relations were a pervasive feature of children's lives together. For example, they were on display during the familiar practice of oral storytelling rounds. As people do across cultures, the children told stories about the remarkable and the unusual, sometimes performing a story with dramatic flair in order to wrap others into their social space (Bauman, 2004; Ochs & Capps, 2001). One story could engender others' stories; "I hear you," listeners seemed to say, "and something like that happened to me."

Rounds of storytelling occurred in both Mrs. Bee's and Mrs. Kay's rooms. And, in both, children could slip into a more performative mode. In the following oral vignette, Alicia takes her narrative cue from her kindergarten tablemates, responding to the evolving talk (even though she had never attended preschool, the setting of her peer Odette's initiating story); in turn, Odette takes narrative license with a plot element of Alicia's story—that of flying:

Alicia, Odette, and Della are completing a reading activity centered on the phrase "A cat scared of a bat." They share stories of seeing bats, and then Odette recalls seeing birds in an odd place:

ODETTE: Guess what? In preschool, there were some birds in the lunch room. . . . I seen some birds on my food, and they go, "Peep peep peep."

DELLA: Guess what? I seen some birds in a store.

ODETTE: Oh my goodness.

ALICIA: Me too [facing Odette]. They were way up on the ceiling "Peep peep
   . . ." And they were—came flying down. I tried to catch it but it flew
   back up.

ODETTE: (continuing her story by building on Alicia's) And then I was starting
   to fly, and I tried to catch one. . . .

ALICIA: (apparently responding to Odette's location of her story in preschool)
   What school was you [Della] in?

DELLA: A preschool.

ALICIA: I was in a preschool! (in an amazed "me too" voice, seemingly
   wanting to be included in this experience common in her classroom)

DELLA: I was in a different preschool.

ALICIA: I was in a different preschool. It was far away, real far away.

ODETTE: Mine was like . . . 100 thousand pounds.

ALICIA: Mines too! (in that same amazed voice)

Peeping birds in schools and stores, flying birds and a flying child—when
community participants take a discursive turn, their utterances borrow
from and respond to the texts of others; thus, their turns are dialogically
linked (Bakhtin, 1981).

During writing workshop time, this familiar practice, and its social
relations, provided a well-worn avenue into composing. The children's
oral responsiveness blended with graphic responsiveness, a collegial action that could result in apparent copying. Asked to draw and write a
"real" story, children did not necessarily have *a* topic but, rather, an evolving conversation and a play with ideas; individual productions could link
together and then veer off.

In the kindergarten, this spontaneous linking of discursive turns led to
Mrs. Bee's first discussions of keeping stories real and not copying somebody else's real experiences. To illustrate, consider the following vignette,
from September of the kindergarten year, featuring Alicia's peers LaTrell,
Cici, and their tablemates:

Mrs. Bee has just interrupted the children's composing of a "true" story to
reiterate that the children were to sketch "something that's really real about
you." She cautions against writing about Spider-Man and other "not really
real" characters that only seem to fly because they are attached to strings.
After the children return to their composing, LaTrell has a comment about
flying—but not a superhero flying:

LATRELL: I seen a balloon when I went on my—

Cici: I seen a air balloon! It was up in the sky.
LaTrell: It was the color blue. Yeah, it went all the way in the sky.
Cici: It was over by my day care. (raising voice) Ms. Bee, we seen the air balloon!
Della: Me too! I saw the air balloon.

As "Me too's" arise from the room, Mrs. Bee comments:

Mrs. Bee: Everybody didn't see an air balloon now. ("I did"'s can be heard all around.) Only the things you really did see.

At his table, LaTrell draws a flying balloon.

LaTrell: I'm gonna make a air balloon.
Cici: I seen an air balloon. Red, yellow, different colors!

Now other children are making air balloons. Cici notes that she and LaTrell stand out among the crowd:

Cici: You all got one. Me and him got two.
LaTrell: I got two air balloons!

Soon, though, one of LaTrell's air balloons sprouts petals and becomes a flower, and another grows appendages and becomes him flying in the air, propelled by his mother:

LaTrell: This how I went up in the sky when I was a baby. My mommy throw me up in the sky. I couldn't come down. I didn't know I couldn't come down. A robot catched me [in my pictured adventure].

In the end, children at LaTrell's table had drawn air balloons because they had seen them or, perhaps, wanted to see them. And LaTrell, whose products were fluid, moved from a flying air balloon to his own flying through the air, saved by a conveniently located robot. In a similar way children exchanged varied kinds of stories, including recurring ones of getting bitten by sharks in the lake, the pool, or even the bath tub! In this mode, the children did not copy in the official sense; they conversed, and that conversing shaped their composing.

The described collegiality seems similar to that reported by Matthews (1999), based on his studies of young children drawing together; across cultures, children's evolving productions were linked through their conversational topics and rhythms. They seemed attuned to their peers as well as to the possibilities and constraints of the page. Thus, children's symbol-making became a "spatio-temporal theater of symbolic play" (Matthews, 1999, pp. 9–10).

Collegial talk, though, could entail more than an interest in one another's stories. It could, for example, include a kind of supportive "I gotcha" talk, to quote Alicia's friend Ella—a providing of help, for example, mutual assistance in sounding out a spelling, a content suggestion, or an inquiry about *sense*. This occurred despite the official position that children should spell independently. For example, in the following brief vignette, Alicia is talking with Ella and Denise about how Tinker Bell dresses. (Her ideas are based on toys she has seen at a large discount store, not on the then current movie, which she has not seen.)

ALICIA: Don't Tinker Bell have dresses?

ELLA: Yes, 'cause I watched the movie.

DENISE: Me too. I watched the movie.

ALICIA: Ella, no Tinker Bell has no pants on, girl.

ELLA: I know that. But they fly. So you might wanta draw fly. And you might wanta do dots.

DENISE: Tinker Bell don't have no dots. (a situated fix-it based on shared knowledge, Figure 5.1, IID)

ELLA: Yeah she do.

ALICIA: On their dresses they do. Sometimes on their nails they do. Sometimes they don't.

ELLA: "My cat is white"—(rereading her own piece)

ALICIA: (rereading) . . . "My Tinker Bell is" cute. I forgot to write *cute*!

ELLA: And you said *pretty* too! (potentially a hierarchical fix-it about a planned detail, [refer to Figure 3.1 IIB], although it is situated in a discussion of shared knowledge, [Figure 5.1, IID]; Alicia does not write *cute* but tries *pretty*)

ALICIA: How you spell *pretty*?

ELLA: "My cat is" pretty. How you spell *pretty*?

ALICIA: P-E

ELLA: /Pre/ /ty/, pretty

And together the girls came up with *prety*.

ALICIA: Oh, you, me, and Denise lost two teeth.

The girls' shared interest in Tinker Bell couched their talk about hierarchical concerns, like graphological conventions, as well as situated ones, like being accurate in their shared knowledge of that popular figure. More complex concerns about both hierarchical and situated fix-its are evident in the following vignette featuring 1st-graders Tionna and Ezekial. Still, the mode of participation—the easy collegiality—is similar.

Tionna and Ezekial are sitting side-by-side as they work to complete an assigned worksheet template that reads: *A ____ is a house for a ____.* The children are to "think" before they write, says Mrs. Kay. And there should be "no talking" adds her student teacher Ms. Hache. But talking there is.

TIONNA: (to Ezekial) You know what I wrote? *A school is a house for a teacher.*
EZEKIAL: You know what I wrote? *A heart is a house for Jesus.*
. . .
TIONNA: O::! You just gave me a idea, Ezekial. (erasing her words) You know what I'm gonna write? "The sky is [a house] for Jesus."
EZEKIAL: No, you mean heaven. (Tionna has a fix-it, in his view; her content needs adjusting, given their assumed shared religious knowledge [Figure 5.1, IID])
TIONNA: No, sky. You don't say heaven. . . . You say he lives in the sky. He's the one who gives you lives. . . .
EZEKIAL: Jon, you should put, "A heart is for—a house for Jesus."
JON: "A bed is a home for me!" (Jon is attached to his planned text.)

Tionna has started to fill in the template. She reads *A* and writes *ski*. She reads *is a home for* but does not read the next word [*a*]; instead, she offers pedagogical insight to Ezekial:

TIONNA: If you want to do something else, all you have to do is cross it out. (She crosses out *a* and writes *god*. "A god" does not seem to sound right.)

Ezekial has his own pedagogical insight to share:

EZEKIAL: It's a little tricky. You have to put a capital *Go* for *God*. (This was a hierarchical fix-it—Figure 3.1, IIIA, graphological conventions.)
TIONNA: I know. . . . (adjusts her *g* and starts drawing God as a little dot in the biggest cloud) I'm gonna draw a little spot for God. This is gonna be the biggest cloud, 'cause God lives in the biggest cloud, doesn't he? . . . I have . . . a hair tie that say, "I love Jesus". . . . I got it at my church, 'cause they said that I was—I was the best kid at my church 'cause I was singing. And I had to go up on the stage.
EZEKIAL: Me and [my sister] Amy sing a song like [humming a song]. (Ezekial is saying he sings church songs too.)
TIONNA: Here's God. And I'm about to put—draw Jesus 'cause Jesus his son. See, they both live in the sky. But that's not funny that—but that's not funny that God died and Jesus did too. My cousin—my cousin he was laughing at Jesus and he died.
EZEKIAL: Tell him not to say it.

TIONNA: He already died 'cause he was laughing at Jesus. . . . They put him
     [Jesus] up on the cross and they stabbed him. But that wasn't—
EZEKIAL: . . . That's gotta hurt. . . .
TIONNA: (rereading her text) The sky is a house for God.
EZEKIAL: AND JESUS!

Tionna accepts this fix-it, situated in their ongoing relationship as
knowledgeable church-goers (Figure 5.1, IID), and she adds the suggested
words.

This lengthy excerpt richly illustrates collegial relationships based,
in this instance, on a comfort with religious discourse, rather than with
a media figure. Ezekial and Tionna's collegiality led to a shared topic
and mutual advice, grounded in a common desire to appropriately represent God through iconic signs (pictures) and discursive, orthographic
ones—God does not follow an article, nor is a deity dressed in lower-case
garb.

Such easy collegiality was evident in both classrooms and helped situate writing within the relations and practices of the children. Thus it was
foundational to all other modes of participation, including the one considered below: the deliberate, rather than spontaneous, coordination of
children's productions.

"Hey You Guys": Coordinated Actions

"We haven't done Boom Chicka in a long time," said Tionna to her good
friends Mandisa and Janette one day.
     "Let's do it," responded Mandisa.
     "Let's do it," confirmed Tionna.

And Tionna, Mandisa, and Janette all began to coordinate their words
and actions, doing the Boom Chicka play, a clapping, dancing game involving parodies of family members who, for example, fumble with canes
and glasses or flirt with members of the opposite sex.

Such coordinated action, when individual children become an in-
synch group, is akin to the hand clap game that began this chapter (and
the one referenced in the opening of Chapter 3). These language plays
are a cross-cultural occurrence and a marker of childhood-in-motion (e.g.,
Dyson & Dewayani, in press; Opie & Opie, 1959; Powell, 2012). Like storytelling rounds, coordinated play could also provide familiar relational
ground for children's early composing. Consider, for example, Tionna's
enthusiastic "let's-do-it" issued to her peers during a writing time:

"Hey you guys!" says Tionna, looking up from her journal. "We can write about we miss Miss Hache [her class's former student teacher]. . . . Tomorrow we can write about we miss Miss Hache."

"Yeah," agrees Mandisa.

Tionna's suggestion of a writing topic was not a spontaneous linking of texts but a deliberate plan to share a topic. Efforts to coordinate composing through direct suggestions and ongoing negotiations were linked to children's recruitment of others for play. "Hey you guys," Tionna called; here is a plan for tomorrow's writing.

Such coordination was common in Mrs. Kay's room. From early in the year, regular companions coordinated both drawing and writing. Although the official emphasis was on writing life stories, they invented seemingly mundane but shared outings. For example, as noted in Chapter 4, early in the school year, Tionna and Lyron went to the store together, according to their texts—although they did not even know where one another lived.

This coordinating of topics—which led to a sharing of words and of spelling challenges—could become a social obligation among friends. To fail to comply, could be, from the initiator's point of view, an occasion for a fix-it (Figure 5.1, IIB, reciprocal obligations). In the following example, Lyron asks (to put it mildly) if other children are going to write about a favorite pastime—floor hockey, a kind of hockey where you "don't need ice skates . . . just regular shoes" but still can play like those professional hockey players appreciated in this northern U.S. state:

LYRON: Janette, write about floor hockey!
JANETTE: I *am*. (irritated, as in "I already said I was," so there is no need to monitor my compliance)
LYRON: Jon, are you?

Lyron now adds classmates to his own text about who is going to be playing field hockey.

LYRON: I'm writing Janette first. (He has her name tag.) Jason, your turn. . . . Here you go, Jason.

As Lyron added each name, his voice was full of anticipation, seemingly assuming others' pleasure at being included. In this, he recalled Mrs. Bee's Ella, exchanging birthday invitations for representational inclusion. But Lyron had organized for his own inclusion, as he and his peers were writing about a shared after-school activity—floor hockey—and the composers were expected to name names.

This deliberate coordination was less common in Mrs. Bee's kindergarten; not only were her children less experienced composers, but Mrs. Bee tended to follow closely her teachers' guide, which emphasized that children should be independent. Moreover, because her children needed much help forming letters and encoding messages, Mrs. Bee monitored them closely. She was relatively more aware of each child's product and, thus, of any apparent copying of topics, or when topics were assigned (e.g., "Thanksgiving plans"), of textual content.

Still, coordination could occur, although usually quite subtly and, relative to Mrs. Kay's children, less verbally anticipated. For example, as readers may recall from the earlier vignette in this chapter, Alicia was quite into Tinker Bell's appearance. However, when the episode continues, her friend Denise begins writing about her baby doll, and Alicia begins writing about a baby Tinker Bell. The two girls' papers contained a footprint of this coordinated choreography in their common spelling of baby (*Beiby*), for which Alicia had taken the lead. In this event and others, the girls referenced their writing as what "we" are doing. From their point of view, "we" were not copying one another, but "we" were writing together about pretend babies.

Similarly, after Mrs. Bee had discussed how poems sometimes rhyme, like songs they knew, tablemates Ernest and LaTrell sang "Ms. Mary Mack" and then "Twinkle Twinkle Little Star." The boys then worked on writing the latter song, their mutual efforts reflected in the common beginning found on each child's paper: *TwecGo TwecGO*. As stars filled the boys' papers, LaTrell thought Ernest's stars did not look too good. When Ernest asked for help, LaTrell temporarily moved from coordinated action to pedagogical assistance, carefully modeling for Ernest how to make better looking stars (Figure 5.1, IC, having to do with aesthetic judgments):

LATRELL: OK. Follow me. Follow me. Just follow me, ok?

(He begins to draw a star, describing his movements as he does so.) . . . Like a triangle, and goes like that (draws the first two lines of a triangle). And go this way, then go down this way, that way. . . . (As he talks, LaTrell draws the last three lines of the star.)

ERNEST: Now I have to write a better star.

Despite LaTrell's careful instruction, Ernest did not achieve a better star, try as he did. Still, he persisted with his writing for days until he had written the whole "Twinkle Twinkle" song. (LaTrell did not persist beyond "twecGo TwecGo" and drawn stars galore). Ernest even followed that with an original song (see Chapter 8). The boys' coordinated efforts thus led to mutual engagement in a task that not only contextualized efforts to encode (which had been challenging for both boys [see Chapter 3]) but also led to a new compositional interest for Ernest ("It's all about songs now").

The most elaborate coordination in the kindergarten occurred the previous year on a day when Mrs. Bee was not at school. Kindergartner Ra'mell had had a difficult time the day before, when he had struggled with encoding during an assignment to write about what the children had seen when their student teacher took them on a pretend trip to the zoo via a slideshow. Ra'mell had tried to just copy somebody else's words, and that sort of copying—copying outside a social relation—was rare but uniformly criticized. Ra'mell did not deny his troubles: "I don't know what I'm doing!"

On the day in question, the substitute teacher had told the children to write anything they wanted. Ra'mell had begun to write on a familiar topic—about seeing a fish in the ocean (seemingly inspired by a science unit about the ocean, a place Ra'mell had never actually been). As it happens, Ra'mell's peer Simeon started to copy Ra'mell's paper. A tablemate, Sadie, noticed this and accused Simeon of copying. Like Ra'mell the day before, Simeon said, "I don't know what I'm writing," with evident frustration in his voice.

Ra'mell was sympathetic. "You can write what I'm writing," he said, allowing Simeon relational ground for his copying.

Initially, Simeon *did* copy, making his letters match his classmate's as closely as he could. Ra'mell, though, wrote loudly; that is, he orally monitored each word that he wrote, which allowed Simeon to know what he was writing. When the boys began a second story, they related to one another differently. They began to actively coordinate their texts, each contributing ideas and even spelling suggestions. Simeon no longer assumed a passive role, as illustrated below.

Each boy now draws a car on a new paper. Ra'mell proposes that they write "A [said but not written] car can drive." They do so, but Simeon is no longer just copying. The shift in participant mode from pedagogic to coordinated is marked in the boys' very letters: Ra'mell continues his usual pattern of capitalizing the first letter of each word, but Simeon stops doing this. Rather, he capitalizes most letters, as is his usual pattern. Moreover, Simeon now has his own content and spelling suggestions to make. Indeed, he is affronted when Ra'mell does not write his ideas (Figure 5.1, IIB, reciprocal obligations.) The boys, after all, are supposed to be writing the same letters:

SIMEON: Cars can drive DOWN! (Simeon suggests the word *down*.)

RA'MELL: Cars can drive down. (writes Di)

SIMEON: Erase that I. /da/ /n:uh/. Put an A [after the D]. (writes DA and then adds NU). . . . Erase that [I]! You won't listen to me!

RA'MELL: (erases the I and writes an A as Simeon has suggested) That what you want (gesturing toward his paper). That what you want!

Ra'mell then suggests an extension of the sentence: "Cars can ride down *the road*," and the boys finish their piece.

They then decide to write yet another story, but the substitute teacher tells them that they are not allowed any more paper. The boys are not deterred; they erase their writing about cars and, on the same paper, write about going to the zoo (exactly the assigned topic that defeated Ra'mell the day before). Then they erase the zoo piece, planning to write yet another text, one about money: "Money, money, money," says Ra'mell, "money on the floor."

In the meantime, Sadie seems inspired to join in the social action: "We're [me and my tablemate are] gonna write another story [too]." Just then, though, the substitute announces the end of writing workshop; it is time to clean up and get in line for lunch.

Thus ended a burst of writing. For the boys, writing together was, at first, a potential source of pride for Ra'mell, who was able to help Simeon. But soon both boys were contributing to the coordination of their texts; indeed, their mutual contributions even revealed one source of Simeon's encoding difficulty (i.e., a distortion of a phoneme's sound, as in "nuh" for /n/). The boys' stretching out of their sentences, their audible efforts to spell, their oral monitoring of their words—all were useful in managing the difficult encoding task, and all made a difficult task a fun project with a newly accentuated friendship.

When he had some choice, Ra'mell usually sat by Yashaun, a close relative; but the very next day he told me that his best friend was Simeon. In his responsiveness to Simeon, especially in his move from a pedagogic to a more mutually contributive stance, Ra'mell showed himself to be a responsive peer, indeed, an ethical one who sympathized with a friend's distress and, then, adjusted his participation mode when Simeon bid for a more active role. Both boys were sustained in their writing by the pleasure of one another's company. Indeed, their coordinated action inspired the girls.

Like kindergartners Denise and Ella, who indexed their mutual affiliation by planning to wear the same dress and the same hair style for Denise's birthday, children could deliberately coordinate their composing to mark, sustain, and support their connections with one another. At the very same time, their coordinated actions could support their engagement with written language itself. Coordinating actions did not involve unidirectional helping but joint participation, as children fulfilled their obligations to one another through the activity at hand and, no less important, had a good time doing so.

THE RELATIONAL LANDSCAPE FOR TEXTUAL PLAY: SITUATING OLD BASICS IN CHILD SPACES

Excuse me. Hello. Talk!

So said Alicia to her friend Ella when the latter child offered no response to her comment about Tinker Bell, the subject of her ongoing composing. "Respond! Don't ignore me!" she seemed to say. "That is not nice. I'm sitting right here."

Alicia's evident discomfort marked the atypical absence of peer talk during writing time in Mrs. Bee's classroom, as would have been the case in Mrs. Kay's as well. Through talk, social expectations were built, relationships were enacted, and composing became a potential mediator of children's lives together.

The talk-filled paths into written composing were well-worn, as they were grounded in childhood relations and practices. This chapter has featured two fundamental ways in which children's social participation in composing was organized. One mode involved informal collegial responsiveness, the other, the more deliberate coordination of actions.

Collegial relations were most vividly displayed in conversational storytelling, when children responded to another's story with a related one of their own. These collegial relations, with their expectation of responsiveness, also could occur during composing. As the children's talk choreographed that composing, the resultant texts could suggest illegal copying in the official world; although, in the unofficial one, the children were an interconnected "we" telling about, say, balloons or a life with Jesus.

A participation mode involving coordinated actions was more deliberate, as illustrated most vibrantly by the children's impressively intricate hand-clapping games. During composing time, a call for coordinated play could provide support for meeting the challenges presented by the symbolic intricacies of written language. Children could be quite subtle in their coordination, writing just outside the curricular lines, as when Alicia and Denise jointly wrote about babies . . . but their "Beibys" differed in nature.

Even though the children's actions were not consistent with the official notion of writing as a strictly individual affair, they were consistent with the ethos of their larger classroom cultures, where children were encouraged to be thoughtful and inclusive. Writing is a situated, dialogic happening, as the children have illustrated; thus, writing "basics" can already be stretched to include social responsiveness across participatory contexts.

This social responsiveness will become more complex in Chapter 7. It will be organized within more intricate modes—complementary and improvisational in nature—and realized in solidified practices that are appropriated and spread by the children themselves. In this way, the children will illustrate more explicitly how social and textual attunement may give rise to participatory childhood cultures.

As the unofficial classroom world continues to unfold, the children will index a more explicitly complex world. In ways both mundane, like imagining fun weekend plans (with their embedded notions of social class), and dramatic, like managing who loves whom and who is allowed to play war (with their interrelated notions of gender, race, and sexuality), that complex world will come to the foreground. The children, after all, were located in particular geographic and societal places in a stratified world, and those places permeated the classroom and the relational landscape upon which they carved out textual playgrounds.

It is time, now, to stop explaining the action to come and to let the children get on with it. It is time for Chapter 7 to begin.

Complementary Relations and Improvisational Play

On Matters of Birthdays, Love, and War

It is mid-afternoon in Mrs. Kay's room, and the children are immersed in activity time. (Mrs. Kay herself is meeting individually with children to correct an assignment.) Tionna and Lyron are sharing the box of Legos, finding their way into collaborative play. Tionna begins by building her house. Lyron seems to assume that she is a grown-up woman living with a grown-up Lyron.

"Soon as you walk in [my house]," starts Tionna, but Lyron interrupts.

"My picture's on the wall, when you walk in," he says, a big grin on his face.

"This is *my* room," Tionna says firmly, "and this is my living room."

"Where's my room?" Lyron asks.

Tionna says that she'll make him one, but he is *not* going to be her boyfriend. *She* owns that house; *she* controls that house; and, moreover, *she* controls Lyron. She names him "son." And when Ezekial joins the play, she deems him her son's friend. Friends are not allowed in her kitchen unless they are accompanied by her son.

"If—if you bring Ezekial, he can—he—if you all go in my kitchen with Lyron, I don't care," she tells Ezekial. "But," she adds, turning to Lyron, "don't let them go in the kitchen by themselves. 'Cause you don't know what they be doing."

"OK, Mom," says the obedient Lyron.

And with that final response from Lyron, Tionna completed her successful negotiation of her role as homeowner and mother (although, before long, she would become Lyron's wife, but that's another story [transcript of Lego event in Genishi & Dyson, 2009, pp. 68–69]).

Negotiating with her "son" and his friend required that Tionna reason within the parameters of her chosen role in the play. In so doing, she appropriated sociolinguistic resources—particularly the voice of a mother, which led to syntactically complex speech: Tionna explained that one could do this or that if, and only if, certain conditions applied, and these conditions mattered for such and such reason. Her in-role voice sounded as if it could be that of her own grandmother (her "mom"). "You don't know what they be doing," said Mama Tionna. For their part, both Ezekial and Lyron responded appropriately, as they slipped into their own roles. A responsive choreography of words and actions allowed the children to join together in an imagined world.

Complementary actions among role-playing children are common in child cultures. Like engaging in collegial rounds of storytelling and coordinated handclaps, role play may provide familiar relational grounds for composing. Indeed, from a Bakhtinian perspective, all language users engage in complementary actions. In enacting varied kinds of communicative events (or genres), language users reach out to others with their words. They shape those words on the other's "conceptual horizon," anticipating—waiting for—a response (Bakhtin, 1981, p. 282). For an academic like me, this can be an abstract process; but, for young children, it is experienced in the give-and-take of human encounters, including in peer play slowed down, stretched out, and played on a textual playground.

On such a playground, children experience what seem to be basic, authorial skills: They not only respond to one another, but they adapt relevant symbolic material, assume complementary roles, and, thereby, construct a textual encounter—a literacy event (Heath, 1982, who builds on Hymes, 1974). This chapter features young children organizing their composing within complementary relations and more intricate collaborative improvisations. Sometimes their playful composing was copied by other children, and as an activity was repeated, a schematic writing practice took shape across classroom space and time (Hanks, 1996). These emergent practices were more common in Mrs. Kay's room; her children *were* more experienced, but they also had more time and space within which practices could spill beyond writing time, give rise to related practices, and thus contribute in observable ways to the evolving peer culture. For that reason, Mrs. Kay's children will dominate this chapter, even though complementary and improvisational practices appeared in nascent form in Mrs. Bee's room.

As will be illustrated, emergent practices involved more than a participation mode. They involved children sharing a sense of the game being played (Hanks, 1996, building on Bakhtin, 1981, and Bourdieu, 1977). The game involved certain defined roles, schematic textual content and structure, and normative and ethical expectations for how players should behave. Indeed, cultural matters of birthdays, love, and war were played out in imaginary, pleasurable worlds, but they could also lead to hurt feelings, aggravated actions, and even critical encounters with the status quo. I begin below with complementary relations involving valuable and potent negotiating capital: birthday parties.

COMPLEMENTARY RELATIONS AND BIRTHDAY PARTIES

Birthday parties are a part of popular culture in the United States, even for children who do not have such parties. Indeed, birthday parties involving children's friends or classmates have become a major ritual for consumption, particularly among the more privileged (McKendrick, Bradford, & Fielder, 2000). Commercial establishments entice young children with happy images of pizza, balloons, and music, or special treatment at an ice skating rink, a miniature golf course, or maybe a bowling alley.

In their unofficial worlds, children commonly use even pretend parties to mediate relationships, as Alicia's peer Ella illustrated when she told the children around her, "Whoever got me in the[ir] picture will come to my birthday. . . . It will be in Chicago" (Chapter 6). Indeed, the appeal of birthday parties was clear very early on in Mrs. Bee's kindergarten. Readers may recall how hard (and unsuccessfully) LaTrell worked to get his name on Ernest's paper about a birthday sleep-over (Chapter 1).

In Mrs. Kay's room, unofficial birthday practices became highly developed (early analysis of party data, like war data, presented in Dyson, 2007). The beginnings of these practices, though, were in the official world of school composing and in children's efforts to *regularize* their texts in ways that conformed to Mrs. Kay's lessons—lessons, it seems, that she did not even know she was teaching (Hanks, 1996).

The Official Roots of Birthday Play: Having Fun Plans

As described in Chapter 2, when Mrs. Kay modeled writing, she adopted a conversational voice, writing about anticipated ("I am going to . . . ") or completed ("I went . . . ") events. These events were always relative to the present moment, but they referenced out-of-school places and, especially, family plans. She thus modeled the value of a busy life filled with plans for fun events.

Like the players they were, Tionna, Ezekial, and their peers were alert to Mrs. Kay's voice during writing time, that is, to her social stance toward others and toward the world in a communicative situation (Bakhtin, 1981). Thus, they too began to anticipate fun weekend plans. But the children lived in very different socioeconomic circumstances than did their teacher.

Mrs. Kay's plans involved disposable income, however modest, for a weekend trip and a nice hotel, a meal at a restaurant, and a movie out. The children, though, had no control over how time and money were spent in their households. Moreover, their households had less disposable income. The children talked mainly about watching movie videos, not about "going to the movies" (unless they went through an after school program). They talked about, played roles as workers in, and at least one (Lyron) had a parent with a job at a fast food place, not the sort of restaurant Mrs. Kay referenced. Further, their reported birthday parties were family affairs, with a cake and a gift. Their planned ones, though, were quite different.

Children's written plans involved special events with one another, not their families. These plans were a part of present-moment play, not anticipations of actual future happenings. The planned events never became reported past events because they never happened (as children would admit if I asked them, which was, I quickly realized, quite rude of me). The children were adept at assuming new roles through dramatic play. Instead of becoming, say, mom and kids, principal and bad children, or fast food counter clerks, cooks, and customers, the children could be party givers and invitees.

The success of the writing time party play was dependent on children's complementary roles and reciprocal actions; good players, like good friends, "build action together" and thereby make a coherent if invented world (Goodwin & Goodwin, 2006, p. 225). That description, though, sounds too benign; as in any human relations there was always the possibility of someone violating expectations of inclusion. This was possible because the children's planned parties, like Mrs. Kay's planned events, were imagined as private, not public, affairs. This in and of itself was in some tension with the classroom ethos of inclusiveness.

The Differentiation of Unofficial Private Parties from Official Public Ones: Negotiating Geographies of Identity

In Mrs. Kay's room, birthday parties were a regular feature of official classroom life, and birthdays themselves were a common topic of children's official writing book entries. (All but three children wrote about birthdays.) Children's birthdays were listed by month on a classroom bulletin board. Moreover, the class celebrated each child's birthday with a rendition of the happy birthday song and a special treat. If a child's parent(s) so desired, they could send along cupcakes and punch for the celebration, but they had to send enough for *everyone*.

Children's writing on official birthday celebrations indexed this inclusiveness in some way. For example, note Tionna's use of "we" and "our" in the piece below:

> today we are going to selbrat mannys [Manny's] Birthday we are go[ing] to eat cupcakes with spreackls [sprinkles] on thim thay will tast very good we will brobby [probably] not have a nof [enough] time to read are [our] writings.

Her writing was inclusive and true . . . even if her picture (see Figure 7.1) was not (i.e., there were no balloons hanging from the classroom ceiling; that was an image appropriated from her student teacher's modeled text about a roommate's party).

Official class parties were for "everyone," but this was not the case for planned parties to be held outside of school. Because of this, writing about the latter parties opened up communicative space for children's imagination and their *social work* (Dyson, 1993). Children's named invitees could be close friends, just boys or just girls, everybody in the class, or an evolving cast of characters.

In Mrs. Kay's racially and ethnically diverse class, girls' close friendships were primarily homogeneous in declared racial identity and, among boys, primarily homogeneous in gender. Still children were assigned seats around two worktables (formed by pushing together smaller tables). This official geography of children could lead to unofficial negotiations of inclusion and, thereby, to social and textual changes, as will soon be seen.

The Evolution of Birthday Party Practices

Birthday party play started modestly, with one child, Ellie, drawing and writing a sentence or two about an upcoming birthday party (e.g., held at a pool, a hotel, even the state of California) and then announcing who would come. As this topic spread in a collegial way, party planners followed a schematic structure—they declared the existence of an upcoming party and named the invitees in their texts. Those invitees could then write, in complementary fashion, that they would be going to so-and-so's party, adding a comment or two on their anticipation of a fun time. The opportunity to read publicly one's text—to declare oneself as an invitee—may have helped fuel this writing action (and could have led to an official discussion of public reading about private parties, since not everyone was included).

Figure 7.1. Tionna's Anticipation of Manny's Party

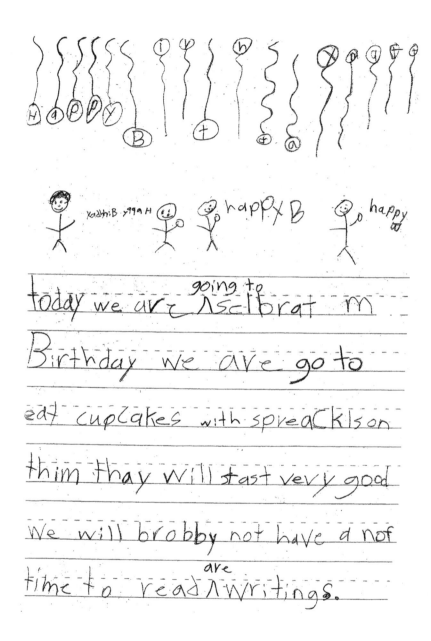

This basic reciprocal process led to oral negotiations, as unlisted children announced their desire to come to the party (i.e., to be in the planner's text). The planner could write again about the party, this time with a revised list of names. Once the planner heard the desire, there was a social expectation for inclusion (refer to Figure 5.1, IIA). Once, though, Mandisa, apparently overwhelmed by all the children desiring to come to her party, wrote that she was "sorry" but there were not enough "prizes" for everybody.

Although the parties were fictional, their "realness" was never questioned in the official or unofficial worlds. Moreover, the dialogic nature of the party planning practice gave rise to other, interconnected practices, appropriated from in and out of school. The official social and material organization of writing (i.e., individuals produced texts in bound journals) worked against the use of varied genres; for example, party invitations required distribution. But, in Mrs. Kay's free activity period, children had access to paper and pencils and ample time and space to venture into new textual experiences; they composed brief invitations, made straightforward lists of invitees, exchanged phone numbers on bits of paper, and orally negotiated who was going to pick up whom on the big day. A lively network of practices, contributing to a complex peer culture, thus took shape.

Listen, for example, to Ezekial's and Tionna's peer, the "stylish" Jon:

Hey Janette! You going to my birthday party?

Although Jon's birthday was 4 months away, he shouted out this request during activity time. The time lag between anticipated and at least possible party date was not unusual. As already noted, out-of-school birthday parties were future affairs in which fun was anticipated—and that anticipation was itself the fun. In fact, Jon's query to Janette may have been his response to the lists of invitees that she, Tionna, and Mandisa were each making during activity time for their parties. Their own birthdays were months away, but that did not stop the party play. The girls included one another on their lists and, also Lyron. But they had not included Jon.

Ezekial spent that same activity time making his party list. He walked around the room with a sheet of paper, inviting children and, usually, asking for their phone numbers. Ellie, witnessing his actions, offered a very pleased (and widely grinning) Ezekial a written invitation—and a polite request—to the current form of her anticipated party (a trip to California):

Ezekial Plese
come
to
Califony

These brief vignettes of children planning for their birthdays illustrate that officially modeled life stories became reframed as peer play. Moreover, that play spread out over time and space and beyond the curriculum itself, which did not envision interconnected fields of communicative practices. The children appropriated from the landscape of voices—of kinds of communicative practices—surrounding them at home and at school. In so doing, they stretched beyond their own power to control their socioeconomic circumstance, and moreover, they gained some power over one another, given the non-inclusiveness of unofficial parties.

In the next section, I will briefly tell the story of the last week of Jon's birthday party play. In this way, I illustrate the complementary relations at the heart of birthday play and, moreover, the ethics of inclusion that arose.

Jon's Birthday: A Textual Slip from Fiction to Life Story

Jon's planned birthday had initially been a contained, managed affair. He wrote about his upcoming party with his regular male companions in the class—Brad, Manny, Joshua, Ezekial, and Lyron:

I am going to have
fun at my brfa [birthday, i.e., birthday party]
Brad and/mAnny and/Joshua and.
Ezekial are coming/to my brfa [birthday, i.e., birthday party] it will/ be
fun and LYron will cum. . . .
(written by Jon in March)

However, pressure came to bear from the girls who sat around him in his table cluster, particularly Mandisa and Elisha, and also from Ellie, who "liked" Jon. As these children began to write their plans to go to Jon's party, Jon reacted in a complementary way: as party host, he included them in his texts:

Ezekial is kuming / and Joshua/ Elisha/ Ellie and
Mandisa are / kumying / to my bira [birthday]
Tomorrow. And / Manny it will / be fun and wey [we]/
will have kedy [candy].

In the imaginations of his invitees, party plans were detailed and made ever so appealing. For example, Elisha wrote about how she was going:

to Jon's Birthday, and / we will git to hit the
pehota [piñata]. And I will give it
my best hit. And I will / git all the candy out and.
I wish there will be mony / in it.

On the day of Jon's actual birthday, the negotiations and anticipation reached unusual intensity and spilled beyond the borders of the imagined world—a singular event. As composing time ended, the school's closing bell sounded, and the children were sent by table cluster to the hallway to retrieve their coats, hats, and gloves from their lockers. However, once in the hallway, children gathered around Jon. They were anxious to ride home with him to his birthday party.

Jon listened quietly and then said that his little brother would be in the car with his mother when she came to pick him up. There would be no room for extra children. But those extra children persisted. Jon said he thought Ezekial and Janette could maybe squeeze in the front seat. Elisha started to cry—she had been *invited*. Jon had said she *was* coming. She should be in that car! Under pressure, Jon said he thought they could all squeeze in the car.

The indignant claims for inclusion continued as ever more children came into the hallway to get their winter garb. These claims, though, were not the sort Jon ultimately could grant. He could put them on his textual playground and keep them there, thus fulfilling his ethical obligations, his promises to others. However, getting them in the car was a different matter altogether. In the adult-governed world, his power was limited. There was, after all, his mother, who did not even know of this party.

Jon went back into the classroom and directly asked Mrs. Kay, "Can I call my mom to see if some of my classmates can come to my party?" It was too late for that, his teacher said.

"You should have given out invitations," said Mandisa, and Elisha agreed. Jon went home, and the disappointed others eventually went to the after school care program (but only after a couple had phoned their mothers in the office and, unsuccessfully, sought parental permission to go over to Jon's house, wherever that was).

Curricular Boundaries

The children's participation in birthday party practices illustrates the complex interplay between official and unofficial worlds. The children drew from the official world, but the reverse was not the case. For Mrs. Kay, these birthday texts elicited the usual matter of editorial help with "the basics" (e.g., capitalization and punctuation, spelling, usage). Moreover, since in Mrs. Kay's room, like Mrs. Bee's, the curriculum dictated the kind and nature of texts to be written and the skills thereby practiced, there was no recognition of the children's social organization of writing (i.e., it remained officially an individual task), nor were genres recognized beyond those officially privileged (e.g., no birthday cards, invitee lists, invitations). For this reason, the latter received no instructional attention (e.g., a genre name, a discussion of features, opportunities for official use).

And yet, viewed over time and from the vantage point of the unofficial world, each text was a written anticipation embedded within a complex of peers' oral and written events aimed at securing inclusion in the anticipation of fun. Indeed, during official sharing time, children unmentioned in a given birthday party text—even if they had not made any attempt to gain inclusion—tended to remain ostensibly passive or otherwise occupied (with a neighbor, a scratch, a shoe), unlike the attentive interest of those included. Thus, in a classroom where inclusiveness was an official value, children read about private parties that were, in fact, not inclusive, and this received no official discussion.

Birthday party play was complicated. Children experienced the complexities of public and private events, felt the social pressures of obligations to others, often initially structured by gender or race, and played beyond the limits of their socioeconomic circumstances and their age-related power. They grappled with the basic communication skills of responding to others in the appropriate social role, articulated with an appropriate voice, and using relevant symbolic material. Moreover, they negotiated with others through their writing, revising the social boundaries of their textual playgrounds and, thereby, letting others in. Similar skills were called upon in an even more complex kind of play—that of love.

COMPLEMENTARY RELATIONS AND THEIR LACK: THE COMPLEX GAME OF LOVE

Young children may join together in cross-gender groups in neighborhoods and homes, but, in the more public world of school, they tend to construct gender borders: Girls associate most with other girls, boys with other boys (Thorne, 1993). When they do play together, children may reinforce borders, as Mrs. Bee's and Mrs. Kay's children did in girls-chase-the-boys (and vice versa) games.

These chase games entailed complementary relations; they could occur only if people agreed to take gendered roles whose subsequent actions were seemingly straightforward—chase or be chased. Still, even this play could carry complex semantic overtones. Tionna's peer Lyron illustrated this early in the school year. He told me that "Ellie likes B-R-A-D." Ellie nodded in response.

"She likes me too," Lyron then added. Ellie shook her head no, but Lyron persisted: "I think she's being jealous, 'cause I know she likes me. She keeps on punching me and chasing me."

Lyron references the other dominant gendered game—the game of love. As a game, it had clear participant roles (most important, boyfriend, girlfriend), familiar plots (e.g., planning dates), and a consistent theme linked to larger ideological structures (e.g., dominant beliefs about who should love whom), often complicated, though, by everyday realities.

Ideally, the central roles of boyfriend and girlfriend were complementary, the declared affection reciprocated. But, of course, this was not necessarily the case. Moreover, the game had to be willingly played; sometimes even a regular participant, like Tionna, just plain old "didn't want to do that" game right then. As in any play situation, the game of love could induce hurt feelings, along with those of amusement and connection.

As a point of access to the children's game of love, I begin below with its language—the ideologically charged word *love*, its less intense companion *like*, and its wordless but linked image, the heart ♥, which means love, as Tionna explained to me one day.

The Language of Love

Sitting around a table during writing time, Brad remarked that he loved his baby sister, which led Tionna to comment, with a giggle, that he should marry her then. Brad called her "nasty," and Manny, also concerned, said, "You suppose' to love people."

"You're not suppose' to *lo::ve* people," Tionna countered.

As the children's talk suggests, even within child culture, *love* can be a complex minefield. Is it a "strong affection," or maybe "a sexual desire," both possibilities listed in my *Merriam-Webster* (2008, p. 737)? (For the children, the latter seemed captured by the notion of kissing, which invariably inspired giggles.) Then again, perhaps, as Manny implied, love is a caring regard for humankind. I myself am confused by the word *love*; my aim here is strictly ethnographic: to probe how language, particularly written language, mediated the game of heterosexual love. The children's talk and texts displayed their expectations for, and the ideological ramifications of, textual choices in the playing of this game. As chosen words, *love* was the most predictably charged, but the meaning and reception of *love* and *like* depended on the discursive context. (See Chapter 5 for a discussion of the complexities of same sex affection among boys, who were "friends.")

Most of the children attended church and heard that, as Manny said, you were "suppose'" to love one another . . . but, situated in young children's relational worlds, *love* (and its iconic image ♥) was a precarious affair. In both Mrs. Bee's and Mrs. Kay's room, one could safely write for official display that *I love my* family (including *my* pet), *my* teacher, Santa Claus, and God. There were a few written declarations of material *loves* (e.g., Aaron loved baseball, Brad loved soccer, and Mandisa loved cookies and Cocoa Puffs). Still the written declaration of one's own, or the reporting of another's, directed *love* was usually limited to family members.

In their official written products, girls and boys did not usually *love* one another. In Mrs. Bee's kindergarten, writing about boyfriends or girlfriends was kept from official display; a heart and an accompanying name might be found on the back of a writing paper or it might be briefly displayed on the front, in the margin, before being erased. If one failed to erase, one might "get in trouble," as a child explained.

In Mrs. Kay's 1st grade, though, there was a whole lot of text-mediated *liking* going on. By the winter months, the practice of imagined get-togethers had developed new variants: the planned date (with its discourse of "going out") and anticipated "marrying" (interchangeable with "living together" in the children's texts). A picture accompanying marriage plans might contain a boy asking via a dialogue bubble the fabled question "Will you marry me?" Despite this traditional nod to the male power to "pop the question," both girls and boys could anticipate marriage, and both held the power of rejection.

You, my readers, are already familiar with one complex relationship, that between Tionna, Lyron, Janette, and Mandisa. After the Lego play that began this chapter, Tionna wrote the piece featured in Part II's introduction. That piece was about "cute" Lyron and included Tionna's plan to live with Lyron when she, and Janette, grew up. (Later she could not believe she had left Mandisa out.) As seen in Figure 7.2, the picture portion of the text portrays Tionna and Janette wearing dresses adorned with hearts. Lyron has a deck of cards, since the ongoing date (spoken and drawn, but not written) involves walking with Lyron to a friend's house, where they will all play cards. The "true" multimodal text (about present feelings and future plans) includes a "fake drawing," to quote Tionna:

TIONNA: (in the midst of drawing) Look Lyron! You got some *cards* up in your hand. . . . We walking you up to your friend's house so you got them cards, in your hand.

Figure 7.2. Tionna's Shared Liking of Lyron

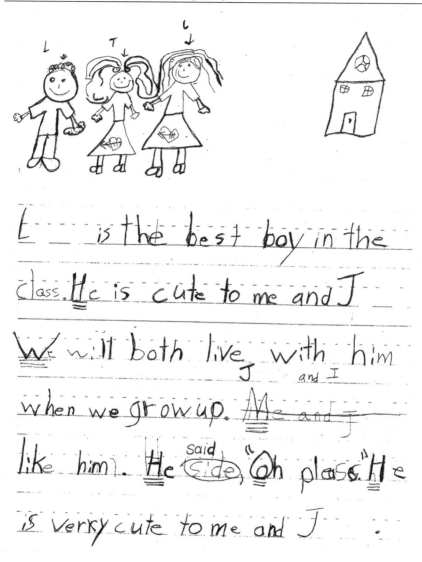

L___ is the best boy in the class. He is cute to me and J___ will both live with him J and I when we grow up. Me and J___ like him. He said "Oh plase." He is verky cute to me and J___.

LYRON: . . . Oh! We're gonna play cards?
TIONNA: Yeah . . . We gotta meet your friend. So you're taking us to his house.
LYRON: Wanta know his name?
TIONNA: What's his name?
LYRON: Mmm. Manny.

TIONNA: OK. We're going to Manny's house.

LYRON: And Jon. Jon lives with Manny.

MANNY: No he don't!

TIONNA: No! We're fake drawing, OK? . . . But when we grow up, this is really gonna happen, OK?

Tionna's piece, then, was situated within, and a part of, her easy-going play with Lyron, who slipped effortlessly into the designated role. When Tionna read the written text to the class, she garnered much appreciative laughter. Indeed Tionna herself began to giggle as she read. (Venturing into the game of love often evoked laughter on the public stage.) Mrs. Kay laughed too; she remembered her own plans to marry:

> You know what? You never know who you're gonna marry. I always thought I was gonna marry this boy that lived behind me. . . . Sure of it, sure of it. But you know what? Never did marry this boy that lived behind me. . . . We're still friends though.

Mrs. Kay did not like children to fixate on topics, including those involving boyfriends and girlfriends. Still such relations struck her as a common part of childhood. Like her children, she distinguished between anticipated marriage partners and those who were "just friends." In her official curriculum, Mrs. Kay was directed to attend to the coherence of, and basic skills displayed in, each child's text individually; my job here is to illustrate the cultural work of the discursive field of love and writing's formative role in a local child culture.

Written Practices in the Textual Choreography of Love

In Mrs. Kay's room, love as a discourse game became visible in the expanding repertoire of game practices. Girls were the more prolific writers about romantic boy/girl relations (all but Brittany wrote of such relations, compared to a third of the boys—Lyron, Brad, and Jon). Still in the 1st grade, as in Mrs. Bee's kindergarten, boyfriend/girlfriend relations were common knowledge in the children's worlds. There may well have been secret affections, kept to oneself and out of the unofficial public of the children's worlds. But it is the public knowledge, mediated by and commented on in texts, that entered into the cultural enactment of heterosexual love in those worlds.

The earliest writing practice linked to the game of love was a straightforward declaration of "liking"; one wrote the other's name, added a ♥, and, perhaps, one's own name. Kindergartners put hearts and names on scraps of paper and backs of writing pages. First-graders did the same but also could embed such images in the picture portions of their texts; since pictures were never read during sharing time, any declarations so positioned were useful for unofficial play but could remain private during official public readings. In Figure 7.3, Ellie has written a date plan; however, it is the imagined *love* letter in the picture that is literally at the heart of an ongoing drama (soon to be recounted).

Figure 7.3. Ellie's Plans for Brad (and Jon)

More elaborate declarations of liking could be written, all of which included references to physical qualities. As readers might recall, Tionna wrote of Lyron's cuteness and Jon's "style." Both Jon and Brad wrote about Ellie, each describing her as "coot," with her red hair; indeed, Brad wrote that she was "like a jrim [dream]." Ellie herself never wrote of a boy's appeal, nor did Lyron write such a text about a girl. Both seemed to like being liked; and Lyron had *three* "girlfriends"—his three friends who were girls (Tionna, Mandisa, and Janette) reframed as "girlfriends," but only for the game of love.

Figure 7.4, a sociogram of 1st-grade players of the game, conveys which child authors declared cross-gender "liking" or "love" for particular others who were not "just friends" (indicated by solid lines affixed to arrows). As the game of love became more widespread, children wrote reports of who liked whom—a practice akin to gossip but lacking any malicious intent, moral outrage, or for that matter, secrecy (Goodwin, 1990). (Such reports are indicated in Figure 7.4 with hyphenated lines; the reports' authors are provided in accompanying boxes.)

In the game of love, an ethical obligation prevailed to be accurate in one's gossip-like reports, unlike in one's imagined date planning (Figure 5.1, IID, on accuracy in group knowledge). One could be melodramatic and funny, but one could not just make up who liked whom. Mandisa grinned as she theatrically read a hybrid love text—a declaration of love and a report of its lack of reciprocation (indicated in Figure 7.4 by solid lines that ended, not in arrows, but in large periods or stops):

> Me, Tionna, and [left blank]/ reaily like Jon./ He does not like us./ But we like him. O.K. heres the/ deail We like Jon/ O.k. people spred the word.
> [accompanied by picture of a distressed Jon saying "Oh No," as Mandisa and Tionna profess their liking, which Mandisa found funny]

Mandisa's text showcases the link between reports and gossip, even as she pokes fun at the whole game of love. Mandisa's piece also suggests that, although complementary relations—that is, reciprocated love—was the recognized ideal, much of the drama came from the lack of such relations.

This lack of reciprocity did not mean a lack of collegiality or of collaborative play. For example, as suggested by Figure 7.4, Elisha was particularly active in declaring and reporting unreciprocated liking. She even reported liking boys who never played the game of love. Nevertheless, she *was* included in boys' and girls' texts as a participant in other games. Indeed, as just illustrated, she was included in Jon's birthday texts; he was even going to squeeze her in his car (until reality set in).

Figure 7.4. Sociogram of Writing in the Game of Love

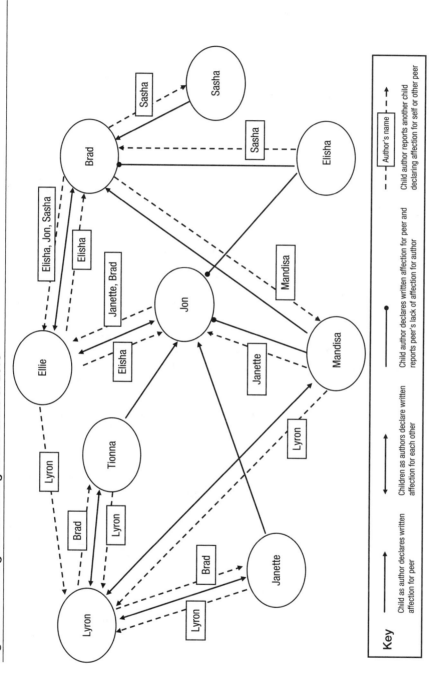

The equivalent of the planned birthday party in the game of love was the planned date. In written form, it never began with an *I* or a *my*, as in *I am going to have fun* when my birthday comes around. A date began with a *me* and somebody(ies), who were going to do this or that. It was about a *we*, usually a known *we* consistent with the ongoing talk about who liked whom. (That "me and somebody" was, of course, subject to a grammatical fix-it in the official world.)

This listing of practices—the names and hearts associated with declarations of "my" affections, the reports of who likes whom (and who does not), the planned dates with their cozy "me and so-and-so's,"—cannot capture the dynamics of the game of love, its ethics, and the choreography of textual actions. For that, we need a story. So below I include the dramatic break up of Ellie, Jon, and Brad, along with Tionna's use of the discourse of love to bring some kind of peaceful resolution to the turmoil.

Connections and Break-Ups in the Game of Love

As already noted (and surely experienced), physical qualities matter in the game of love (see also Dyson, 1997). This emphasis may help explain why the initial reciprocal players shared racial identity. For example, Tionna's closest friends were Black, and they reconfigured themselves (as three girlfriends and a boyfriend) to play the game of love, despite her temporary "crush" on Jon, who identified as "Mexican." Ellie, whose best girl friends were white (Brittany and Sasha), declared herself "Irish" and chose first the fair-haired Brad as "boy-friend."

These racialized relations in no way defined the breadth of children's textual choreography with other children. Depending on the referenced activity (e.g., planning birthday parties or anticipating activities in the after-school program), children constructed shared identities as, for example, birthday-party attendees, moviegoers, or street-hockey players (the latter involving both boys and girls in an activity sponsored by the after-school program).

Moreover, the game of love itself was neither static nor conventionally organized in pairs. For example, Ellie took the initiative in adding Jon as "boyfriend" along with Brad. Jon reciprocated. This did not upset Brad, nor did it interfere with the two boys playing together; the linking of these three children was a matter of common knowledge and the subject of written gossip.

Brad himself tried to add other players in the role of his "girl-friend," although with less success than Ellie had had. For example, in January, a month before the game of love became most intense, Brad said to every-one at his worktable that he liked Tionna. In turn, Tionna (who sat at that table) teased him through her writing. As he looked on expectantly, she wrote on a scrap of paper *I love you*, paused, and then wrote the next word: *Mom*. Tionna smiled, and Brad gave an exasperated sigh—a complemen-tary relation not realized.

Brad, like Jon, *was* successful in declaring affection for Ellie. In re-sponse, Ellie planned dates. Beginning in February, she included one boy, the other, or both, as in the following text:

> Tomorro me 8 [Ellie's ampersand]/ Jon 8 Brad/ are going to/ a chines/ buffay. We will have fun There. (accompanied by a picture of a girl, two boys, and a giant heart)

Ellie, Brad, and Jon did not play all the time, but when they did, all seemed peaceful and, for Ellie especially, fun. She laughed as she wrote. Love was just another game . . . until it got out of hand.

When I arrived one day in March, trouble seemed to be brewing. It was social studies time, and the children were working on a map work-sheet. I noticed, though, that Ellie was tearing up as she sat by Janette near the end of the long worktable. Tionna noticed too. "What happened?" she asked, as she looked up from her place across from Lyron and kitty corner from the sheepish-looking Brad.

"Brad dumped me," said Ellie, bringing in another named action from the discourse of love.

This was new, this public display of distress. It was a form of role play—the weeping, wronged woman. (In fact Ellie had confided to me once that, in her world, Brad was a "jinx," which meant he "was not that good at things.")

Still, Ellie had real tears in her eyes, and the children at the table seemed to hold Brad accountable. This was, after all, a known, reciprocal relationship; it had been a mainstay in peer culture since early fall. And now Brad was "dumping" her, saying, in effect, that he would not include her in his game of love. This was not nice.

Brad reacted defensively:

Brad: I never do anything to her. . . . I'm not gonna marry Ellie. I'm gonna marry somebody else. . . . "
Janette: You always say something to make somebody sick.
Tionna: When she—when you grow up you probably gonna marry Ellie 'cause you gonna think she cute.

BRAD: No I'm not gonna marry Ellie.

TIONNA: Yes you are.

BRAD: The only thing I like to do is play video games all day.

TIONNA: When you're a dult, you're not gonna play video games all day.

BRAD: I'm not gonna be a dog.

TIONNA: I said a *dult* (emphasis now on the T). . . .

Tionna now slips into the role of helpful friend, appropriating the relevant symbolic material, that is, the discourse of break up and reconciliation, with its vocabulary, its sad reflections, and its vague apologies:

TIONNA: (to her table companions) [Ellie]' s thinking about all the days that she having fun with Brad. . . . That has changed. She want that to go back together. She don't want that to break up.

BRAD: (quietly to Tionna) I still like Ellie.

. . .

TIONNA: Just say um, "Ellie, I didn't mean to say it. I was just in a bad mood." I say it for you. (louder voice) Ellie, Brad say, he was just in a bad mood.

In the choice activity time that followed, Ellie, still in the discursive field of love, wrote her first observed declaration of affection in the form of a note on a paper scrap:

To Brad
From Ellie
[inside a large heart] I love you Brad
From Ellie

Moreover, during writing time, Ellie wrote the piece in Figure 7.3, which contained a love note she anticipated getting the following year on Valentine's. She was giggling again, no tears (although a small male figure was crying in the picture).

The incident had passed. Jon declared in writing his liking of Ellie (and his need for her phone number), and Brad anticipated that he and Ellie would have a "rel good hosm [home (with an *s*, a graphic connection to *house*)]." Brad thereby assumed his, by now, group-prescribed identity as Ellie's boyfriend and his reciprocal obligations to respond to her affectionately. Still, after the "break-up" and its resolution, the three children did not play love again. Perhaps, having slipped out of play into the awkwardness of hurt emotions, the game lost some of its appeal. Nevertheless, in the classroom gossip, the three remained linked until the end of the year.

Curricular Cubicles

Every child, whether a kindergartner or a 1st-grader, had a folder, just as directed in the mandated curricula. Each child's progress was monitored against the basic skills being taught. It was as if each child wrote in his or her own cubicle. But it takes at least two, a me and a you, to play love.

Love was but one game; it did not define relationships between girls and boys (and, in this, it differed from other reported class studies [Blaise & Taylor, 2012]). Moreover, it stressed just one kind of love. The children played with sibling love (you may recall Alicia and Willo "playing sisters on paper" [see Chapter 4]). Both boys and girls also demonstrated if not love at least a valuing of friends and classmates; both kindergartners and 1st-graders put others' names in their texts, planning (and imagining), like Alicia, joint trips to the swimming pool, or, like Ezekial, afternoons playing video games or going to somebody's birthday party. And Brad, who struck me as a bit of a romantic—in love with love—once put hearts on drawings of his male friends.

Most important, the children's games of love involved play with family love, as they experienced it. Ezekial lived in a home that included his two parents, but Tionna, Alicia, and LaTrell did not. Their family situations could be reduced to mere statistics swallowed up in divorce rates and marriage rates, as they relate to income level (Kreider & Ellis, 2011); their families too could be simple indexes of the racialized and disproportionate rates of incarceration, related not only to income but also to race (Mauer & King, 2007).

When the children played love, though, they were doing more than responding to some abstract societal ideology of heterosexual love or to the media's reinforcement of that ideology. Their play was also a response to an idealized family. There were "true" stories of families behind the play with boyfriends, girlfriends, dating, marrying, and breaking up.

For example, the discourse of love was there in the details of LaTrell's repeated drawings of houses:

All year long, whenever LaTrell has drawn his house, he has included a window for each family member, mom, dad, himself, his brother. This, as it turns out, is more dream than fact, as the collegial talk reveals this day. The talk has been about crying. Cici, unnerved by the loud thunder and lightning outside, has become teary; she wants her mommy. In response, Ernest says that he does not cry except just "one time. I cried about my daddy," who recently and unexpectedly died. (His t-shirt displays a picture of his missed daddy.)

I interject that that *was* upsetting and express how sorry I am that that happened. LaTrell now turns to me:

LATRELL: I'm upset because my daddy has a baby.
MRS. D: Your daddy has a baby. (echoing him)
LATRELL: And my daddy has a girlfriend. (irritated)
MRS. D: That's upsetting.
LATRELL: Yeah, I'm mad at him. But (tone changes to a warm one) every day
    on Friday he will always pick me up. So I'm not mad at him . . . now.
MRS. D: You decided—
LATRELL: to be nice. . . . He's my daddy.

Families break up. One can, like Brad, end up with two dads, one "fake," or, like Jon, two moms, one fake. Moreover, like LaTrell and Tionna too, one can learn of a new baby that is not your mama's baby. The dream of reciprocated love is one shared by many people and kept alive despite the reality that love can be a struggle, especially when times are hard. For the children, the extended play was about their imagined lives as "dults," to again quote Tionna, when they would have reciprocated love that might go on till death do us part, or so the saying goes.

This complex game of love was visible in writing time. In Mrs. Bee's room, it was there in pictures and erased notes, in Mrs. Kay's, in an expansive network of literacy practices that was interconnected with activity time play. To see such games, though, we need to view children, not as workers in cubicles, but as participants using whatever symbolic tools are available "to make sense and to make relationships" in a shared world (Nelson, 2007, p. 15).

Certainly children deserve some privacy—they do not need to have their love notes read to the class, unless they so choose. But, once again, some interplay between children's worlds and the official school world seems critical. As for written communication itself, an awareness of children's worlds may lead teachers to an appreciation of children's discursive flexibility, their capacity for appropriating language for a social practice they understand—a communicative skill that seems "basic" to writing. As for love, such an awareness may open the classroom floor to children's experiences with, and worries about, all kinds of *liking* (Boldt, 2011); and it may thus support teachers' and children's efforts to push against the boundaries of superficial gender images and stereotypical gender roles that inform games of love.

Moreover, through such official classroom talk, we may help children to articulate the many kinds of love they experience now, not when they are "dults." Letters of gratitude, of well wishes, of farewells, and, indeed, of happy birthdays are all variants of love letters in a sense, potential official opportunities to express affection. Sometimes, in the observed children's products, little notes to others would be embedded in children's official life stories—hints at discursive purposes with no official textual place (Dyson, 2008).

Most challenging of all for a small child may be the kind of love necessary for an inclusive classroom community; this is that love Manny referred to when he said "you suppose' to love everybody." That kind of love is a caring directed toward humanity, which leads us to treat others like we would like to be treated (a mantra of both Mrs. Bee and Mrs. Kay [see Chapter 2]). Such caring sometimes seems in short supply, particularly because this is a world of war as well as love. War is present as a metaphor (in games), as an adventure story (in media), and as a human tragedy (in the experiences of families all over the world). I turn now, in the last section of this chapter, to children's war play, which led to the most socially complex textual play.

FROM COMPLEMENTARY RELATIONS TO COLLABORATIVE IMPROVISATIONS: THE PINE CONE WARS

Children's imaginative play with physical power—be it that of human soldiers, policeman, or superheroes—has long troubled teachers of young children. The play is associated with aggressive male violence (Holland, 2003; Paley, 1984). But children play with the world as they experience it, given their complex gendered, racialized, and classed identities. In the time of this project, in the years immediately after 9/11, war filled the local news channels, as did talk of soldiers deployed or returning home and of families worrying and grieving.

Actual war, though, was only one influence on the war play of interest in this chapter. Indeed, the practice began as a team chase game ("The Pine Cone Wars") on the 1st-graders' playground. The game had no "good" guys, no "bad" guys; there were, though, projectiles—pine cones and wood chips tossed at the other "team" (never referred to as "armies"). There were two versions of this game, whose players were mainly but not exclusively boys. In one version, being tagged (by person or projectile) meant that one had to join the other team; in another version, being tagged led to being down for 2 minutes and then rejoining one's team. When this playground chase game was reorganized as composing time play, it became a collaborative improvisation—the most complex participation mode.

In improvisational collaborative composing, children had complementary roles in joint play, *and* their graphic turns built on one another's,
evolving dialogically. The most elaborate collaborative practice, the written version of The Pine Cone Wars game, yielded ethical issues of inclusion and exclusion in the unofficial world. Moreover, in the official world,
it yielded an unusual situated fix-it. That official fix-it, like an unofficial
one, was based on the prescribed identities of boys and girls (Figure 5.1,
IIC). Ironically, as I will illustrate, those identities led Mrs. Kay to ban the
topic of war, but they led Tionna to argue for the right to play.

The Evolution of Symbolic Wars

By late winter, The Pine Cone Wars dominated when Mrs. Kay's class
went out for recess. One day, though, the children were not allowed to
walk, much less run, in the playground's open field; it was deep in snow.
Everyone had to stay on the blacktop area. Lyron and Manny, though,
transformed the chase game into one involving *manipulatives*. Informed
(or so they said) by a cartoon with castles on a strange planet, the boys
designated as their castles two huge snow mounds left by the snow plow
on the edge of the blacktop. Their teams did not consist of children running wildly about but of small wood-chip "men" in the boys' respective
castles (a symbolic move that linguistically eliminated the girl players).
And then the boys' battle began, as each hurled projectiles at the other
team's men, in a kind of inanimate dodge ball.

This symbolic transformation of The Pine Cone Wars, from being to
representing team members, yielded a greater role for narrative turn-
taking during play (i.e., for each boy to say what was happening, since
the teams no longer moved under their own power). Such a movement
among symbolic media is common among young children; it allows them
to examine both experience and semiotic possibilities (Dyson, 1989; Kress,
1997; Matthews, 1999; Pahl, 2005). Herein, such multimodal movement
is an aspect of the history of a practice. When Lyron and Manny began
to engage in writing time war play, the war being graphically enacted
was linked to the chase game through the mediating step of narrative talk
about manipulatives in the snow mounds.

During composing time, drawing, not bodily movement or manipula-
ble objects, became the key symbolic tool as war transformed once again.
The boys' wood-chip "men" became tiny stick figures on paper, and the
castles were rendered as large structures with towers, each castle usually
topped with a flag marked with a boy's initials. The battles unfolded in a
cartoon-inspired alien land, where men fought with swords, bombs, and
lasers and flew about in helicopters and rocket ships that came from and
soared into outer space.

The oral narration continued, as it accompanied the unfolding drawn action. Indeed, a collaborative improvisation was enacted: Each child had to take into account the ongoing story and, more particularly, the just completed move of the other child before making his own next move. The children did this, of course, in dramatic play, but their representation was now one step removed, so to speak, enacted in talk and in the "deliberate semantics" of graphic action (Vygotsky, 1962, p. 100; Vygotsky, 1978). The details of the boys' graphic duel were realized in visual conventions related to direction and movement—arrows to indicate path, multiple lines in back of rocket ships to indicate energy and motion, and dense scribbles to convey chaotic action. Following is a brief excerpt from Lyron and Manny's talk while drawing (see Lyron's picture, Figure 7.5):

Figure 7.5. Lyron's Written War Games

Manny and Lyron, seated kitty corner from one another, are doing their respective quick sketches. They each have their own journals, they each are drawing, but they are clearly playing together:

LYRON: Manny, your men and my men are fighting with their swords.
MANNY: Well I still got men up here on Earth. Lyron, look it! . . . Look how many people that are from Earth.
LYRON: Manny, here's me and you on the bridge fighting, on my bridge. . . . I kicked you off the bridge. . . . [omitted data] . . . Here's where one of your guys jumped one—one of my guys . . .
ELLIE: (who has been listening) Lyron, you better watch out and you better not cry because looky what he [Manny] has coming.

And thus the battle continued in talk and drawing. The talk served to guide the drawing and, at the same time, to commandeer the other's attention.

After drawing the boys turned to writing. That writing, though, had a different history than the drawing and, at least initially, was not a collaborative improvisation. It was a new variant of fun plans; that is, the texts were typically about anticipated playground fun, akin to the earlier surfacing plans for weekend get-togethers (like birthday parties). In time, the texts settled into a basic genre: a statement of the game to come, an optional description of anticipated action (e.g., what or whose men would be crushed), and a declaration of who would win, as in the following text by Lyron:

> Manny I [*and* written over *I*] are going to
> have a war I am going to / winn Manny is goin to
> los I am going to winn.

Both boys' texts anticipated the action (e.g., the "going to" frame), named the players, and proclaimed who would win (in *Manny's* text, *Manny* wins). Unlike the social organization of the drawing (a collaborative improvisation), the written texts were produced within complementary relations of two opposing warriors.

The Spread and Variation of Textual War

Composing-time war play became known in the class through collegial interest and sharing-time presentations. On occasion, almost all boys claimed their own teams, or joined with others, to engage in such play. And one day, in early May, at the work table parallel to Lyron's and Manny's, Elisha and Mandisa began to join the play.

As authors, though, the girls' multimodal texts rendered war as comic theater—as an individual performance designed to elicit laughter. To this end, the girls introduced new discursive and symbolic possibilities into the production of textual war. For example, in her text, Mandisa used dialogue bubbles in her pictures, in which feisty selves proclaimed their power:

> I will beat
> you gus
> and win

Mandisa read her piece in the daily sharing time (although she told me that she did not get the laughs she expected). Still, that reading may have peaked Tionna's interest. The next day, as Mandisa began to organize teams for war play, Tionna turned around at her own table and asked her good friend across the aisle, "Can I play?"

"Sure," came the response. But that was not the response of the boys at Tionna's own table.

Sexism and the Ethics of Textual Inclusion

Girls playing war elicited no objection at Mandisa's table, but this was not the case at Tionna's table. When Lyron overheard Tionna's and Mandisa's talk about war, he objected quite firmly on the basis of their prescribed identity as girls (Figure 5.1, IIC):

LYRON: Me and Manny have our own war. You guys [in other words, "you girls"] don't even know about war.
TIONNA: Yes we do. I watched the war on TV.
MANNY: You're just copying offa us.
TIONNA: We got the girl war. No boys are allowed.

As people do when they are excluded, Tionna claimed her own story (cf., Dyson, 1997). Having been excluded from "the men's" war, Tionna declared the "girl war" and proceeded to rule boys out:

JASON: (makes battle sound effects, aiming an invisible weapon at Tionna and then Janette [who has no interest in war play]). . . . Kill them!
TIONNA: Jason, we're not playing in your war. We're not playing with you, in a war with you.

JASON: You are.

TIONNA: So you can kill us by yourself. You might be killing us, but we're not killing you and we're not on your team and we're not playing war with you guys. . . .

JASON: OK. (resigned)

LYRON: No! We're *letting* you guys [girls] play with us.

JASON: No man. A girl army's strong.

Lyron may have "let" the girls play, but Tionna reacted with aggressive drawing and writing. She abandoned the war games on Mandisa's table. As a "girl," Tionna led a drawn team in a collaborative improvisation of war, primarily with Lyron and Manny (the most verbal players). All three children began similarly by drawing "their" side pummeling the other with lasers and, in the boys' case, with one visible tank. And all declared that "we" would win.

However, Tionna made semiotic moves that the boys did not. She responded to the boys' claims with more complex drawn plots that went beyond pummeling others (e.g., she and her team found the boys' hidden treasure and stole their money). Moreover, she responded to their moves in writing. As already illustrated, Tionna could slip into familiar voices with relative ease. In her war play, she wrote as a woman warrior leading her "tofe girls." Thus, her writing was not only about plans to play war; it was a reasoned, dialogic argument for why her team would win.

Thus, when Manny and then Lyron drew a cannon-like missile, she switched from anticipating the future when they would play war, "girls a gints the boys," to the present tense, arguing that

> . . . nobody can stop the girls because
> we have a 1,0000001500000
> of misssl and the boys
> oldy have one misssls noway
> the boys can bet the girls thay
> can't laya ton [lay a hand] on us no you can't
> stop us not a bit because thay
> don't have a nofe things
> to getaditus [get at us] we are tofe girls . . .

However, Manny wrote, *We have two big casle. They have ten little tents.*

But Tionna claimed, *Thay oldy have one tent we have a lot of cacle.*

Despite the furious burst of writing, this day marked the end of textual war. Mrs. Kay, responding to an ethical concern of her own, decided to summarily ban texts about war play. The improvisational collaboration, the push for female inclusion in the male-dominated games at Tionna's table, the play with the genre at Mandisa's table, all came to an end.

Curricular Possibilities

Mrs. Kay viewed boys' plans for war play as just part of being a boy. But on the day that Jason, in his loud monotone voice, proclaimed that the boys should "kill" the girls, she was taken aback, as was I, truth be told. There is something disturbing about that word, which was only used in that exchange between Jason and Tionna. Mrs. Kay said that she did not want to have boys writing about killing girls (although Tionna herself was textually armed against the boys). Mrs. Kay told me that she was going to tell the children that they could not write about war any more. There would be no discussion, she said. She wanted to be clear. She viewed that response as part of her ethical obligation as a teacher, triggered by a concern about the inappropriate verbal aggression of boys against girls.

So Mrs. Kay told the children that they were not to write about war. As she spoke, her tone was firm, just like when she disciplined the children. In real war, she said, people are killed and that is that: "They are put in a box and buried." That latter comment seemed to seize the children's attention; as a group, they had experiences to share about dead people they had known and, moreover, they had questions and comments about burials themselves. (When the ground is full, Ellie explained, people are put in the water [i.e., burial at sea]). Given the community ethos of the class, this evolving discussion was unsurprising, despite Mrs. Kay's initial decision to avoid it.

Mrs. Kay's move to ban the topic of war play was not unreasonable; we as educators do have obligations to make our classrooms safe, supportive places for children. Still, her banning of war precluded the children's engagement in critical discussions of their own texts (Dyson, 1997; see Comber, 2003, for discussion of such pedagogy). After all, Mrs. Kay was not the only one who did not like war play (Janette had explicitly said she did not like war). Moreover, the ethical issues of the children, those of prescribed and limiting identity, of inclusion and exclusion, were not addressed. Textual war stopped because, explained Lyron, Ezekial, and Tionna, Mrs. Kay was thinking about "real" war, not fake war. Fake war no longer occurred on textual playgrounds, but it continued during recess as a chase game among friends.

THE BASIC DRAMAS OF CHILDREN'S TEXTUAL PLAY

The underlying point of this portrayal of parties, love, and war, is that the complex social dynamics of children writing were unremarkable within the mandated curricula. And yet, collegial peers, complementary role players, and collaborative dramatists were all on display. These relations gave evidence of the social agency of children, of their exercise of both camaraderie and power, and of the dialogic dynamics contributing to a participatory childhood culture. Moreover, they evidenced as well children's power to slip into a practice-appropriate role, to adapt relevant material, and when dialogically engaged, to give voice to their positioned subjectivity—their complex, emergent selves. This situated agency is at the heart of the basics of learning to write. The spirited Tionna and some verbally playful kindergartners will help me underscore this point in Chapter 8, as my own "basics" drama approaches its final act.

Performers on a Moveable Stage
On the Malleability of Voice and Image

It is the 100th day of school. In Mrs. Kay's room, the children are happily engaged in celebratory activities. They are making hats adorned with a hundred stickers and necklaces strung with a hundred cereal O's, perfect adornments for a 100-day march through the school. As the children fold, stick, and string, they talk and sing. On this February day, surrounded by heart stickers, their talk turns to boyfriends, girlfriends, and the then popular media stars—the kid rappers Lil' Romeo and Lil' Bow Wow. Tionna has a story about Lil' Romeo. She takes and then maintains center stage among her peers:

TIONNA: I went to uh the [Lil' Romeo] concert . . . I told him that I wanna be his girl friend. He said, "Uh::. I gotta think about that real quick." I think when I go there again I'm gonna ask him, and he'll probably say yes. . . .
LYRON: My cousin went to Lil' Bow Wow's concert. It was fun.
TIONNA: He ugly. On my birthday I will say that—I will say it on the radio. [in high pitched voice] "Lil' Bow Wow is *so ugly. Yes he i::s.*"

Storytelling was a regular practice among the children featured in this book. Typically, one story begot another in a collegial round of storytelling. Sometimes, though, a child took ongoing control of the storytelling, the stage, and the audience as Tionna did with her imagined encounters with rappers. As she illustrates, storytellers do not necessarily use language in unique ways (Pratt, 1977) but, rather, in decidedly more performative ways, using, for example, exaggerated plot action, rhythmic language, or vividly portrayed dialogue—Tionna's forte. In the above vignette, Tionna stretches out vowels, allowing Romeo time to think (Uh::) and, combining vowel duration with a raise in pitch, allowing herself time to stress her distain for the competing star.

How, one might ask, does a child accomplish such manipulation of sound, such capturing of the situated human voice, when the story is mediated by a blank page? Learning to perform through text entails something other than the official concerns that children become productive by drawing less and writing more details.

This chapter features two interrelated aspects of this "something other" required for performance. One aspect is children's linguistic flexibility, undergirded by the social knowledge that allows us all to use language appropriately in situations we understand. Indeed, language in use is always a kind of performance, so said Hymes (1972) in making elbow room for social knowledge in our understanding of "communicative competence" (p. 281). We know the generic or type of voice that usually accompanies a familiar situation. This knowledge helps us reach beyond words to social worlds and, thus, to make judgments about what's going on and what, then, we might say (Bakhtin, 1981; Blommaert, 2005).

The other aspect is multimodal flexibility; this flexibility depends upon, and is fed by, an understanding of the respective powers of one's semiotic tools (e.g., spoken word, visual image, music, animation). This differentiation of powers potentially allows performers rich resources for responding to the situation at hand. The use of semiotic resources, including but not limited to language, is sometimes referred to as *design* rather than composition (Kress, 2003, 2010). As the children will demonstrate, this aspect of performance actually helps them craft voices on paper. (FOR HEAVEN'S SAKE!!!!)

Through these means, children as performers use word, sound, and image to capture the subjective nature of experience (i.e., the feelings entailed); that experience is thus made material and put on display to garner others' attention and appreciation. This is the traditional meaning of *performance*, which brings to fore the aesthetic aspect of our lives (Bauman, 1992, 2004). Herein performance functions as a mode of child participation in social worlds.

In Mrs. Bee's mandated curriculum, there was no regular daily sharing and, thus, no opportunity for children to come to anticipate a potential audience response. This was not the case in Mrs. Kay's room, where audience response during the daily sharing time could be anticipated and commented upon. Listen, for example, to the exasperated but amused Mandisa:

> I did a knock knock joke once in my book. They [the class] didn't get that. It was like [makes a dead pan face]. . . . Nobody got it but me. It was the funniest joke. Ms. Kay wasn't even laughing. She was like (makes deadpan face [I laugh, clearly enjoying the performance]). And when Brad did um a knock knock joke we was all like [dead pan face]. And he was like, "What?"

Child performers manipulated resources in their linguistic and multimodal repertoire when they engaged in story composing, rhyme, and song writing, and, as Mandisa noted, even in writing knock knock jokes (for illustrations of the latter, see Dyson, 2006). In this closing chapter to Part II, I begin with children's performative prose, deemed by them "stories"; I stress children's use of malleable linguistic and multimodal resources. I then turn to children's deliberate writing of rhymes and songs.

I shine the spotlight most brightly on Tionna, whose performative efforts were particularly rich in linguistic and multimodal flexibility. Moreover, she highly valued performance in the daily sharing time; readers may recall her frantic efforts to remove the date from her Super Duper Man text so that she could share it as "today's story" (see the introduction to Part I). Nevertheless, Tionna will have to move over at times, so that other children from both Mrs. Kay's and Mrs. Bee's rooms can take the stage as they manipulate voice and image. Inside all their childhoods-in-formation is found the communicative flexibility central to this book's rethinking of the basics.

STORYTELLING:
COMMUNICATIVE RESOURCES AND SOCIAL STAGES

Oh, it is an unseasonably warm March day, and the afternoon sun is streaming through the window, smack dab in children's faces. Ms. Hache, the student teacher, pulls down the shade.

"*Thank* you," says Ellie. "We were melting!"

The children laugh, especially Tionna. When writing time begins, Tionna uses Ellie's appealing language and extends it, having Ellie hold forth on melting, ice cream, and good taste. Tionna giggles when she rereads the following text to the curious me, a text she will soon read to the class (after practicing its reading by herself for a bit).

M.s.s. H pull
down the shass [shades] Ellie
said we are mellting overe
here we are mellting like
Ice cream on a tree.
We fill [feel] like Ice cream
we have chodleita [chocolate] in the
outsid and vnedad [vanilla] in the
inside [Taste us] it will be good

you will sade [say] I won't [want]
some more of that.
(Bracketed words are those Tionna planned and/or read; they are
provided for ease of reading.)

Tionna was enacting a performative participation mode, manipulating the aesthetic aspects of language in order to garner others' appreciation (Bauman, 2004). Like other performative texts, Tionna's has
rhythmic repetitions, vivid images, and engaging dialogue (Tannen,
1989). From Tionna's point of view, she had written a funny story; it
would not be complete until she shared it (Bakhtin, 1986). Then the written text would be infused with life by the oral word, and the audience
would respond.

As she did in composing this poetic piece, Tionna, throughout this
book, has appropriated ways with words and, thereby, situated herself
in a world of voices. In interrelated oral and written modes, she has per-
formed appropriately as a firm mama and a consoling friend, an admirer
of a cute guy and a tough girl warrior, a coordinating player of childhood
clapping games, and finally, as an artful story composer. Tionna, then, is
the perfect guide to the first subsection below, with its focus on the linguistic repertoire. She will share the spotlight with others when the focus
moves in the second subsection to the multimodal repertoire.

A Linguistic Repertoire

For Tionna and her friends, as for children generally, words and how
they are arranged and articulated seemed inextricable aspects of how varied "we's" talk, that is, of situated voices. In childhoods, these are show-
cased in dramatic play. Children assume roles inaccessible to them as
"real" children; to do so, they deliberately manipulate not just words but
qualities of voices, such as volume, rhythm, vowel duration, and pitch—
"Uh::" (Garvey, 1990; Genishi & Dyson, 2009; Goodwin & Kyratzsis, 2011;
Minks, 2006).

As evidenced particularly in Chapter 7, Tionna and her peers could
adopt participant roles in diverse writing practices as well. These extended beyond those of writing time into free activity time, when the children
could, for example, make birthday lists for pretend parties and write and
deliver love notes.

These variations were clearly realized through children's textual
choices, as they enacted the speaking and writing ways associated with
particular situations. Such child variations may also involve the very languages and language variants that exist in a child's linguistic repertoire.

Vernacular voices and child writing. The link between assuming a social role and the variable use of one's languages has been dramatized primarily in studies of multilingual children (e.g., Long, Volk, & Gregory, 2007; Moll, Saez, & Dworin, 2001; Reyes & Azuara, 2008; Samway, 2006). But this link may be evident too in a child's differentiated use of the syntactic and semantic choices of AAL (African American Language).

AAL has grammatical options (e.g., in certain contexts, to use a *be* verb or not), some of which overlap with regionalized "standard" and "nonstandard" Englishes (Green, 2011). In the schools described in this book, the systemic grammar of AAL was unrecognized. Rather, it was deconstructed into a series of correctable errors. Thus, the way that manipulating languages themselves indexes social situations—the mark of a sophisticated communicator—was not an identified composing skill.

Indeed, AAL-speaking children—and all children who did not speak "standard" English—were potentially at a disadvantage. Teachers officially modeled conversational storytelling (as demonstrated in Chapter 2). In turn, the children were asked, first, to think about what they wanted to *say*, second, to *stretch* out their words, and third, to put their words on paper. This official directive, though, was deceptively simple ("as easy as A, B, C"); conversationally *saying* one's message would systematically render some children's texts as prime candidates for fix-its.

So it is in the society as a whole. Official language "basics" index a language variety (the "standard") that is objectified, rigidified, and normalized. Language users seen as deviating from that standard can themselves be objectified, racialized as the disorderly "other," and in school, marked as not measuring up (Dyson & Smitherman, 2009; Genishi & Dyson, 2009; Miller & Sperry, 2012; Urciuoli, 1998).

Still, children's use of AAL did seem to give rise to contradictory feelings in Mrs. Bee and Mrs. Kay, who very much enjoyed their children's writing. When Mrs. Bee read aloud a child's text she found appealing, she never changed the grammar. And, as readers may recall (see Chapter 3), in fixing Alicia's text, Mrs. Bee identified herself as part of the "we" who sometimes "talk like that" (i.e., deleting the *be* verb). As for Mrs. Kay, despite her consistent grammatical fix-its, she in fact thought Tionna became an unusually strong writer precisely because "there's lots of talk" in her home. Indeed, Tionna did rely increasingly on revoicing talk in her own progressively longer, more elaborate texts (which, in the last half of the year, averaged 52 words, almost twice the class average). Below, I sample these written voices.

Tionna and the written voices. Tionna was socially attuned both to the generic ways with words used in particular situations (e.g., the discourse associated with having a "crush" [on Jon]) and to particularly appealing utterances, often associated with appealing or at least interesting people (like Ellie). She wrote about what her dad or her grandma said; she replayed the words of her classmates, and also those of her close friends, aunties, and cousins—and even of Mrs. Kay. As these situated voices changed, so too could the grammatical features of her language. In one entry, for example, Tionna slipped into a performative voice, writing about a cousin who

> all ways copy cat me and I say aret [aren't] you tier [tired] of copycating me she say no am [I'm] not that is my favord [favorite] so plese stop ascking [asking] me mame [ma'am] I get tier of that[,] calling me mame so I will call her mame

The assertive back and forth of Tionna's expressive dialogue, her explicit feelings and conversational present tense ("she say" and "I say") contrast the syntactically "standard" and straightforward prose of the following text, closely modeled on her teacher's talk:

> Yesterday Mrs. Kay wint to the doctor she had to leav for the rest of the after non because she said her son Kelly had a bump on his arm she said they had to remove it thay had to give him a shot in his arm to numb it so he won't feal it.

The above text did not seem aesthetically performative. Tionna was retelling a narrative she had heard with everyone else in the class. Moreover, she was not joining in on some coordinated peer replaying of the text. She seemed, rather, to be socially, perhaps collegially, aligning with her teacher; she retold her teacher's story in her teacher's narrative voice.

Not all official voices were straightforward in nature. To illustrate, I inject a poem into this consideration of Tionna's prose. The poem was not an official assignment, but it was based on an official text Tionna had read during a reading group meeting. The text was a Mother's Day poem; it read, in part, "above the rest we think you are the best mom there could be." The day of this reading lesson was the same day that, during the later free activity period, Mandisa had shown Tionna and Lyron how to make pop-up books (having learned herself, she said, from her grandmother). Tionna decided to make one for her grandmother. She wrote the Mother's Day poem on the book. She explicitly tried to remember the poem exactly, to get it "right." In so doing, she preserved the formal tone of the original, even using an archaic-sounding "be":

Out of all the moms there be
you are the best one
There is in live.
Happy mothers day love mom.

Although Tionna's striking changes in voice were atypical, her so-cial orientation to language use was not. The notion of manipulating a text in order to better suit a situation was common—it was at the heart of dramatic play and, more broadly, of the relational ideology dominant in children's worlds. In early schooling, children's linguistic repertoire can be named, maintained, and stretched, a point that will inform Chapter 9's consideration of re-imagined basics. Or, as was the case for Tionna, it can be narrowed in school; by the end of the 2nd grade Tionna felt that a book for children written in AAL was full of grammatical fix-its (Dyson & Smitherman, 2009).

A Multimodal Repertoire

As we toured the neighborhoods in Chapter 1, we noted some of the written language displayed on the streets. That print never made mean-ing on its own—it was always located in particular spaces and most often intertwined with other symbolic modes. Children themselves—and, most vividly, kindergartner LaTrell and 1st-grader Ezekial—borrowed this styl-ized and spatialized print, reproducing street signs, building labels, score boards, toy product boxes, and even television screens (as in LaTrell's *CN*, which turned his paper's drawing space into a television screen for Car-toon Network).

Similarly, the child products featured in the pages of this book could not be understood only by examining written language. The children's stories, plans, and reports were often interwoven with the semiotic stuff of talk and drawing, as well as writing. These differing symbolic modes were not necessarily closely aligned: Mrs. Bee's children especially drew and talked much more expansively and, sometimes, more fluidly than they wrote (cf. Dyson, 1989); Mrs. Kay's children sometimes operated in shifting space/time places, as when they planned war games that were enacted in talk and drawing. Nevertheless, productive children were ex-pected to write at least the minimal number of sentences or pages (three). The assumed path of progress was from drawing to writing.

This official path was constructed by official benchmarks, focused solely on children's writing. However, if the unit of study is not a child's written text but a situated production and a multimodal whole, the path of writing development and the repertoire of symbolic resources become more complex, as explained below.

Places, action, and drama through semiotic flexibility. The less-experienced kindergartners used drawing and accompanying talk as sole forms of composing, at least until the pressure to write increased. Still, as children gained experience, the representational strengths of drawing vis-à-vis writing became clearer.

First, drawing was particularly useful for the location of figures and objects in space (cf., Bezemer & Kress, 2008). This was so even for Alicia and LaTrell, neither of whom had consistent baselines in their early school drawings. For Alicia, so intent on managing social relations, family members, friends, and classmates were drawn close together in bounded space—parks, pools, cars, and buses. Often they held hands as hearts floated above their heads. For LaTrell, writing time initially was a collegial site for scary happenings. Creatures in close proximity—especially when one was distinctly larger than others—signaled danger ahead. Among the 1st-graders, particularly detailed drawings were produced in The Pine Cone Wars. Inevitably, an initial step in the play was locating the opposing teams' castles and warriors on the page. Without such marked space, there could be no attacking warriors violating space, no defending warriors protecting space.

Second, drawing was sometimes critical to, sometimes an augmentation of, movement. In fact, the depiction of movement is perhaps the earliest visual meaning-making of the very young. Lines, curves, and dots do not necessarily represent shapes but sensorimotor qualities (Dyson, 1989; Mathews, 1999; Smith, 1983), including the speed or nature of movement, its force and direction, its duration. "I don't know what it is," a preschooler commented about her quick circular scribble to a long-ago student of mine; but, whatever it was, "it's going fast." The Pine Cone War players were particularly vivid in their use of drawing for movement. In their collaborative improvising, they drew the dense scribbles of destruction, lines of exhaust from jets, and, animation-style, repetitions of small projectiles, tracing out their movement in space, all the while commenting on the unfolding action.

Both space and movement mattered in Tionna's semiotically complex rendition of a traffic accident, which had led to an ambulance ride for her and her grandmother. Even fairly early in the school year (December), Tionna was more given to writing than drawing. In this event, though, she uncharacteristically ignored Mrs. Kay's urgings to start writing and, moreover, she broke the rule against writing-time coloring. In order to narrate the drama of what happened, she needed the referential power

Figure 8.1. Tionna's Traffic Accident

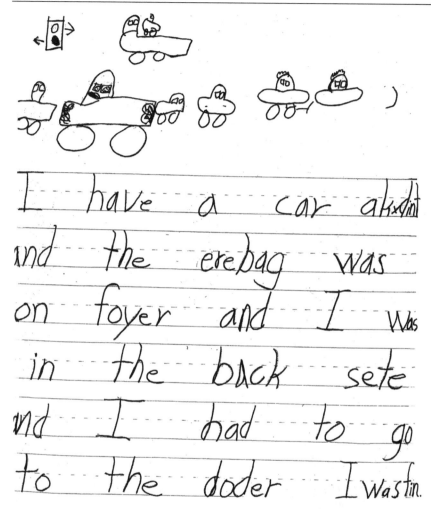

of marked space. (One could imagine Tionna as lawyer, calling the jury's attention to her displayed figure [in my Perry Mason-shaped mind], making clear who was the victim and who "came from *nowhere*" and broke the law.) An excerpt follows from the production of Figure 8.1:

Tionna is drawing and talking, as I listen. Next to her is Jon, whose collegial attention is soon piqued, and Tionna becomes performative in word and image, keeping Jon's interest.

TIONNA: (talking and drawing) Here's our truck. A little dent up in it and stuff, lights all bent up, and scratched up. . . .

And here's the truck that's in front of us. . . . There's the [other] truck that hit us. And here's the air bag, that—it's got on fire.

And that's all the cars in front of us . . . And this one crashed in the back of us. In the back of us, all dent up and scratched up and crashed in. And I was right in the back seat. Just cars hitting us and stuff.

Here's the light. The light was green. I gotta color it. . . .

(In the background, Mrs. Kay is telling children that they should be writing by now. Tionna keeps coloring.)

And the other light was red. And the other guy he just came from *nowhere* and hit us. Red. Our light was green. And that was that side. (making an arrow from red light to the offending guy's "side")

. . .

And here's the police car. The police car was there and the ambulance.

. . .

JON: Were you hurt?

TIONNA: I had to go to the hospital. The ambulance was there. The police was there. . . . Oh:: I know! The tow truck. He was towing our truck. . . .

JON: It got hit right there? (pointing to the front of Tionna's truck) [Tionna: No.] That was like that?

TIONNA: That was a airbag got on fire. . . . It goes inside a car, a truck. You know the air bag?

JON: Yeah. It comes out of the steering wheel.

TIONNA: It was in the front seat by my mom. It was *right there*. My *mom* was sitting there.

The interaction continues, as Tionna tells what happened to her grandmother at the hospital.

I bet more than a few readers are thinking, "What happened next?" Tionna involved you in her story with her visual and oral symbolizing. (Her grandmother had to be treated at the hospital and sustained long-term back problems, but Tionna, as she says, "was fine.")

Tionna did provide some spatial information in her text (*I was in the back sete*), but the positioning of the cars, trucks and her "mom" (*so dangerously close to the fire*) and the assigning of fault ("Red.")—both were much more easily conveyed in a drawing, rather than in prose (whatever the skill of the writer). The suddenness of the accident was in her narration ("from *nowhere*"), but the chaotic scene of cars, trucks, and blaring sirens was in her drawing.

As image, sound, and animation become increasingly important in contemporary texts, writing remains important but it does not remain singular. The direction of growth does not involve simply the abandonment of drawing and talk but the more differentiated use of semiotic tools, given the task at hand.

The depiction of human voices. In early schooling, teachers guide children to stretch and listen to the sounds of spoken words. Still, as human utterances, the same words sound quite different, depending on speaker and context. This knowledge is basic to dramatic storytelling, and evidence of that knowledge can be found in young children's multimodal composing.

Drawn characters may speak in children's pictures; words, encased in dialogue bubbles, can be central to a story's action. Moreover, children may visually represent speech, including its paralinguistic features, like VOLUME, duraaaation, and affect!!!!! Throughout this book, children's use, or non-use, of capital letters and periods bespeaks the difficulty of these seemingly simple punctuation "basics." However, both dialogue bubbles and exclamation points (placed after a word or a line) could appear well before a child could be relied upon for an accurately placed period. Unlike periods, these conventions were clearly tied to meaning and (quite literally) to voice.

Such visual resources were particularly evident in Ezekial's composing. Breaking the usual conventions of spelling, he married visual play and qualities of voice to YELL in his writing or to stretch out a sound in a drawing, like the distressed coach's *boo* (see Chapter 3) or his own *zzz*'s when sleeping in his bed. His texts themselves were simple, straightforward sentences (e.g., *I will be sleepy*), but he sometimes acted them out when he presented them. He could join sound effects found in his picture ("zzz . . . ") with bodily movement (a cocked head) for an oral reading that yielded appreciative laughter.

In the kindergarten, LaTrell was a detailed storyteller, sometimes a performative one (he was attacked, I note, by a shark which bit his leg in the local pool). But, as earlier discussed, LaTrell tried hard to follow the directions in writing workshop—eventually writing a sentence on each of three pages, which ended when he took a shower, ate, and/or went to bed. His cousin Charles, though, never abandoned his adventurous life that year. His peers, and I, were an available audience for his stories, which, by the end of the year, took shape in image and voice on the page.

A Midwest child, Charles, as readers may recall, had a house that was destroyed one night by a tornado in Florida (see Chapter 4). His father was in jail but, nevertheless, was a spaceman. Charles' mother gave him a long pet snake, which was prone to attack and had to be kept in a cage. Among his other animals was "a cat that's gonna grow up to be a cougar." He had a dog, but it was killed by a lion.

Although Charles had, in my view, a fabulous imagination—and a deadpan way of sharing his truths—he found both handwriting and drawing a challenge. His people, for example, remained circles with appendages for the entire year. Nevertheless, he was drawn to expressive images. His walking circles were involved in "awesome" adventures; and, despite his awkwardness with a pencil, his racing cars had exhaust out the back end, his basketballs were repeatedly drawn so that they moved through space, and his snake sunk his teeth into a shark loose in the local pool.

As for writing, Charles was attracted to dramas in which he could insert the self as victim and, ultimately, survivor. To mark the excitement of happenings, by February he made use of the exclamation point, as in the following example:

> I hit! / ThAT BAes! [Base!]
> BIl Sow [So] hRod [hard]
> I got FoR / Ho res [home runs].

As just suggested, Charles was interested in conventions he saw as tied to meaning-making. The first time Charles put a dialogue bubble in a picture, he used a proselike phrase: *O my gish [gosh] I sid [said]*. (In his story, the power had gone off in his home.) The next time that he included dialogue in his picture, he abandoned the dialogue bubbles but also the "said." Rather, Charles placed the dialogue near the depicted characters— himself and his big sister (see Figure 8.2). The spoken words were mainly in the picture.

On the day in late May when Figure 8.2 was produced, Charles was surrounded by children reporting that they would go swimming this summer. In their pictures could be found named friends and family members in a city pool. True to form, Charles did not merely report his intention but told a story (a fictional one, or so he said when I visited him in the 3rd grade). In his picture, Charles and his sister stand side-by-side, their respective identities indexed by the length of their appendages, not their hair. (Charles did not do hair.) *Jup!* ["Jump!"] says his sister. *No* says Charles at first. He relents, though: *Oka* ["OK"].

Then Charles jumps in and moves through the water (depicted by a succession of images across the bottom of the picture border). At the beginning of the succession, he says *hop I no* [know] *ho* [how] *to swim*. At the end, he says [How] *osum* [awesome] *is that*.

Figure 8.2. Charles' Jump in the Water

In the bottom half of the page, Charles' writing indirectly reports his sister's speech [*My./SustR!/ tod* [told] *me to Jmup/iN to the wot* [water]!*] and narrates his subsequent jump, each event linearly following the other. Still, Charles' picture, augmented by dialogue, conveys his tense approach to the water, his movement through it, and his concluding pride in his accomplishment. Awesome differentiation of semiotic powers!

When Mrs. Bee came by to listen to Charles read his writing, she asked him to redo his illegible name and, also, to add the necessary periods. Charles responded with tears spilling down his face. There was no need for that, explained Mrs. Bee; it was her job to teach him how to do things better. After she left, Charles commented to me, "Mrs. Bee didn't like my writing."

I pointed out that that was not what Mrs. Bee said; she had just wanted him to fix a couple of things. Still, Charles was a performer in need of an audience, and he seemed to approach Mrs. Bee as such. Children in such need may be particularly vulnerable to others' comments, precisely because they are performers (see the performative Jameel in Dyson, 1993). Tionna did not react in such ways to Mrs. Kay, but her major anticipated audience was her peers during whole-class sharing time. Without a predictable time for an audience, it may be hard for a performing child to differentiate a pedagogic from an audience role.

Moreover, Mrs. Bee's curriculum did not support her appreciation of multimodal efforts. Charles's story, as well as his learning, was not graspable through the writing bounded by the lines on the lower two-thirds of his paper. For example, Charles was differentiating the conventions for dialogue in different discursive conditions. There is, for example, no "[somebody] said" in his picture. Moreover, he was exploring, not only dialogue, but also spatial detail and old-style animation (i.e., multiple pictures that combine to convey movement) to communicate his feelings, in this case, his tentative beginning and his prideful ending.

As all the productions presented in this subsection have suggested, the direction of written language growth is not necessarily a linear progression through forms, leading to the pinnacle—written language. Rather, it is a more complex differentiation, as children situate newer tools within existent symbolic repertoires (Dyson, 1989; Kress, 1997; Stetsenko, 1995; Vygotsky, 1978).

The manipulation of varied symbolic material, including language, was central to children's composing of performative prose, particularly dramatic or funny stories. Less pervasive than stories but also fundamental to human experience, perhaps especially to children, are rhyme and song.

RHYMING AND SINGING:
NEW WRITTEN VENUES FOR PLAY AND PERFORMANCE

Both Mrs. Bee and Mrs. Kay enjoyed singing with their children. Mrs. Kay worked it in by choosing a children's book with songs to share. (You might recall from Chapter 2 when Ezekial located the class's old friend—*Take Me Out of the Bathtub* . . . [Katz & Carrow, 2001]—in the basement book fair). Mrs. Bee wrote the children a song (also in Chapter 2) but, in the main, she left her considerable singing skills with her family and church.

None of Mrs. Kay's children engrossed themselves in song writing—it was never presented as a viable option. For most of the year, none of Mrs. Bee's children did either. In Mrs. Bee's room, though, rhymes and songs did become viable options, and it all began when Mrs. Bee made an unmandated response to a mandated poetry unit in the early spring; that unit took up weeks of class time but, nevertheless, was not successful.

The official unit was quite structured, and Mrs. Bee initially followed the required lessons carefully. As directed, she had her children look at objects and describe them in detail, she talked about how language is like music (stressing repetition), and she read the children suggested poems, changing their rhythm with different line breaks. In the end, though, most every child's poem consisted of brief sentences about some favorite object, written with a great deal of teacher guidance on details and encoding.

One day, Mrs. Bee abandoned the required lessons. She told the children that they actually knew lots of poems. She heard them say poems when they were waiting to line up for lunch or during transition times between lessons. Moreover, she knew many of the same poems from when she was a little girl, and she knew some that they did not.

Then she led the children in these known poems, like "Shame Shame Shame" and "Miss Mary Mack Mack Mack." These were the children's hand clapping games, or as some called them, "songs." Every child was now attentive, alert, and reciting loudly. The rhymes and songs (like "Twinkle Twinkle Little Star") took over the lesson; everyone was having such a good time. Mrs. Bee even taught her children a rhyme most did not know, an old favorite from her own childhood—"Ride, Sally, Ride"—which was, she said, about singing for the one in the middle and awaiting your turn.

Mrs. Bee had the children listen for those poetry qualities she had taught: They were moving to the music, the rhythm, of the poem; they were repeating words; and, in fact, they knew all about rhyme. When the handclaps and singing stopped, Mrs. Bee suggested that they make their own rhyme or poem; it could even be a different version of one they knew.

Recalling Part I's conundrums, I note that this is not, though, what the children did. Many children (half the class) had a go at writing a song or a rhyme they knew. They were not, however, going for their "own" individual version but, rather, for accuracy; they corrected one another if they got a line wrong (refer to Figure 5.1, ID). After all, these were social games for coordinating their efforts, not for individual display. Some children, though, were cognizant of the rule against copying, and so they wrote different lines of the same poem, although all could join in on the reading.

As described in Chapter 6, Ernest first attempted Twinkle Twinkle as a coordinated effort with LaTrell. Ernest was a small, thin, agreeable child; an easy conversationalist; and a language player, especially with LaTrell. "Yipeo, jibeo, jibeoo," said LaTrell as he wrote Twinkle Twinkle.

"Cheerio, cheerio, cheerio," answered Ernest.

Viewed as a sweet "fake daddy" by Alicia and her friends, who would pat him on the head on occasion, Ernest initially had a difficult time grasping the alphabetic system (see Chapter 3). By now, though, he had some orthographic insight into the system, and he persisted in his effort to spell the words of Twinkle Twinkle over a 2-week period. In the midst of this effort came that day of thunder and lightning, when Cici was scared and teary, but LaTrell and Ernest were not (see Chapter 7). In fact, this was the day that Ernest interrupted his Twinkle Twinkle writing to compose an original song about the storm. After all, as he said, "It's all about songs now." He began by commenting to LaTrell:

ERNEST: I'm gonna make a song outa that. I'm gonna make a song outa what it's doing. "It's raining."

Ernest starts his first line (*its RiE* [It's raining]), but then begins to draw. At first he puts raindrops all over the drawing space on his page, but he changes his mind; the drawing space is divided into three sections: the raindrops interrupted by lightning. Ernest explains to Cici:

ERNEST: There's a storm here. (pointing to the drawing in Figure 8.3) There's lightning here. (pointing to middle section) I'm making a song.
CICI: Oh. That's pretty smart.
ERNEST: I let you see it.

Ernest wrote his poem on "it's raining and stormy." He knew he was "repeating," just like a poet does, and he hoped to end with a rainbow, but he ran out of time. Still, inspired by the moment, and informed by a new possibility for composing, Ernest got a good start for his song and, indeed, he had a potential audience in Cici.

Figure 8.3. Ernest's Storm-Inspired Song

Mrs. Bee used known poems to situate children as knowledgeable about, rather than failing at, poetry. Those poems came within a participation mode involving social play. The children took to that new form of an old social play, and many wrote long pieces, working hard to represent a familiar rhyme or song on paper that peers could unofficially read together. This was the dominant child response to Mrs. Bee's response to that mandated poetry unit.

From within a familiar social play, Ernest thought of himself as a composer of songs—"it's all about songs now." In the midst of talk about rain, thunder, and lightning, he was decidedly not going to cry. He was going to play with the weather on paper. That is, he was "gonna make a song out of what it's doing." Pretty smart. All he needed was a proper stage, and, then, the song might have been sung and maybe taken a place with Mrs. Bee's "Wake Up, Sleepy Heads" (see Chapter 2).

ON CHILD PERFORMERS

In the common sense guidelines for teaching children to write, the teachers were to help children learn the basics, the ABC's and their sounds, the periods, the grammatical niceties as they are so defined. Moreover, the teachers were to have children reflect on experiences and detail them in increasingly more elaborate ways on paper. Writing was thus an individual act.

But these young children were not withdrawing from the world but borrowing from, and responding to, the articulated world around them. In this sense, their performative moments were undergirded by their alert collegiality, their coordinating moves, their complementary responses, and the urge to "be on" for their peers (Bauman, 2004, p. 9). Tionna's elaborate metaphor of melting ice cream, inspired by Ellie and, perhaps, the receptive response of the class; Charles's efforts to convey his tension about actually swimming like his big sister, not just going to the pool as his peers planned; Ernest's confident intention to make a song out of the storm that Cici found so scary—all these responses to the voices surrounding them evidenced some deliberate effort to craft a world.

Moreover, composing—performing—a world with words and images went beyond the basics of text production: focus, add details, and simply write more. It entailed exploiting one's linguistic and multimodal repertoires to capture the feelings of things. Alicia conveyed her social belonging and affections by stringing hearts over her hand-holding family. LaTrell initially made jagged lines, connoting a dangerous world in which a small child could save the weak. By the end of the year, Charles combined image and dialogue, portraying himself as capable of overcoming danger with courage.

Most sophisticated was Tionna, who on occasion could embed her feelings in the very structure of her prose (Labov, 1972; Toolan, 1988). No simple "it was fun" for her. She drew our attention to the uniqueness of people and events—her cousin was "the best cousint in the hole wide world"; Ellie-as-ice-cream tastes so good, you will "won't [want] some more of that." And one day, in the after-school garden club, the snacks were such that even though she and Mandisa "was *verey fool[full]*," "*nobody could stop us from eating it thats how good it was*" (emphasis in original).

The children's efforts were supported by their teachers, who, in one way or the other, widened the universe of textual possibilities beyond the narrow and monitored literacy curriculum. Those children with a guaranteed daily stage had opportunities to anticipate their audience and, moreover, to learn about the varied roles participants in literacy events might share (e.g., not only collaborator but also pedagogue and audience).

If linguistic disrespect had not been a school basic (i.e., the notion of a homogeneous "correct" language), the children could have also begun to learn explicitly about making social and aesthetic decisions in the use of a language repertoire. If the basics of text production and productivity were not so exclusively tied to language, children might also have begun to appreciate their differential use of a multimodal repertoire.

Indeed, a furthering of children's communicative flexibility is dependent upon a rethinking of the basics themselves. With the help of Mrs. Bee, Mrs. Kay, and their children, this has been the work of this book, which culminates in Chapter 9. Off in the distant echoes of this just-finished chapter, I can hear Charles reading his written rendition of a locally well-known hand-clap game, based on an old disco-era song. He is getting me in the mood for the work to come, when I discuss guidelines for basic composing programs that make sense to me:

> that!/The!/WA!
> Uh uh!/I LiKe it!
> Uh Uh!

We had best move on.

Re-Imagining
Writing Basics for
Contemporary Childhoods

"So," said Tionna, big grin on her face, "What do you think of our pic-nic?" I was walking up to the park's shelter, where the children were enjoying the hot dogs Mrs. Kay was fixing at the grill for this end-of-the-year event. Mrs. Kay waved hello and motioned for me to come get a hot dog and to help myself to the chips, pickles, and kool-aid. As I readied a plate, Tionna finished up and made her way over to a patio chaise lawn chair. She stretched out in that chair, then sat up, placed her imagined drink in the chair's cup holder, and adjusted her pretend TV. "Ah::," she sighed as she laid back down and folded her arms behind her head. This was the life.

That day at the park, I first saw children from afar, sitting in a concrete area in a treeless spot. Not so great, I thought. But when I moved closer, was queried by Tionna, heard the children chatting and then, after eating, laughing and chasing one another on the open field, my view began to change. And when I saw Tionna stretched out on that lawn chair watching the invisible TV, well, I knew I had not been seeing the picnic from children's points of view.

In a similar way, through this book, I have aimed to get another angle, not on settings for school picnics, but on the matter of school basics. My tack has been to re-view school writing "basics" by situating them within the life spaces of young children. The goal was, in some ways, akin to that of psychologists Chabris and Simons (2010), who study selective atten-tion. "Did you see the gorilla?" they ask at the end of their short video, os-tensibly on ball passing. The researchers use the video to illustrate how a narrow focus can make invisible what might, in retrospect, seem obvious. Viewers of their video are asked to count how many times three people in white shirts (as opposed to three people in black shirts) pass a basket-ball. Viewers may be so intent on counting the balls that they do not see the large gorilla that saunters across the screen and even stops to face the audience, pounding on his chest.

In this book, official curricula channeled professional attention to "the basics." Those basics were located within interlocking sets of spaces and times: on individual child papers and, more particularly, on the lines on those papers; within time units set by institutional ways of organizing academic calendars, school-reporting periods, grade-level objectives, paced teaching materials, and benchmark assessments. Those institutional ways themselves fit within federal funding requirements and, more broadly, within societal narratives about how to make sure the "all" children measure up (*all* meaning the *some* children schools consistently fail [Dyson, 2003b]). *All* children receive the same instruction, an ambition that confuses uniformity and equity. How could every child in our socioculturally diverse society possibly make the "same" sense out of the "same" lesson (Genishi & Dyson, 2009)? What are "the basics" anyway?

To get another view, I moved in close to the children in Mrs. Kay's and Mrs. Bee's rooms, especially during writing time. I observed the children's unofficial actions and interactions, heard their fix-it concerns, and studied how they organized themselves within social relations and emerging but unofficial practices. Composing continued to pose graphological and content challenges (refer to Figure 3.1). However, it did not remain solely a school task; rather, it became a complex of communicative events and practices, within which children orchestrated, and sought out, knowledge and know-how. Thus, I re-imagined the basics, as I followed the children into their childhood times and spaces.

In this final chapter, then, I begin by summarizing the work of contextualizing and stretching the traditional basics and use two such basics to illustrate this re-imagining. I close with guiding principles for "basic" composing programs for the very young.

I have no intention of dismissing the efforts of dedicated teachers like Mrs. Bee and Mrs. Kay, or of ignoring children's need to learn letter names, to gain insight into the alphabetic system, and to make sense of punctuation. Further, I have no desire for the official world to colonize children's unofficial worlds—an impossibility in any case. But I do aim for the official world to learn from unofficial worlds. The children's actions and reactions inform a re-imagining of the basics and of academic resources. That re-imagining might itself further writing programs that are open to children's diverse communicative experiences and, at the same time, geared to expanding children's possibilities in ways that are compatible with human sociability and ethical responsibility.

I begin, then, with the "basics"!

CONTEXTUALIZING THE BASICS

In official worlds, the conventional basics are a set of technical skills, often listed on a report card. In the kindergarten, for example, the child "prints capital and lower case letters correctly," "hears and records sounds in words," "communicates ideas by writing words," and "stays on topic when writing a story." In 1st grade, the child "writes three or more connected sentences," "writes with complete sentences with grade level appropriate grammar, usage, mechanics and temporary spellings," and "reads drafts of their work to clarify meaning and attempt some revision." (Objectives from districts' standards-based reporting guidelines for parents.)

The children, though, were not so much learning skills as figuring out how to participate in the socially organized world of school. Over time, they built expectations for official school practices, which they conformed to (or negotiated around). Moreover, the children were not only socialized into official practices, but they also exercised agency; they used familiar frames of reference—familiar practices—to give these new school demands relevance and meaning in their ongoing lives. Indeed, when faced with new demands, we all use familiar frames of reference. Otherwise, we would have no basis for acting (Bakhtin, 1986). Collectively, the children, however new to school writing, knew about collegially making meaning on paper through drawing and talk, about playfully interacting in complementary ways, and about joining in the improvisation of ongoing action (cf. Sterponi, 2011).

In this situated view, children were being socialized into school writing practices, but they were doing so as people with a communicative past, with agency in their own life spaces, and with connections and obligations to others with whom they shared aspects of their identities, including friends and other kids or classmates, as well as players, churchgoers, and fans of varied cultural happenings. Moreover, even as children situated writing within familiar ways of interacting, they also recontextualized or borrowed voices, images, themes, and intentions initially associated with other practices (cf. Dyson, 2003a). These allowed them linguistic and semiotic resources for the composing task at hand.

The children found resources in varied aspects of local (if globally influenced) child cultures, like birthday parties, chase games, playground handclaps, after-school sports programs, popular songs, familiar video games, and many TV shows, including cartoons, sports shows, news reports, weather forecasts, and music programs. This cultural material included voices, from homes and neighborhoods, that differed from those that sounded right in school. It included as well images, including de-signed print that could contradict school spelling and punctuation rules (the latter of which were not clear to most children in any case). Capital letters played off one another's size on building fronts; sports heroes had names written "the short way," to quote Ezekial (i.e., in abbreviations); S's turned into $'s on a dollar store's signs; and speech bubbles could show up most anywhere, not just in comics but also on posters and ads, and in picture books (as in the popular *Pigeon* books [e.g., Willems, 2003]).

As a consequence of such gaps between school rules and experienced diversity, official "basics" are set against the symbolic displays of chil-dren's everyday worlds. If these gaps were to be visible or even acknowl-edged in the official world, then traditional writing "basics" would be transformed from following rigid surface-level rules to flexibly adapting linguistic and semiotic resources (e.g., choices of content, text features, or symbols) for participation in the event at hand.

Just as the ABC's are differentially appropriated for encoding particu-lar words, words themselves and other kinds of symbols are differentially arranged to enact a practice in a particular event. For example, within an event, isolated elements—a repeated letter (*boooo* . . .), a repeated phrase (*it's raining, it's raining, it's raining*), a punctuation mark (!), an image (♥), a wording (*I am going to win*), a topic (birthdays), even a grammatical usage (*she say* or *she said*)—may become communicative options in service of, or against, social expectations, efficiency, or aesthetics.

This transformation would also stretch "the basics," because it would make relevant children's use of basic communication actions: appropri-ating and adapting relevant symbolic resources, slipping into practice-appropriate roles, and responding in relationally attuned ways (e.g., collegially; complementarily; in coordination, improvisation or perfor-mance; or even pedagogically). These are sociolinguistic skills central to relationships and to social play, and they are central too to relations and practices mediated through composing.

In the vision of child writing arising from this book, then, learning to write involves learning how to manipulate symbols to participate in varied kinds of composing practices and in the larger worlds of values and beliefs (Bakhtin, 1981). Because they draw on familiar practices and tools in the writing-focused contexts of school, children confront the "op-tions, limits, and blends that are acceptable to oneself or others" in varied practices (to stretch the words of Miller and Goodnow [1995, p. 12] on development).

Taking the long view across the school years, children differenti-ate the multiple dimensions of textual communication (e.g., the varied symbol systems involved, typified communication genres or practices, punctuation and formatting possibilities) and the flexible use of those dimensions given the constraints and possibilities of practices (including their structural expectations, social relationships, and ideological underpinnings). Thus, children are not envisioned herein as climbing up the proverbial ladder of success but as maneuvering on an expanding landscape with more flexibility and more deliberateness in their decision making.

As for Mrs. Bee's and Mrs. Kay's children, they were already adapting their symbol-making to the situation at hand. For example, even before Alicia understood the alphabetic system, she understood how the use of children's names (and that potent heart image) mattered socially, and she revised even her wavy-line cursive when she worried Regina might read it. In Mrs. Kay's 1st grade, child voices, articulated in choices of words and text structure, shifted as children moved among unofficial practices of parties, love, and war.

Moreover, children were also experiencing ideological differences, that is, official and unofficial worlds' differing notions of what a desirable story is, what wording sounds right, what is ethically right, and I dare say, even what is fun. Such gaps in the use of written language in official and unofficial worlds—and in and out of school—*may* raise children's awareness of situated options, but, without official acknowledgment, it may also lead them to view their own linguistic and semiotic experiences as irrelevant to schooling. The worry, then, is that children's resources and communicative skills will be lost to the official world if that world's composing constraints and possibilities are too narrow.

To illustrate the re-imagining of the basics, and the attendant possibilities and worry, I highlight below two key basics: making one's text "sound better," focusing on *adjusting Standard English usage*; and "being productive," focusing on *writing more/drawing less*.

Linguistic Flexibility: Rethinking "Making it Sound Better"

As noted early on in this book, official curricula were undergirded by a valuing of a homogeneous language, a one best way with words, the "standard" way. Certainly the children in both rooms had a sense that they needed to be on their "best" language behavior during writing. For example, the children used "ain't" orally among themselves, but they never wrote the word.

No one would argue that children, including Tionna and her peers and bookmates, should not learn the societal variant of "standard" English, deemed the Language of Wider Communication (LWC) (Fishman,

1972). Still, it is not clear what these young children were learning through the fix-it corrections of their grammatical usage. Perhaps they were learning to denigrate their vernaculars, the languages that "throb vibrantly" with everyday life and, as for Englishes, languages that are multiplying in these postcolonial times (Ahmad, 2007, p. 17; Dyson & Smitherman, 2009). After all, young children do not learn language as a matter of correction (Chomsky, 1965); it is a matter of situated construction over time, given interactional opportunity (Clark, 2003). If it were mere habit, Ezekial would have found consistent success with his eventual strategy of substituting "so-and-so and I" for "me and so-and-so," even when the latter was "better" (e.g., *Jon likes Joshua and I for friends*).

If the basic is not to use Standard English but, rather, to flexibly adapt and stretch one's linguistic resources to expanding social practices, then what "sounds better" is a matter of situational context, of social convention, and of power (i.e., of who gets to say what is "better"). This newly imagined basic would support a curricular valuing of different registers, vernaculars, and languages as options and resources for literacy learning. This would allow all children to benefit from equal access to familiar voices for entering into literacy, a point frequently made by scholars focusing on our multilingual student population (e.g., Genishi, Stires, & Yung-Chan, 2001; Reyes & Halcon, 2001). Young children are, after all, just getting their feet on the ground as writers; why pull their linguistic rug out from under them?

The re-imagined basic would also support educational curricula and instruction that build on children's knowledge, evident in their play, of language variation (Anderson, 1992; Genishi & Dyson, 2009; Zentella, 2005). As they proceed through school, children would not be asked to master the "correct" usage but to expand their linguistic resources in ways that are flexible and socio-politically adept. (Those who speak *only* the regional "standard" may need particular guidance in figuring out that all speakers vary their language and in understanding why some sound noticeably "different.")

Within the context of diverse literacy practices, young school children can listen to, read, talk about, enact, and compose a diversity of texts—playground rhymes, comics, and literary dialogue—and, in so doing, appreciate others' ways of talking, make use of their own everyday vernaculars, and, of course, continue their experience with LWC (Delpit & Dowdy, 2002; Goodman, 2003). Children expand their ways of talking when they assume new roles; as Tionna suggested in Chapter 8, those roles entailing institutional authority—talking like the teacher, for instance—may entail their most formal and "standard" speech (Adger, 1998; Steinberg & Cazden, 1979).

For children like Tionna and Ezekial, who are comfortable with the alphabetic system, this concern with communicative options and linguistic flexibility could extend to variation in spelling. Books (like commercial signs [*Come and Get 'Em*] and t-shirts [*WAZZUP*]) try to capture the sound of talk by spelling "incorrectly" (e.g., Lucille Clifton's many books for children incorporating AAL). For talk about such a phenomenon to occur, though, teachers must be provided information on developmental, sociolinguistic, and political aspects of language use (Adger, Wolfram, & Christian, 2007; Genishi & Dyson, 2009; Hudley & Mallison, 2011).

Interestingly, one scripted lesson in Mrs. Bee's room did feature a poem written in AAL by Eloise Greenfield. The poem in question repeatedly uses the line *Ain't got it no more* to refer to ephemeral pleasures like sweets and sandcastles (Greenfield, 1978, n.p.). The provided lesson, though, makes no comment on the poem's language nor on that *ain't*. Yet the curriculum is supposedly for all children. The word is not only differentially part of children's everyday speech but, as noted, children in this project did not write it. Even Mrs. Bee's young entrants to formal schooling seemed to know that that word was ideologically marked as not school smart, so to speak.

In the poem, *ain't* (and the double negative construction *ain't got it no more*) helps construct the rhythm and rhyme of the poem; moreover, it captures an important message—that poetry can be a lasting part of everyday lives. A teacher who had the benefit of professional information on variation could use the poem to discuss such matters; indeed, such a teacher (like 1st-grade teacher Ms. Rita [Dyson, 2003a]) could so use the entire book, *Honey I Love* (Greenfield, 1978), whose poems are not all written in AAL. Without official school recognition, though, the linguistic repertoire of young children may be dismissed; indeed, the pedagogical insights of teachers themselves may be unexploited, particularly those of teachers who speak more than one language or language variant, like Mrs. Bee.

In sum, the "basic" is not to master the singular way to write and speak. This basic promotes linguistic ignorance, since there is no one English (or French, Spanish, Korean, and so forth; for discussion, see Blommaert, 2005). Moreover, denying the legitimacy of a child's home variety furthers inequality in academic access. *The re-imagined basic is linguistic flexibility, a basic that builds on the familiar practices and situated voices of children's lives.* In their play, children know, however unconsciously, that appropriate language—language that sounds right—depends on social role, social occasion, and power. This is the foundational backdrop against which children may construct new voices on their textual playgrounds, including those articulating the Language of Wider Communication.

Normalizing Multimodality: Rethinking "Being Productive"

In both Mrs. Kay's and Mrs. Bee's rooms, drawing was a problem, a fix-it concern. The very paper children were given conveyed that there was a space for drawing and another for writing. Except for Mrs. Bee's children early in the year, children were not to spend the *writing* period *drawing*. Drawing was to be just "a quick sketch." (The sense of asking small children making tadpole people and fast-moving lines to make "a quick sketch" escapes me.) The assumption seemed to be that, unless forced to abandon drawing, children would not write.

Cross-culturally, given a marking tool and a canvas of some sort (be it pencil and paper or stick and dirt), very young children do tend to participate in the cultural activity of making meaning through drawing. However, in print-saturated societies, children draw letters as well as actions and images, and they grapple with the relationship between drawing and writing as symbol systems, as a means of representing and communicating meaning (Dyson, 1982; Eng, 1931; Matthews, 1999; Stetsenko, 1995).

All of the children who have taken the stage in this book have regularly gone about their composing with multiple semiotic tools. Moreover, children used voice, image, and print in ways suggestive of at least an emerging if unconscious knowledge of the strengths of varied media. Consider, for example, how in Chapter 8 Charles used written dialogue to construct a conflict with his big sister who wanted him to just jump in the pool *and* old-school animation to indicate his successful movement through the water (imagine what he might do with digital tools); or recall, also in Chapter 8, Ezekial's use of voice and movement to transform an un-amusing text to a laugh-inducing one about being sleepy.

However, in Mrs. Bee's and Mrs. Kay's classrooms, highly regulated by "the basics," the official focus was on print alone; other media were invisible, unless they occupied too much time. This official focus unraveled children's *symbol-weaving* (Dyson, 1990). Pulling print out from the larger story-making event eliminated any talk about how varied semiotic tools—how drawing, writing, and performance—figured into the meaning-making. And yet, image and word were interwoven in the multimodal texts that comprised children's school materials (e.g., textbooks, storybooks, posters [cf., Bezemer & Kress, 2008; Hull & Nelson, 2005]). Indeed, it is precisely multimodality that defines many contemporary literacy practices and will surely do so in the children's futures (Jenkins, 2009; Kress, 2010).

If we do not unravel children's weaving, if we consider, not just the words, but images and even performative voices, we can re-imagine the basic of being productive (i.e., of writing ever more words). The basic is not simply to write more but to exploit multimodal tools to produce texts appropriate for the circumstance, that is, for the situated literacy practice.

This re-imagined basic would support talk about children's productions that highlights the strengths of diverse media, including words and pictures, with their differing ways of handling space and time (Kress, 2010; Siegal, 2006). For example, it would support teachers including in their instructional repertoire writing down young children's dictated stories about their drawing or play. In so doing, teachers not only collaboratively construct and encode meaning with those needing help but also support children (through comments and questions) as they tell stories to accompany, transform, or discursively comment on drawn and/or enacted tales (Cooper, 2009; Dyson, 1989; Lindfors, 2008).

Another illustrative pedagogical move involves acting out children's stories in Author's Theater (Dyson, 1997; Paley, 1981, 2004). In this practice, child composers learn that stories with action and dialogue are more fun, as they lend themselves to peers' acting out. They thus experience stories as a sort of script for a play (or a "movie," as a child I once knew called them). Child actors interpret child composers' words with gestures and movement that may surprise those composers. Words are slippery, open to interpretation. Some stories (perhaps those to be developed for an outside-of-class audience or, indeed, for a movie) may lend themselves to designed sets or props and to accompanying music.

Finally, such a multimodal basic, with its emphasis on adapting to situated practice, suggests that contexts matter in expanding writing's place in children's symbolic repertoire. The intention to join in, to participate in a communicative practice, compels young children to orchestrate their knowledge and know-how about writing (and other modes), to become aware of their need for help, and even to seek out an audience. Indeed, the enactment of any symbolic act involves grappling with the connection between symbolic vehicle (e.g., the graphic), intended meaning, and the relationship between self and other (Bakhtin, 1981; Werner & Kaplan, 1963).

In Mrs. Bee's and Mrs. Kay's classrooms, even the least experienced composers were interested in writing as a means of social connection. For example, early in her kindergarten experience, Alicia not only explored the look of writing—its linearity and directionality, its lines and curves (cf. Clay 1975), she also knew that letters mattered. For example, they were needed to put one's "play sister" on paper. She drew her "sister" Willo into her family, but she also put Willo's letters—her name—into her writing. Mrs. Bee worked to make sure the children learned the letters of their own names, but friends need to know how to do one another's names right.

Mrs. Kay's children also illustrated the intensity of child composers when engaged in compelling practices. Recall, for example, how their own expectation of reciprocity among friends helped transform the writing of personal plans into intense social play. This planning play, particularly about birthdays, generated a diversity of related practices (e.g., making lists of addresses, phone numbers, invitees; oral negotiations of who was picking up whom; composing written details of what would happen at the get-together). In so becoming a field of interrelated practices, planning get-togethers contributed to and drew from a peer cultural world. It was as if the children were taking information from in and out of school to make a study of the intertwined practices of social engagements.

In short, the basic is not to move from drawing pictures to writing a certain number of sentences. Rather, the basic is to produce texts—deliberately organized constructions of meaning—through the use of symbolic modes appropriate to the circumstance, that is, to the social situation and the cultural practice. Children do draw before they write. But a shift from drawing images to writing words is not a matter of abandoning drawing. It is a matter of differentiating the representational nature and the material and social affordances of these symbolic modes (among others). Modes are not in opposition but rather play off one another, not only on a single page, but also in a field—a playground—of interconnected practices.

In Sum: Contextualizing the Basics in a Stratified World

The ABC's are not easy, except as a song to sing. But, when they become a means for belonging and for meaning, they are worth trying to corral. And then the struggle and the fun unfolds. As our most important educational theorists have noted, among them Vygotsky (1978) and Dewey (1916/1944), when energized by intention—by some purposeful effort to accomplish some act—children mobilize resources, seek out assistance, and even practice necessary skills.

From one angle of vision, highlighting the children's unofficial responses to official opportunities, writing did seem to be "founded on the needs of children"; it grew on, and interwove with, children's existent capacities to "speak" through play and drawing (Vygotsky 1978, p. 105). Indeed, within the children's world, writing was socially organized in familiar ways tied to children's storytelling, drawing, and dramatic play practices; at the same time, the tool posed new challenges and suggested new possibilities for making use of drawing, for telling stories, and for playing games on new kinds of playgrounds.

The children were not all equally experienced with print, versatile as communicators, or engaging as storytellers, but they were all social beings who wanted companionship and meaning in their lives. Writing practices—social activities imbued with shared values and beliefs—were their metaphoric mailboxes for venturing into new symbolic and social ground. As I focused on their efforts, the basics were re-imagined as resources for participation in relations and practices that mattered. They were stretched to include the social skills of slipping into social roles, appropriating and adapting sociolinguistic and multimodal resources, and attuning themselves to others. Children's choices of words, their adjustments of content, at times even their graphological decisions were situated and relational.

If the angle is changed, though, from the children's unofficial world to the official world, then children's social relations, multimodal tools, and inclinations to play and imagine disappear and, at times, become downright troublesome. This was not simply because of *classroom* conditions; rather each classroom was itself situated in, and constitutive of, broader institutional and societal discourse about the "at risk" and related ideologies about language itself (Goodwin & Duranti, 1992; Gutiérrez & Orellana, 2006; Miller & Sperry, 2012).

Children are deemed "at risk" because of their very being: they are categorized as low-income and, disproportionately, as "minority." Stereotypes about their families, whose boot straps seem broken, and about children themselves are related to the flight of the more economically privileged from the public schools (a phenomenon in both Mrs. Kay's and Mrs. Bee's districts). The worry about getting these "at risk" children up-to-snuff on a linear line to skill mastery contributed to the highly test-regulated worlds that Mrs. Bee, Mrs. Kay, and their children lived in. This perception that the "at risk" need a tight, direct focus on "the basics" (Ladson-Billings, 2005) has been the case since the beginnings of interest in children's literacy during the War on Poverty (e.g., Bereiter & Engelmann, 1966; for a discussion of this interest relative to learning to write, see Dyson, 1999; for a recent discussion of the re-emergence of deficit views of children, see Miller & Sperry, 2012).

Given the sense of urgency about the "at risk," time was in short supply for children's exploration of the written system and for easing their way into its use through familiar social practices and multimodal tools. There was no curricular nod to children's identities as friends, neighbors, cousins, players, singers, sports enthusiasts, Spider-Man fans, and on and on. They were to be *writers*. Moreover, the basics made problematic children's very voices, which reverberated in a stratified, polyphonic world and, thus, positioned them as out of place in school (Bakhtin, 1981). Finally, the emphasis on individual and literal truths, in the context of writing your *story*, clouded out the varied social arrangements of composing time and, also, the children's often playful and imaginative intentions.

More particularly, as friends and peers, and as experienced players, children situated their ventures into writing in the relational ethics of childhood cultures, where children sometimes wanted to be named, to get their turn, and to be included in the fun. The ideology of individualism worked against official recognition of the relational dimension of writing and, indeed, of the meanings these young children were drawn to. This did not necessarily stop the children from reaching out to others, but it did make children's intentions and multimodal resources invisible in the official world.

Thus, official extensions of child practices could not occur, practices like designing birthday cards or books for and about class members, mapping out the neighborhood (with paths marked between children's houses) or maybe a cross-country trip (like to Ellie's California birthday party), and designing those homes for the homeless that Mrs. Kay's children wanted, whatever the social studies text said. (For powerful examples of children's actions on local school and neighborhood spaces, see the work of Comber and colleagues [e.g., Comber, 2011; Nixon & Comber, 2008].)

Moreover, sometimes children were left on their own in dealing with unanticipated responses to their efforts. Help was needed, for example, in understanding how a group's private fun could do public harm (as in reading private party plans in the classroom public), how their own visions could limit "the other" (as when Lyron tried to keep Tionna from playing the Pine Cone game), or even how their choices (including of topic, like that of war) could reverberate in a public with differing values.

The experiences of Mrs. Kay, Mrs. Bee, and their children were not unusual. Internationally, there is a push toward standardization and regulation in schooling (Comber, 2011). Young children are expected to bring "the basics" (e.g., letter names and sounds) to kindergarten, as part of their cultural backpacks, as it were (Genishi & Dyson, 2009; Hirsh-Pasek et al., 2009). But in our economically and culturally diverse society, children bring differing experiences as communicators to school.

Indeed, as Miller and Sperry (2012) discuss, we as a profession know a great deal about the cultural and linguistic possibilities of young children from many "non-mainstream" communities. Among these possibilities are experience with the nature and functions of storytelling (e.g., Michaels, 1981; Michaels & Sohmer, 2000; Miller, Cho, & Bracey, 2005), the capacity for linguistic flexibility and cultural brokering (e.g., Orellana, 2009; Vasquez, Pease-Alvarez, & Shannon, 1994), and, herein, the potential for flexibility in social organization and social appropriation of voice and image. But these potential capacities can become invisible, in part because they are fluid and contextualized and, thus, not easily converted to test scores.

The current resurgence of barebones "basics" education is, I suggest, spreading a kind of ignorance. When we teach children that writing is only a set of skills or a means of individual expression, we misrepresent the dialogic nature of writing. Even those of us who sit alone, late at night, trying to corral our words into sense, are doing so as members of some community in which we want to have a say. (And sometimes, of course, we share our push toward sense with others who "author" with us.) Even when engaged in some academic practice, like I am right now, we play with our words, negotiating with our addressees, who are not really absent. We have heard their words before in similar practices, and perhaps we are trying to head them off at the pass in our own version of The Pine Cone Wars.

Children, of course, do this sort of playing with images and voices much more literally. If we are not to make childhoods themselves a deficit condition, we need to rethink "basic" education in a way that welcomes children in all their diversity, with their strengths as well as their needs. I close with key pedagogical principles on how that might be done.

TOWARD A RE-ENVISIONED BASIC EDUCATION

The preceding section has been a review of the path this book has taken in contextualizing and stretching the basics. Implicit in that review are key principles for easing children into the use of writing. (Descriptions of specific instructional alternatives include Pahl and Roswell's [2005] broad pedagogical visions and exemplary particulars for literacy education; Marsh's [2005] depictions of new media possibilities; and Wohlwend's [2011] portrait of a kindergarten that officially supported play as an approach to literacy.)

With an overriding concern for the marginalization of childhoods in low-income schools, I emphasize "basics" principles that will need to be locally interpreted but that, nevertheless, should open up the composing program to child strengths. These principles aim to situate the writing period (or workshop) within the inclusive communities that both Mrs. Bee and Mrs. Kay valued (see Chapter 2).

Of course, a school, no more than a symbol system like literacy, is not a decontextualized force. Mrs. Kay's school was in a hard pressed economic neighborhood in a city that itself was struggling. Mrs. Bee's was in an area that was effectively formed by an "American apartheid" (Massey & Denton, 1993). A school cannot provide a house for those who are homeless; it cannot bring children's parents home from jail, nor provide those parents with good-paying jobs. It can do nothing about manufacturing plants that have closed, nor the absence of wealth that allows families to comfortably traverse economically rough times. All these conditions can threaten children's access to outside places to play, the stability of their families, their home access to school-valued media, including books and computers, and their sense of possibility in the larger world.

But my goal is to look at school from children's perspectives. And from that view, there is no child without school resources, among them, communicative experiences, a tendency to play, an appreciation of song, and engagement with storytelling. The following principles are offered in the spirit of allowing children to bring their strengths as children in particular times and spaces to the official world of school:

Writing programs for young children should rest on the foundation of play, talk, and social relations. It is in play that children venture into new social roles, try out new discourses, and negotiate their own possibilities in a world of others. Entering into writing practices entails imagining oneself as having some agency, some resources, and some companions with whom to venture forward. (Pardon my prescriptive bent here but) every early childhood classroom needs official places for social play and, particularly, for making worlds out of words and actions.

In making such worlds, children engage the basic composing skills of assuming appropriate social roles, being responsive given the participatory frame, and appropriating and recontextualizing relevant cultural content. When written texts are conceived of as yet another place for play, children may experience the transformation of meaning across media, as themes and play practices travel across—and rework—borders of time, space, and media.

Children attend to their everyday environment, and, to build on their knowledge, so too should we as teachers. It is the everyday worlds of children that provide the representational and communicative diversity that problematizes rigidity in language use, including in grammatical usage and in graphological conventions. Indeed, as children gain experience, spellings may grab their attention precisely because they contrast the usual consistency of spellings across contexts. Hence as a second grader, Tionna objected to author Lucille Clifton's (1992) spelling, *'bout*: "It's supposed to be *about*" (see Dyson & Smitherman, 2009).

Everyday texts are typically multimodal in design, may use capitalization and punctuation in non-prose ways, and thus potentially further semiotic flexibility. Scoreboards with team names and numbers are potentially children's first efforts to organize print on paper, as are signs on important buildings (like LaTrell's *Boys and Girls Club*). Important names and numbers (sometimes arranged vertically) index people, houses, and streets; dialogue bubbles are a common occurrence. (For a teacher and child's rich discussion of traffic sign numbers, apartment numbers, and building numbers, see Genishi & Dyson, 2009, p. 89).

Children, like teachers, should have opportunities to experience a curiosity about, and an appreciation and critical understanding of, language variation. That is, classrooms should explicitly construct a language ideology that entails a conscious awareness of language variation across situation and tied to identity, geography, and history. This principle implies that we as teachers should attend to children's own language variation across situations and, as already discussed, provide them with opportunities to enact, discuss, and appreciate language variation.

Contemporary literacy practices should entail the deliberate design of complex texts, thereby normalizing multimodality. Initially, children are not so deliberate in their symbol weaving. Teachers, though, can work toward such deliberateness. As earlier noted, they may specifically organize for children to pay attention to the voices and the texts in their lives, and they may also take advantage of children's interesting productions (like LaTrell's *CN*, for Cartoon Network, and Ezekial's *.C.O.O.L*).

The composing "tasks" we offer children should be ones "with scope" (Clay, 1998, p. 237; see also Love, Burns, & Buell, 2007). The more restrictive the curriculum, the more opportunities children have to fail to conform. In contrast, writing events "with scope" allow children to participate in different ways with different resources. Such tasks also allow teachers to observe what children attend to and, so informed, to extend their knowledge and know-how (Rogoff, 2003; Vygotsky, 1978).

We must recognize that children's composing actions vary across communicative situations. "Do the tasks just like this," we might say as teachers. But, of course, children will do the tasks "just like this" only if they are imitating the surface structure of what we are about. If they are to make sense of composing tasks, they have to situate them within practices that they understand. That switch from *task* to *practice* is important, because an enacted practice (i.e., a communicative event) has multiple and intertwined properties that matter (Hymes, 1972); among them are children's intentions, their participation modes, their symbolic tools, and their sense of appropriateness. Moreover practices may be hybrid, in that they are formed in the intersection of official and unofficial spaces (Bakhtin, 1981).

In response, we as teachers have to both complicate the linear progression of skills that inevitably dominates formal literacy assessments *and* observe across kinds of writing events in order to uncover the breadth of children's practices, the contents of their semiotic repertoire, and their capacity for communicative flexibility. To begin, children's behaviors may vary from day to day, not simply because some days they try or concentrate, and some days they do not (although we all have our problem days); they vary because of the particular demands of the participation mode and, more particularly, the practice they are participating in.

For example, Alicia initially made wavy lines and letter-like shapes when dashing off comments about peers. It could seem as if she knew little about letters; but Mrs. Bee knew that Alicia could write her friend Willo's first and last name—and Alicia did this when she was playing with Willo through her text. Indeed, despite grade-level benchmarks and curricular scripts, which positioned stretching and listening to words' sounds as *the* first step to participation in writing, Alicia's steps were constructed with friends' names. There is no one pathway into use of the written system. After all, names too share letters with phonological features (e.g., both *Alicia* and *Willo* have that dependable *L*).

Moreover, a mark of a growing young writer is sensitivity to the social occasion and the enacted practice being negotiated, as well as becoming more deliberate, more thoughtful, about textual features that might vary. In Mrs. Kay's room, the daily sharing-time practice was implicated in this growth, because it was so highly anticipated (and the response could be disappointing, as Mandisa pointed out—even Mrs. Kay did not get her written joke, which Mandisa deemed "the funniest"). With thoughts of Alicia's unofficial intentions intersecting with official occasions and of Mrs. Kay's children's beloved sharing time, I turn to the last principle.

To support an intellectually- and ethically-informed dialogue between the official and unofficial world, a public forum for child writing should exist in the classroom community. We as teachers are busy in a classroom filled with young school entrants during composing time. Sylvia Ashton-Warner summarized the pedagogical situation best: After about 30 minutes of "bending over the children writing at their low desks," it's "backache time" (1963, p. 55). We are so engaged with this one and that one, that it can be hard to see the big picture: the diversity of child intentions; the choreography of child players and texts; the matters of inclusion, exclusion, and representation that drive the sometimes passionate talk; the ways in which repeated topics may be favorite games played over and over (like "parties"); and the tenuous line between *truth* and *fiction*, especially when a performance is going on. Without knowing what is happening, it is hard to build on what the children are doing; hence the great value of the daily time to talk about children's texts—a kind of public forum.

During this forum, the *centripetal* or unifying forces of official expectations are complicated by the *centrifugal* and *stratifying* forces of children's interpretations and intentions (building on Bakhtin, 1981). For this complexity to be audible, the social expectation for the forum would be that every child (or every participant in the event of interest) will talk about their production, in all its modalities. That is, all class members would be responsible and responsive to one another: Children would be responsible for sharing and explaining their efforts; and teachers would be responsible for building on what children bring and connecting it to the official school agenda (Souto-Manning, 2010). Such a forum would make for a *permeable* curriculum (Dyson, 1993); it would not eliminate official expectations or unofficial, even hidden ones, but it would bring the official and unofficial worlds into mutually expansive interplay.

In this way, variations in participation modes may surface, as may varied authorial and, in fact, ethical issues. In a democratic society, a major purpose of common schooling is, at least ideally, to engage children in just such discussions (Shipps, 2000). For example, in Mrs. Kay's class, the children's responses during the daily sharing time—their mumbled indignations, their laughter or its lack—were potentially instructional material for collective reflection. Moreover, if enacted curricula do not take official account of children's situated fix-its about social inclusion, obligation, and identity, then children are left on their own to grapple with the social and ideological ramifications of authorial decisions.

Mrs. Bee and Mrs. Kay were given, in different ways, to such conversations; they simply did not see them as tied to the basics. But social attunement *is* a basic composing skill, and the children's situated fix-its made it clear that relational and ideological matters were central to their composing lives together. Composing is not only about producing a text, but also about composing a complex, responsive self in a world made with others.

SO, WHAT DO YOU THINK?

"What do you think of our picnic?" Tionna had asked before she went to have a relaxing moment stretched out in an old lawn chaise like it was the best sofa in town. Through this book, I have asked, in effect, what do you think of our children and those writing "basics"? Are the basics stark matters of linearly mastered skills, best applied in life stories where an old lawn chaise is just an old lawn chaise? Such an anemic view of "the basics" is undergirded by an anemic view of composing and, moreover, of our children. Following Tionna and her bookmates into their everyday worlds dialogized—situated and problematized—those old basics, giving them new vitality. Paying attention as they found social and playful uses for written language stretched those basics to include the social dynamics of childhoods in formation. I close with this image of Tionna because it so clearly displays how children may draw others into a transformed world, finding joy and power in humble circumstances. Imagine what she and all our children could do if we as educators joined together to re-imagine a "basic" education for our young. Let the work—and play—begin.

Reflections on Methods

As an ethnographer, my overriding concern was to understand the ideological—indeed, the ethical—underpinnings of "basics" in the official composing curricula, as materially given and interactionally enacted. Moreover, I aimed to understand how children made sense of what was curricularly on offer in their own times and spaces and, thereby, the language ideology and social ethics governing their actions. These goals were dependent on constructing relationships with teachers and children that would allow me access to the goings on.

In the following sections, I comment on data collection, particularly the roles I negotiated with teachers and children. I also provide a brief overview of the series of data analyses that undergird the assertions and vignettes of this book.

SITUATING TEACHERS

I am not a preacher, an evaluator, or a social worker; I am a researcher. Given my own need to feel useful, I work primarily in classroom settings that are, in my judgment, respectful places for children; in that way, I can concentrate on pushing forward my understanding of children's social worlds and of school literacy learning. If children are treated in ways that are clearly disrespectful (e.g., they and their families are put down, ignored, and insulted), they do not need a researcher.

I was comfortable in Mrs. Bee's kindergarten and Mrs. Kay's 1st grade. Both teachers were respectful of their children and their children's families. They did not doubt their children's capacity to learn, fail to instructionally attend to each and every child, or miss an opportunity to warmly welcome children's relations into their rooms. As is abundantly clear in this book, my project was motivated by a critical stance toward the highly regulated teaching situations in which they, and their children, found themselves. The teachers were no fans either of the test-regulated worlds in which they worked, as noted herein. Many teachers all over the country, indeed, internationally, are facing such "basics" curricula.

I explained to each teacher that I wanted to slide into the children's worlds as innocuously as possible; so I would be of limited usefulness in disciplining and guiding the children. If I was successful, I told them, the children would resist my role violations (e.g., my unsolicited helping might garner child embarrassment, my disciplining might lead to resistance since I'm "not our teacher"). However, the teachers and I found times during and after school when I could listen to their plans, worries, and joys. I also shared selected observations that I thought conveyed the children's sense-making and relations, trying to adopt a consistent tone of enthusiastic inquiry and interest. Both teachers had expressed a desire that I keep coming to their rooms after my initial visits and chats. It is often good to have someone take a respectful interest in one's daily work, whether one is 5 or 50-something.

COPYING THE CHILDREN

RA'MELL: Hey! You copied offa mine! (with pleasure)
MRS. DYSON: I'm seeing what you did.
SADIE: Why don't you see what we [Briana and I] do?
SIMEON: Why you ain't doing mine?

In Mrs. Bee's and Mrs. Kay's classrooms, I constructed my own relationship with the children by copying them. This copying was not viewed as a violation of their ownership but as evidence of my interest in what they did. I could not copy everybody at any one moment, given my ethnographic need for an evolving narrative with some coherence. But I could show an interest in other ways, including by literally (photo) copying everybody's work.

I explained my "job" in both rooms as trying to figure out "what it's like to be a little kid learning to write." I was "too busy" writing—or "copying" them—to be a reliable helper. I aimed to be a nonthreatening adult friend, who never issued directives or "told" on children. Mrs. Kay's children did not ask me for "help," but Mrs. Bee's children did do so at times. If I could respond with a brief bit of help, I did; if children needed substantial help, I reminded them to raise their hand high and help would come (and it did). I also tied shoes, and, in both rooms, tamed wayward zippers and listened to stories told by or read by students. During my time in Mrs. Bee's room, I had a serious fall and ended up in the hospital. Mrs. Bee came to visit me, the children made me get-well cards, and when I returned with a cane, unable to sit in kindergarten chairs, the children made room for my adult-sized chair by their child-sized ones, took control of placing the mic on the table, and retrieved dropped items for me. (They did not understand, though, that all my troubles came from a slip on the ice; they slipped on the ice all the time. LaTrell proposed that I tripped over my shoe laces, which was immediately understood.)

As an older White woman, I understand that age, race, and gender could be constructed as sources of tension between the children and me. However, I was indeed nonthreatening—the children would sometimes hide their behavior from the teacher (e.g., LaTrell's "man with bling" on the back of his writing paper), but I was privy to all manner of action. I was no doubt aided by the children's familiarity with White adults in school, as teachers, administrators, volunteer helpers, and cafeteria workers. I was outside any familiar role, but, nevertheless, the children were accepting. One day in Mrs. Kay's room, Tionna left early for a dental appointment; before she left she hugged her friends—Mandisa, Janette, Lyron, and me.

As the book attests, I copied children by jotting their behaviors in my notebooks as my trusty audio recorder captured their voices. As explained in Chapter 1, I used certain *focal* children as anchors for my observations. I had three focal children in each class, although in this book, I've reduced the number to two in each (the two whose friendship circles collectively extended most widely in the class).

I spent long hours constructing field notes from written jottings, audio recordings, and products. Often one child's production could not be understood without situating it in other children's productions. In each room, I kept up with writing the twice-weekly field notes, but the fleshing out of the notes with audio transcripts occurred after each academic year was completed. I made no attempt to capture the phonetic features of children's speech (unless there were dialect issues with their spelling); however, I carefully transcribed their words, never altering their syntactical features. Transcript conventions include the following:

- Parentheses enclosing text contain notes, usually about contextual and nonverbal information [e.g., "(reading, starts writing)"].
- Brackets may contain explanatory information [inserted into quotations or written texts].
- A capitalized word or phrase indicates increased VOLUME.
- An italicized word is stressed.
- Colons inserted into a word indicate that the preceding sound was elongated (e.g., "Ri::ght!").
- A single slash [/] inserted into a written record of a text indicates the end of a line on the original page.
- Parallel slashed lines (e.g., /u/) indicate that the speaker made the sound of the enclosed letter or letters.

- Ellipsis points (. . .) indicate omitted data.
- Conventional punctuation marks are used to mark ends of utterances or sentences, usually indicated by slight pauses on the audiotape.

CONSTRUCTING ANALYTIC NARRATIVES

Pages of field notes and inserted transcriptions, file boxes of child products, not to mention stacks of state curricular frameworks, district pacing guides and benchmarks, and newspaper articles on school issues—none of these data magically become organized. Constructing this ethnographic analysis of "the basics" from the children's world proceeded through a series of interwoven and recursive steps. What follows is an overview of key steps undergirding this book.

If I was to consider the basics, the first step was to amass official documents detailing the basic skills expected of young children, initially to contextualize Mrs. Kay's teaching situation and, later, Mrs. Bee's. Lists of skills gave way to an ongoing consideration of the underlying definition of *literacy* and of *writing*, the ideology or values and beliefs about language and, also, about child learning.

Teaching these basics was the responsibility of Mrs. Kay and Mrs. Bee. The second analysis step, then, involved identifying the kinds of events (i.e., practices) that comprised teaching the children to write. I inductively studied those events, identifying their focus (i.e., what was explicitly being taught), their routine interactional structure, their thematic content, and their symbolic tools (e.g., writing, talk, and drawing).

Early on, in Mrs. Kay's classroom, I noted the importance of fix-it events, which happened in individual conferences about a child's product; these were prime places for addressing "basic skills" (e.g., punctuation, grammar, spelling). The third step, then, involved examining the data on correcting child writing, not only by the teacher, but also by children themselves as they sat at their tables doing their writing. This analysis revealed the differences between the basic errors that the teacher was sensitive to and those that garnered the children's attention. I carried this analysis to Mrs. Bee's room with me and, based on data from both rooms, developed the official and unofficial categories of fix-it errors presented in Figures 3.1 and 5.1.

Perhaps because Mrs. Bee's children were new to formal schooling, there was a great deal of official talk in her room about "good," or ethical behavior during writing. In the unofficial world too, there were perceptions that others were not being "fair," "good," or "nice" in their composing. I noticed that the unofficial fix-it categories in both rooms were undergirded, not only by different values and beliefs about language, but also by ethical concerns. Moreover, these ethical concerns were related to the ways in which children organized their social interactions during writing, that is, their *participation modes*. Thus, the fourth major analysis involved identifying these different modes.

As a result of this latter analysis, the chapters in Part II are organized according to how the children were unofficially organized during composing events and, therefore, their expectations for both compositions and others' responses. It was this analysis that led more than anything else to contextualizing and stretching the basics so that social responsiveness and communicative flexibility became, in fact, part of the "basics."

There were other ethnographic analyses that occurred, of course. I have, for example, a notebook filled with descriptions of the kinds of play in which the children engaged on playgrounds and in classrooms (including handclaps). In that same notebook, I detailed new kinds of emerging play (like The Pine Cone Wars). In another analysis, I traced variation in focal children's use of semiotic tools across kinds of events so that I could flesh out the notion of *communicative flexibility*. In the end, though, all of these analyses, stretched out in a line, make the doing of a project seem rather anemic and soul-less. Mainly, I think, I started with thin tales about Mrs. Kay's children and then Mrs. Bee's, taking a look at school writing's "beginnings" in contemporary times; as I read helpful others (including long-time intellectual companions, like Bakhtin, and newer ones, like Appiah and Blommaert), as I poured over the same data while sketching out new kinds of analyses, the plot thickened, characters emerged, and this consideration of the ABC's threatened to stretch out to the length of an old Russian novel. I enjoyed the children, the teachers, and the work; and I'm hopeful that you, my readers, will have found yourselves knee-deep in the classrooms with me.

Demographic Tables

Table B.1. Sex and Ethnicity of Mrs. Kay's Children

Sex	Ethnicity
Girls (7)	
Brittany	White
Elisha	Black
Ellie	White/Irish
Janette	Black
Mandisa	Black
Sasha	White
Tionna	Black
Boys (9)	
Aaron	White
Alex	(American) Indian
Brad	White
Ezekial	Mexican
Jason	White
Jon	Mexican
Joshua	(American) Indian/Mexican
Lyron	Black
Manny	Mexican

Note. List includes only those children who attended throughout the academic school year; the ethnicity labels are based on terms used by Mrs. Kay's children.

Table B.2. Sex and Ethnicity of Mrs. Bee's Children

Sex	Ethnicity
Girls (12)	
Alicia	Black
Alexia	Black
April	Black
Cici	Black
Coretta	Black
Della	Black
Denise	Black
Ella	Black
Janelle	Black
Odette	Black
Precious	Black
Soraya	Black
Boys (9)	
Antone	Black
Charles	Black
Chandell	Black
Essau	Black
Ernest	Black
Jamal	Black
Kevin	Black
Lamont	Black
LaTrell	Black

Note. List includes only those children who attended throughout the academic school year.

References

Adger, C. T. (1998). Register shifting with dialect resources in instructional discourse. In S. Hoyle & C. T. Adger (Eds.), *Kids talk: Strategic language use in later childhood* (pp. 151–169). New York: Oxford University Press.

Adger, C. T., Wolfram, W., & Christian, D. (2007). *Dialects in schools and communities* (2nd ed.). Mahwah, NJ: Erlbaum.

Ahmad, D. (Ed.). (2007). *Rotten English: A literary anthology.* New York: W.W. Norton & Company.

Anderson, E. S. (1992). *Speaking with style: The sociolinguistic skills of children.* London: Routledge.

Appiah, K. A. (2005). *The ethics of identity.* Princeton, NJ: Princeton University Press.

Applebee, A. N. (1978). *The child's concept of story: Ages two to seventeen.* Chicago, IL: University of Chicago Press.

Ashton-Warner, S. (1963). *Teacher.* New York: Simon & Schuster.

Au, W. (2007). High-stakes testing and curricular control: A qualitative metasynthesis. *Educational Researcher, 36*(5), 258–267.

Bakhtin, M. (1981). Discourse in the novel. In M. Holquist (Ed.), C. Emerson & M. Holquist (Trans.), *The dialogic imagination: Four essays by M. Bakhtin* (pp. 254–422). Austin: University of Texas Press.

Bakhtin, M. (1986). *Speech genres and other late essays.* Austin: University of Texas Press.

Bakhtin, M. (1990). Art and answerability. In M. Holquist & V. Liapunov (Eds.), *Art and answerability: Early philosophical essays by M. Bahktin* (pp. 1–3). Austin: University of Texas Press.

Barton, D., & Hamilton, M. (1998). *Local literacies: Reading and writing in one community.* London: Routledge.

Bateson, G. (1956). The message "This is play." In B. Schaffner (Ed.), *Group processes* (pp. 145–242). New York: Macy.

Bauman, R. (1982). Ethnography of children's folklore. In P. Gilmore & A. A. Glatthorn (Eds.), *Children in and out of school: Ethnography and education* (pp. 172–186). Washington, DC: Center for Applied Linguistics.

Bauman, R. (Ed.). (1992). *Folklore, cultural performances, and popular entertainments: A communications-centered handbook.* New York: Oxford University Press.

Bauman, R. (2004). *A world of others' words: Cross-cultural perspectives on intertextuality.* Malden, MA: Blackwell.

Baynham, M., & Prinsloo, M. (2009). Introduction: The future of literacy studies. In M. Baynham & M. Prinsloo (Eds.), *The future of literacy studies* (pp. 1–20). Hampshire, England: Palgrave Macmillan.

Bereiter, C., & Engelmann, S. (1966). *Teaching disadvantaged children in the preschool.* Englewood Cliffs, NJ: Prentice Hall.

Berman, R. (1996). Form and function in developing narrative abilities. In D. Slobin, J. Gerhardt, A. Kyrastzis, & J. Guo (Eds.), *Social interaction, social context, and language: Essays in honor of Susan Ervin-Tripp* (pp. 343–368). Mahwah, NJ: Erlbaum.

Bezemer, J., & Kress, G. (2008). Writing in multimodal texts: A social semiotic account of designs for learning. *Written Communication, 25*(2), 166–195.

Bialystok, E. (1991). Letters, sounds, and symbols: Changes in children's understanding of written language. *Applied Psycholinguistics, 12* (1), 75–89.

Blaise, M., & Taylor, A. (2012). Using queer theory to rethink gender equity in early childhood education. *Young Children, 67*(1), 88–98.

Blommaert, J. (2005). *Discourse.* Cambridge, UK: Cambridge University Press.

Boldt, G. M. (2009). Kyle and the Basilisk: Understanding children's writing as play. *Language Arts, 87*(1), 9–17.

Boldt, G. M. (2011). One hundred hot dogs, or performing gender in the early childhood classroom. In T. Jacobson (Ed.), *Perspectives on gender in early childhood* (pp. 77–94). St Paul, MN: Redleaf Press.

Bourdieu, P. (1977). *Outline of a theory of practice.* Cambridge, UK: Cambridge University Press.

Brandt, D. (2001). *Literacy in American lives.* Cambridge, UK: Cambridge University Press.

Brandt, D., & Clinton, K. (2002). Limits of the local: Expanding perspectives on literacy as a social practice. *Journal of Literacy Research, 34*(3), 337–356.

Britton, J. (1970). *Language and learning.* Harmondsworth, Middlesex, England: Penguin.

Britton, J. (1982). Shaping at the point of utterance. In G. Pradl (Ed.), *Prospect and retrospect: Selected essays of James Britton* (pp. 139–145). Montclair, NJ: Boynton/Cook.

Calkins, L., & Mermelstein, L. (2003). *Launching the writing workshop.* Portsmouth, NH: Heinemann.

Chabris, C., & Simons, D. (2010). *The invisible gorilla.* Available at http://www.theinvisiblegorilla.com

Chomsky, N. (1965). *Aspects of the theory of syntax.* Cambridge, MA: MIT Press.

Clark, C. D. (1995). *Flights of fancy, leaps of faith: Children's myths in contemporary America.* Chicago, IL: University of Chicago Press.

Clark, E. V. (2003). *First language acquisition.* Cambridge, UK: Cambridge University Press.

Clark, K., & Holquist, M. (1984). *Mikhail Bakhtin.* Cambridge, MA: Harvard University Press.

Clay, M. (1975). *What did I write?* Auckland, New Zealand: Heinemann.

Clay, M. (1998). *By different paths to common outcomes.* York, ME: Stenhouse.

Clifton, L. (1992). *Three wishes.* New York: Doubleday.

Comber, B. (2003). Critical literacy: What does it look like in the early years? In N. Hall, J. Larson, & J. Marsh (Ed.), *Handbook of early childhood literacy* (pp. 355–368). London: Sage.

Comber, B. (2011). Changing literacies, changing populations, changing places— English teachers' work in an age of rampant standardization. *English Teaching: Practice and Critique, 10,* 5–22.

Comber, B., & Kamler, B. (Eds.). (2005). *Turn-around pedagogies: Literacy interventions for at-risk students.* Newtown, Australia: Primary English Teachers Association.

Cooper, P. A. (2009). *The classrooms all young children need: Lessons in teaching from Vivian Paley.* Chicago: University Of Chicago Press.

Corsaro, W. (1985). *Friendship and peer culture in the early years.* Norwood, NJ: Ablex.

Corsaro, W. A. (2003). *"We're friends, right?": Inside kids' cultures.* Washington, DC: Joseph Henry Press.

Corsaro, W. (2011). *The sociology of childhood* (3rd ed.). Thousand Oaks, CA: Pine Forge Press.

Corsaro, W., & Johannesen, B. (2007). The creation of new cultures in peer interaction. In J. Valsiner & A. Rosa (Eds.), *The Cambridge handbook of sociocultural psychology* (pp. 444–459). Cambridge, UK: Cambridge University Press.

Crystal, D. (1997). *The Cambridge encyclopedia of language.* Cambridge, UK: Cambridge University Press.

Dargan, A., & Zeitlin, S. (1990). *City play.* New Brunswick, NJ: Rutgers University Press.

Delpit, L., & Dowdy, J. K. (Eds.). (2002). *The skin that we speak: Thoughts on language and culture in the classroom.* New York: The New Press.

Dewey, J. (1944). *Democracy and education.* New York: Macmillan. (Original work published 1916)

Duranti, A. (2009). Linguistic anthropology: History, ideas, and issues. In A. Duranti (Ed.), *Linguistic anthropology: A reader* (pp. 1–60). Hoboken, NJ: Wiley-Blackwell.

Dyson, A. Haas. (1982). The emergence of visible language: Interrelationships between drawing and early writing. *Visible Language, 16*(2), 360–381.

Dyson, A. Haas. (1983). The role of oral language in early writing processes. *Research in the Teaching of English, 17*(1), 1–30.

Dyson, A. Haas. (1989). *Multiple worlds of child writers: Friends learning to write.* New York: Teachers College Press.

Dyson, A. Haas. (1990). Symbol makers, symbol weavers: How children link play, pictures, and print. *Young Children, 45*(2), 50–69.

Dyson, A. Haas. (1993). *Social worlds of children learning to write in an urban primary school.* New York: Teachers College Press.

Dyson, A. Haas. (1997). *Writing superheroes: Contemporary childhood, popular culture, and classroom literacy.* New York: Teachers College Press.

Dyson, A. Haas. (1999). Transforming transfer: Unruly children, contrary texts, and the persistence of the pedagogical order. In A. Iran-Nejad & P. D. Pearson (Eds.), *Review of research in education* (vol. 24, pp. 141–172). Washington, DC: American Educational Research Association.

Dyson, A. Haas. (2003a). *The brothers and sisters learn to write: Popular literacies in childhood and school cultures.* New York: Teachers College Press.

Dyson, A. Haas. (2003b). Popular literacies and the "all" children: Rethinking literacy development for contemporary childhoods. *Language Arts, 81*(2), 100–109.

Dyson, A. Haas. (2006). On saying it right (write): "Fix-its" in the foundations of learning to write. *Research in the Teaching of English, 41*(1), 8–44.

Dyson, A. Haas. (2007). School literacy and the development of a child culture: Written remnants of the "gusto of life." In D. Thiessen & A. Cook-Sather (Eds.), *International handbook of student experiences in elementary and secondary school* (pp. 115–142). Dordrecht, The Netherlands: Kluwer.

Dyson, A. Haas. (2008). Staying in the (curricular) lines: Practice constraints and possibilities in childhood writing. *Written Communication, 25*(1), 119–157.

Dyson, A. Haas, & Dewayani, S. (in press). Writing in childhood cultures. In K. Hall, T. Cremin, B. Comber, & L. Moll (Eds.), *International handbook of research on children's literacy, learning, and culture.* Oxford, England: Wiley-Blackwell.

Dyson, A. Haas, & Smitherman, G. (2009). The right (write) start: African American Language and the discourse of sounding right. *Teachers College Record, 111*(4), 973–998.

Eng, H. (1931). *The psychology of children's drawings.* London: Kegan Paul.

Feld, S., & Basso, K. H. (Eds.). (1996). *Senses of place.* Santa Fe, NM: School of American Research Press.

Ferreiro, E., & Teberosky, A. (1982). *Literacy before schooling.* Exeter, NH: Heinemann Educational Books.

Fisher, M. T. (2003). Open mics and open minds: Spoken word poetry in African diaspora participatory literacy communities. *Harvard Educational Review, 73*(3), 362–389.

Fishman, J. A. (1972). National languages and languages of wider communication in developing nations. In D. Anwar (Ed.), *Language in sociocultural change: Essays by Joshua Fishman* (pp. 191–213). Stanford, CA: Stanford University Press.

Garvey, C. (1990). *Play.* Cambridge, MA: Harvard University Press.

Geertz, C. (1996). Afterword. In S. Feld & K. H. Basso (Eds.), *Sense of place* (pp. 259–262). Santa Fe, NM: School of American Research Press.

Genishi, C., & Dyson, A. Haas. (2009). *Children, language, and literacy: Diverse learners in diverse times.* New York: Teachers College Press; Washington, DC: The National Association for the Education of Young Children.

Genishi, C., Stires, S., & Yung-chan, D. (2001). Writing in an integrated curriculum: Prekindergarten English language learners as symbol makers. In A. Haas Dyson (Ed.), *Elementary School Journal* (special issue), *101*(4), 399–416.

Goffman, E. (1981). *Forms of talk.* Philadelphia: University of Pennsylvania Press.

Goodman, Y. (2003). *Valuing language study: Inquiry into language for elementary and middle schools.* Urbana, IL: National Council of Teachers of English.

Goodman, Y., & Martens, P. (Eds.). (2007). *Critical issues in early literacy: Research and pedagogy.* Mahwah, NJ: Erlbaum.

Goodwin, M. H. (1990). *He-said-she-said: Talk as social organization among black children.* Bloomington and Indianapolis, IN: Indiana University Press.

Goodwin, C. & Duranti, A. (1992). Rethinking context: An introduction. In A. Duranti & C. Goodwin (Eds.), *Rethinking context: Language as an interactive phenomenon* (pp. 1–46). New York: Cambridge University Press.

Goodwin, C., & Goodwin, M. H. (2006). Participation. In A. Duranti (Ed.), *A companion to linguistic anthropology* (pp. 222–244). Malden, MA: Blackwell.

Goodwin, M. H., & Kyrastzis, A. (2011). Peer language socialization. In A. Duranti, E. Ochs, & B. B. Schieffelin (Eds.), *The handbook of language socialization* (pp. 365–390). Malden, MA: Blackwell.

Green, L. J. (2011). *Language and the African American child.* New York: Cambridge University Press.

Greenfield, E. (1978). *Honey I love.* New York: Harper & Row.

Greenfield, E., & Little, L. J. (1979). *Childtimes: A three-generation memoir.* New York: Crowell.

Gutiérrez, K. D., & Orellana, M. (2006). At last: The "problem" of English learners: Constructing genres of difference. *Research in the Teaching of English, 40*(4), 502–507.

Haberman, M. (1991). The pedagogy of poverty versus good teaching. *Phi Delta Kappan, 73*(4), 290–294.

Hall, N. (1996). Learning about punctuation: An introduction and overview. In N. Hall & A. Robinson (Eds.), *Learning about punctuation* (pp. 5–36). Portsmouth, NH: Heinemann.

Hall, N., & Robinson, A. (Eds.). (1996). *Learning about punctuation.* Portsmouth, NH: Heinemann.

Hanks, W. F. (1996). *Language and communicative practices.* Boulder, CO: Westview Press.

Hanks, W. F. (2000). *Intertexts: Writings on language, utterance, and context.* Lanham, MD: Rowman & Littlefield.

Heath, S. B. (1982). Questioning at home and at school: A comparative study. In G. Spindler (Ed.), *Doing the ethnography of schooling* (pp. 96–101). New York: Holt, Rinehart, & Winston.

Heath, S. B. (1983). *Ways with words: Language, life and work in communities and class-rooms.* Cambridge, UK: Cambridge University Press.

Hirsh-Pasek, K., Golinkoff, R. M., Berk, L. E., & Singer, D. G. (2009). *A mandate for playful learning in preschool: Presenting the evidence.* New York: Oxford University Press.

Holland, P. (2003). *We don't play with guns here: War, weapon and superhero play in the early years.* Maidenhead and Philadelphia, PA: Open University Press

Holquist, M. (1981). Glossary. In M. Bakhtin & M . Holquist (Eds.), C. Emerson & M. Holquist (Trans.), *The dialogic imagination: Four essays* (pp. 423–434). Austin: University of Texas Press.

Hudley, A. H. C., & Mallison, C. (2011). *Understanding English language variation in U.S. schools.* New York: Teachers College Press.

Hull, G. A., & Nelson, M. E. (2005). Locating the semiotic power of multimodality. *Written Communication, 22*(2), 224–261.

Hymes, D. (1972). On communicative competence. In J. Pride & J. Holmes (Eds.), *Sociolinguistics: Selected readings* (pp. 269–293). Harmondsworth, England: Penguin.

Hymes, D. (1974). *Foundations in sociolinguistics: An ethnographic approach.* Philadelphia: University of Pennsylvania Press.

Jackson 5. (1970). The Corporation (Writer). ABC [Record Album]. Detroit, MI: MoTown.

Jenkins, H. (2009). *Confronting the challenges of participatory culture: Media education for the 21st century.* Cambridge, MA: MIT Press.

Jones, B., & Hawes, B. L. (1972). *Step it down: Games, plays, songs, and stories from the Afro-American heritage.* New York: Harper & Row.

Katz, A., & Carrow, D. (2001). *Take me out of the bathtub and other silly dilly songs.* New York: Simon & Schuster.

Kirkland, D., & Jackson, A. (2009). "We real cool": Toward a theory of Black masculine literacies. *Reading Research Quarterly, 44*(3), 278–297.

Kreider, R., & Ellis, R. (2011). *Number, timing, and duration of marriages and divorces: 2009.* Washington, DC: U.S. Census Bureau. Available at http://www.census.gov/prod/2011pubs/p70-125.pdf

Kress, G. (1997). *Before writing: Rethinking the paths to literacy.* London: Routledge.

Kress, G. (2003). *Literacy in the new media age.* London: Routledge.

Kress, G. (2010). *Multimodality: A social semiotic approach to contemporary communication.* London: Routledge.

Labov, W. (1972). *Language in the inner city.* Philadelphia: University of Pennsylvania Press.

Ladson-Billings, G. (2005). Reading, writing, and race: Literacy practices of teachers in diverse classrooms. In T. McCarty (Ed.), *Language, literacy and power in schooling* (pp. 133–150). New York: Routledge.

Lancy, D. F. (2007). Accounting for variability in mother/child play. *American Anthropologist, 109*(2), 273–284.

Lensmire, T. (1994). *When children write: Critical re-visions of the writing workshop.* New York: Teachers College Press.

Levinson, M. (2007). Literacy in English Gypsy communities: Cultural capital manifested as negative assets. *American Educational Research Journal, 44*(1), 5–39.

Levy, A. (2004). *Small island: A novel.* New York: Picador.

Lindfors, J. (1987). *Children's language and learning* (2nd ed.). Englewood Cliffs, NJ: Prentice-Hall.

Lindfors, J. (2008). *Children's language: Connecting reading, writing, and talk.* New York: Teachers College Press.

Loban, W. (1976). *Language development: Kindergarten through grade 12.* Urbana, IL: National Council of Teachers of English.

Long, S., Volk, D., & Gregory, E. (2007). Intentionality and expertise: Learning from observations of children at play in multilingual, multicultural contexts. *Anthropology and Education Quarterly, 38*(3), 239–259.

Lonigan, C. J., & Shanahan, T. (2010). The National Early Literacy Panel: A summary of the process and the report. *Educational Researcher, 39*(4), 279–285.

Love, A., Burns, S., & Buell, M. J. (2007). Writing: Empowering literacy. *Young Children, 62*(1), 13–19.

Luke, A. & Grieshaber, S. (2004). New adventures in the politics of literacy: An introduction. *Journal of Early Childhood Literacy, 4*(1), 5–9.

Marsh, J. (2005). *Popular culture, new media and digital literacy in early childhood.* London: Routledge.

Marsh, J. (2013). Early childhood literacy and popular culture. In J. Larson & J. Marsh (Eds.), *Handbook of early childhood literacy* (2nd ed., pp. 207–222). Los Angeles, CA: Sage.

Massey, D. B. (2005). *For space*. Los Angeles, CA: Sage.

Massey, D., & Denton, N. (1993). *American apartheid: Segregation and the making of the underclass*. Cambridge, MA: Harvard University Press.

Matthews, J. (1999). *The art of childhood and adolescence: The construction of meaning*. London: Falmer Press.

Mauer, M., & King , R. (2007). *Uneven justice: State rates of incarceration by race and ethnicity*. Available at www.sentencingproject.org

McDermott, R. P., & Varenne, H. (2010). Culture, development, disability. In W. Luttrell (Ed.), *Qualitative educational research: Readings in reflexive methodology and transformative practice* (pp. 164–182). New York: Routledge.

McKendrick, J. H., Bradford, M. G., & Fielder, A. V. (2000). Time for a party!: Making sense of the commercialization of leisure space for children. In S. L. Holloway & G. Valentine (Eds.), *Children's geographies: Playing, living, learning* (pp. 100–118). London: Routledge.

Merriam-Webster's collegiate dictionary (XI edition). (2008). Springfield, MA: Merriam-Webster.

Michaels, S. (1981). "Sharing time": Children's narrative styles and differential access to literacy. *Language and Society, 10*(3), 423–442.

Michaels, S., & Sohmer, R. (2000). Narratives and inscriptions: Cultural tools, power, and powerful sense making. In M. Kalantzis & B. Cope (Eds.), *Multiliteracies: Literacy, learning, and the design of social futures* (pp. 267–288). New York: Routledge.

Miller, P. (1996). Instantiating culture through discourse practices: Some personal reflections on socialization and how to study it. In R. Jesson, A. Colby, & R. Shweder (Eds.), *Ethnography and human development* (pp. 183–204). Chicago: University of Chicago Press.

Miller, P., Cho, G. E., & Bracey, J. (2005). Working-class children's experience through the prism of personal storytelling. *Human Development, 48*(3), 115–135.

Miller, P., & Goodnow, J. J. (1995). Cultural practices: Toward an integration of culture and development. In J. J. Goodnow, P. J. Miller, & F. Kessel (Eds.), *Cultural practices as contexts for development, No. 67, New directions in child development* (pp. 5–16). San Francisco, CA: Jossey Bass.

Miller, P., & Sperry, D. (2012). Déjà vu: The continuing misrecognition of low-income children's verbal abilities. In S. Fiske & H. R. Markus (Eds.), *Facing social class: How societal rank influences interaction* (pp. 109–130). New York: Russell Sage Foundation.

Minks, A. (2006). Mediated intertextuality in pretend play among Nicaraguan Miskitu children. *Texas Linguistic Forum (SALSA), 49,* 117–127.

Mitchell, J. C. (1984). Case studies. In R. F. Ellen (Ed.), *Ethnographic research: A guide to general conduct* (pp. 237–241). San Diego, CA: Academic Press.

Moats, L. (2004). *Language essentials for teachers of reading and spelling*. Longmont, CO: Sopris West Educational Services.

Moll, L.C., Saez, R., & Dworin, J. (2001). Exploring biliteracy: Two student case examples of writing as a social practice. In A. Haas Dyson (Ed.), *Elementary School Journal* (special issue), *101*(4),435–449.

Montgomery, H. (2009). *An introduction to childhood: Anthropological perspectives on children's lives*. Malden, MA: Wiley-Blackwell.

Nelson, K. (2007). *Young minds in social worlds: Experience, meaning, and memory.* Cambridge, MA: Harvard University Press.

New London Group (1996). A pedagogy of multiliteracies: Designing social futures. *Harvard Educational Review, 66*(1), 60–92.

Newkirk, T. (2002). *Misreading masculinity: Boys, literacy, and popular culture.* Portsmouth, NH: Heinemann.

Newkirk, T. (2009). *Holding on to good ideas in a time of bad ones: Six literacy principles worth fighting for.* Portsmouth, NH: Heinemann.

Nicolopoulou A., McDowell, J., Brockmeyer, C. (2006). Narrative play and emergent literacy: Storytelling and story-acting meet journal writing. In D. Singer, R. M. Golinkoff, & K. Hirsh-Pasek (Eds.), *Play=Learning: How play motivates and enhances children's cognitive and social-emotional growth* (pp. 124–144). Oxford, England: Oxford.

Nixon, H., & Comber, B. (2008). Redesigning school spaces: Creating possibilities for learning. In P. Sefton-Green, P. Thomson, L. Bresler, & K. Jones (Eds.), *The international handbook of creative learning* (pp. 249–259). London: Routledge.

Noguera, P. (2003). *City schools and the American dream: Reclaiming the promise of public education.* New York: Teachers College Press.

Numeroff, L. (2002). *If you take a mouse to school.* New York: HarperCollins.

Ochs, E., & Capps, L. (2001). *Living narrative: Creating lives in everyday storytelling.* Cambridge, MA: Harvard University Press.

Opie, I., & Opie, P. (1959). *The lore and language of school children.* London, England: University Press.

Orellana, M. F. (2009). *Translating childhoods: Immigrant youth, language, and culture.* New Brunswick: Rutgers University Press.

Pahl, K. (2005). Narrative spaces and multiple identities: Children's textual explorations of console games in home settings. In J. Marsh (Ed.), *Popular culture, new media, and digital literacy in early childhood* (pp. 126–145). London: Routledge Falmer.

Pahl, K., & Rowsell, J. (2005). *Literacy and education.* London: Paul Chapman.

Paley, V. (1981). *Wally's stories.* Cambridge, MA: Harvard University Press.

Paley, V. (1984). *Boys and girls: Superheroes in the doll corner.* Chicago: University of Chicago Press.

Paley, V. (1986). *Mollie is three: Growing up in school.* Chicago: University of Chicago Press.

Paley, V. (2004). *A child's work: The importance of fantasy play.* Chicago: University of Chicago Press.

Paris, D., & Kirkland, D. (2011). "The consciousness of the verbal artist": Understanding the vernacular literacies in digital and embodied spaces. In V. Kinloch (Ed.), *Urban literacies* (pp. 177–194). New York: Teachers College Press.

Park, B. (1993). *Junie B. Jones and her big fat mouth.* New York: Random House.

Philips, S. (1972). Participant structures and communicative competence: Warm springs children in community and classroom. In C. B. Cazden, V. P. John, & D. Hymes (Eds.), *The functions of language in the classroom* (pp. 370–394). New York: Teachers College Press.

Piercy, M. (1994). The low road. *The moon is always female* (pp. 44–45). New York: Knopf.

Powell, A. (Ed.). (2012). "I don't want to go to Mexico no more." Available at http://www.cocojams.com

Pratt, M. L. (1977). *Toward a speech act theory of literary discourse*. Bloomington: Indiana University Press.

Read, C. (1975). *Children's categorization of speech sounds in English*. Urbana, IL: National Council of Teachers of English.

Reder, S., & Davila, E. (2005). Context and literacy practices. *Annual Review of Applied Linguistics, 25*, 170–187.

Reyes, I., & Azuara, P. (2008). Emergent biliteracy in young Mexican immigrant children. *Reading Research Quarterly, 43*(4), 374–398.

Reyes, M. L., & Halcon, J. (Eds.). (2001). *The best for our children: Critical perspectives on literacy for Latino students*. New York: Teachers College Press.

Rogoff, B. (2003). *The cultural nature of human development*. New York: Oxford University Press.

Salvio, P. M., & Boldt, G. M. (2009). "A democracy tempered by the rate of exchange": Audit culture and the sell-out of progressive writing pedagogy. *English in Education, 43*(2), 113–128.

Samway, K. (2006). *When English language learners write: Connecting research to practice, K–8*. Portsmouth, NH: Heinemann.

Schieffelin, B. (1999). Introducing Kaluli literacy. In P. V. Kroskrity (Ed.), *Regimes of language* (pp. 293–327). Sante Fe, NM: School of American Research Press.

Shipps, D. (2000). Echoes of corporate influence: Managing away urban school troubles. In L. Cuban & D. Shipps (Eds.), *Reconstructing the common good in education: Coping with intractable American dilemmas* (pp. 82–106). Stanford, CA: Stanford University Press.

Siegal, M. (2006). Rereading the signs: Multimodal transformations in the field of literacy education. *Language Arts, 84*(1), 65–77.

Slate, J. (2001). *Miss Bindergarten gets ready for kindergarten*. New York: Puffin Books.

Smith, N. (1983). *Experience and art: Teaching children to paint*. New York: Teachers College Press.

Smith, K., & Stock, P. (2003). Trends and issues in research in the teaching of the English Language Arts. In J. Flood, D. Lapp, J. Squire, & J. M. Jensen (Eds.), *Handbook of research on teaching the English Language Arts* (pp. 114–130). Mahwah, NJ: Erlbaum.

Smitherman, G. (1986). *Talkin and testifyin: The language of Black America*. Detroit, MI: Wayne State University Press.

Souto-Manning, M. (2010). Challenging ethnocentric literacy practices: (Re)positioning home literacies in a Head Start classroom. *Research in the Teaching of English, 45*(2), 150–178.

Steinberg, Z., & Cazden, C. (1979). Children as teachers—of peers and ourselves. *Theory Into Practice, 18*(4), 258–266.

Sterponi, L. (2011). Literacy socialization. In A. Duranti, E. Ochs, & B. Schieffelin (Eds.), *The handbook of language socialization* (pp. 227–246). Malden, MA: Blackwell.

Stetsenko, A. (1995). The psychological function of children's drawing: A Vygotskian perspective. In C. Lange-Kuttner, G. V. Kuttner, & G. V. Thomas (Eds.),

Drawing and looking: Theoretical approaches to pictorial representation in children (pp. 147–158). New York: Harvester/Wheatsheaf.

Street, B. (2000). Literacy events and literacy practices. In M. Martin-Jones & K. Jones (Eds.), *Multilingual literacies: Comparative perspectives on research and practice* (pp. 17–29). Amsterdam, the Netherlands: John Benjamin's.

Sutton-Smith, B., Mechling, J., Johnson, T. W., & McMahon, F. R. (Eds.). (1995). *Children's folklore: A source book.* New York: Garland Publishing.

Tannen, D. (1989). *Talking voices: Repetition, dialogue, and imagery in conversational discourse.* Cambridge, UK: Cambridge University Press.

Thorne, B. (1993). *Gender play: Girls and boys in school.* New Brunswick, NJ: Rutgers University Press.

Thorne, B. (2005). Unpacking school lunchtime: Structure, practice, and the negotiation of differences. In C. R. Cooper, C. T. G. Coll, W. T. Bartko, H. Davis, & C. Chatman (Eds.), *Developmental pathways through middle childhood: Rethinking contexts and diversity as resources* (pp. 63–88). Mahwah, NJ: Erlbaum.

Tolchinsky, L. (2003). *The cradle of culture and what children know about writing and numbers before being taught.* Mahweh, NJ: Erlbaum.

Tomasello, M. (2009). *Why we cooperate.* Cambridge, MA: MIT Press.

Toolan, M. J. (1988). *Narrative: A critical linguistic introduction.* London, England: Routledge.

Urciuoli, B. (1998). *Exposing prejudice: Puerto Rican experiences of language, race, and class.* Boulder, CO: Westview.

Vasquez, O., Pease-Alvarez, L., & Shannon, S. (1994). *Pushing boundaries: Language and culture in a Mexicano community.* New York: Cambridge University Press.

Volosinov, V. N. (1986). *Marxism and the philosophy of language.* New York: Seminar Press.

Vygotsky, L. S. (1962). *Thought and language.* Cambridge, MA: MIT Press.

Vygotsky, L. S. (1978). *Mind in society.* Cambridge, MA: Harvard University Press.

Wenger, E. (1998). *Communities of practice: Learning, meaning, and identity.* Cambridge, UK: Cambridge University Press.

Werner, H. & Kaplan, B. (1963). *Symbol formation: An organismic developmental approach to language and the expression of thought.* New York: John Wiley.

Willems, M. (2003). *Don't let the pigeon drive the bus.* New York: Hyperion.

Williams, V. B. (1984). *A chair for my mother.* New York: Greenwillow Press.

Wohlwend , K. (2011). *Playing their way into literacies: Reading, writing, and belonging in the early childhood classroom.* New York: Teachers College Press.

Zentella, A. C. (Ed.). (2005). *Building on strength: Language and literacy in Latino families and communities.* New York: Teachers College Press.

Zickuhr, K., & Smither, A. (2012). Digital differences. Pew Internet and American Life Project report, Pew Research Center. Available at http://pewinternet.org/Reports/2012/Digital-differences.aspx

Index

Adequate yearly progress, 12
Adger, C. T., 63, 167, 168
Aesthetic judgments, 90, 108
African American Language (AAL), 13,
    60–61, 63–65, 147–149, 166–167
African Americans, 11, 14–16, 186–187
Ahmad, D., 167
Alicia (kindergarten student)
    birthdays and, 40–41
    collegial relations and, 101–102, 104
    coordinated actions and, 108, 111
    introduction, 17–18
    mediation of childhood cultures,
        100–101
    performance and, 158, 160
    sibling love and, 79–80, 133
    situated content adjustments and, 91–94
    storytelling and, 71, 77, 78–80, 150, 160
Anderson, E. S., 167
Antone (kindergarten student), tension
    between talking drawing and talking
    writing, 47–48
Appiah, Kwame A., 6, 68, 88, 185
Applebee, A. N., 73–74
Ashton-Warner, Sylvia, 177
Asian Americans, 16
Au, W., 34
Author's Theater, 170
Azuara, P., 147

Bakhtin, M., 6–7, 22, 26, 51, 68, 76, 85, 88,
    93, 102, 114, 115, 144, 146, 164, 165,
    170, 172, 176, 178, 185
Barton, D., 5
Basics of writing, 21–81
    in 1st grade, 34–37
    in case studies, 2–3. See also Mrs. Bee's
        kindergarten class; Mrs. Kay's 1st-
        grade class
    classroom as community and, 25, 26–33,
        57–58, 80–81

contextualizing, 164–174. See also Peer
    relations
critiques of, 5–6
dialogue between official and unofficial
    world in, 177–178
ethics. See Ethics of writing
in hybrid writing programs, 3
isolated versus independent selves and, 6
in kindergarten, 37–41
mailbox metaphor in, 1–2, 3–9
mastering ABC's in, xi, xii, 1–2, 165
multimodal nature of literacy and, 5–6,
    8, 149–156, 169–171
nature of, 163
official writing lives of young children,
    33–41
peer culture in. See Peer relations;
    Relational fix-its
re-envisioned basic education and,
    174–178
re-imagined, 168–171
role of, 1–4, 34
search for relationships and meaning,
    4–5, 7, 44
situated classroom and, 2, 31–33, 89–91.
    See also Peer relations; Relational
    fix-its
social organization of writing time, 23,
    25, 26–33
standards and accountability for, 2, 5–6,
    26, 33–35, 38–39, 45, 51–52, 55–58,
    61, 67, 164, 177
wide-awake children and, 25–26, 41–42
writing out (silencing) childhood and,
    5–9
Basso, K. H., 9
Bateson, G., 70–71
Bauman, R., 85, 96, 101, 144, 146, 160
Baynham, M., 23
Bee, Mrs. See Mrs. Bee's kindergarten class
    and names of specific students

Bereiter, C., 172
Berk, L. E., 5, 173
Berman, R., 62
Bezemer, J., 2, 150, 169
Bialystok, E., 53
Birthdays and birthday parties, 7–8, 30,
     40–41, 50, 52, 67, 78, 95–96, 100–101,
     115–122, 173
  evolution of practices in, 117–120
  fiction *versus* life story, 120–121
  official roots of play in, 115–116
  official *versus* unofficial worlds and,
     116–117, 121–122
  private *versus* public, 116–117
Blaise, M., 133
Blommaert, J., 144, 168, 185
Boldt, G. M., 6, 41, 134
Book fair, 31–33, 157
Bourdieu, P., 114
Boys & Girls Club, 15, 19, 55–57, 175
Bracey, J., 173
Brad (1st-grade student)
  complementary relations and, 127, 128
  cross-gender relations and, 127, 128,
     130–132
  family love and, 133, 134
Bradford, M. G., 115
Brandt, D., 33
Britton, Jimmy, 48, 77
Brockmeyer, C., 52
Buell, M. J., 176
Bureaucratic negotiations, as content fix-its,
     90
Burns, S., 176

Calkins, L., 6
Capitalization, 22–23, 35–36, 65–66, 165
Capps, L., 76, 101
Carrow, D., 27, 157
Case studies, 181–185. *See also* Mrs. Bee's
     kindergarten class; Mrs. Kay's 1st-
     grade class
  constructing analytic narratives, 184–185
  copying children in, 182–184
  situating teachers in, 181–182
  transcript conventions in, 183–184
Cazden, C., 167
Chabris, C., 162–163
Chair for My Mother, A (Williams), 32
Charles (kindergarten student)
  birthdays and, 7–8, 52

performance and, 153–156, 160, 161
  storytelling and, 71, 74, 153–156, 160,
     161, 169
Chase games, 12, 122–123, 135–141
Children at risk, 2, 35, 171–174
Cho, G. E., 173
Chomsky, N., 167
Christian, D., 63, 168
Clapping games, 43–44, 99–100, 106, 111,
     114, 157, 161
Clark, C. D., 71, 72
Clark, E. V., 167
Clark, K., 88
Classroom as community, 25, 26–33. *See also*
     Peer relations
  inclusive classroom, 30–31
  situated classroom, 31–33
  social organization of writing time, 23,
     25, 26–33
  social orientation *versus* individualism of
     writing, 80–81
  storied classroom, 27–30
  writing fix-its and, 57–58
Clay, M., 23, 39, 52, 170, 176
Clifton, Lucille, 67, 168, 175
Clinton, K., 33
Collaborative improvisation, 12, 96,
     135–141
Collegial relations, 95, 99–100, 101–106, 111
Comber, B., 23, 141, 173
Communicative flexibility, 13, 60–61, 63–65,
     147–149, 166–167, 185
Complementary relations, 113–135
  birthday parties and, 115–122
  in complex game of love, 122–135
  nature of, 95–96
Conceptual horizon (Bakhtin), 114
Content fix-its
  adding details, 45, 47–48, 91
  bureaucratic negotiations, 90
  curricular fix-its *versus*, 51–52
  group knowledge, 90, 104, 105, 106, 128
  kindergarten class, 46–52
  organizing text, 45, 47, 53
  prescribed identity, 90, 136, 139
  reciprocal obligations, 90, 91, 93, 101,
     107, 109
  situated, 90, 91–94, 93, 101, 104–107, 109,
     119, 158
  social expectations for inclusion, 90, 91,
     119

writing more/drawing less, 45, 46, 49, 91
Conversational style, 35–36, 39–40, 115–116
Cooper, P. A., 6, 52, 170
Coordinated actions, 95, 99–100, 106–111, 114
Coretta (kindergarten student), writing fix-its and, 87–88
Corsaro, W. A., 85, 94–95, 100
Cross-gender relations, 122–135
    chase games in, 122–123
    class demographics, 186–187
    connections and break-ups in, 130–132
    curriculum issues in, 133–135
    language of love in, 123–126
    in Pine Cone Wars, 139–141, 173
    planned date and, 130
    sexism and ethics of textual inclusion, 139–141
    sociogram of 1st-grade players, 128–129
    textual choreography of love in, 126–130
    Valentine's Day and, 30, 91, 132
Crystal, D., 59
Cultural brokering, 173

Daily sharing time, 51, 70, 76, 89, 96, 122, 127, 138–139, 144–145, 156, 177–178
Dargan, A., 83
Davila, E., 33
Deficit views of children, 172
Delpit, L., 167
Denise (kindergarten student), coordinated actions and, 110–111
Denton, N., 174
Details, as content fix-its, 45, 47–48, 91
Dewayani, S., 106
Dewey, J., 171
Dialogic spaces, 7–8
Dialogue bubbles, 139, 154
Dictated stories, 51–52, 170
Digital technologies. *See* Multimodality
Dowdy, J. K., 167
Dramatic play, 116
Drawing, 35, 39, 41
    labels next to drawn objects, 47
    in normalizing multimodality, 169
    performance and, 150, 153
    in Pine Cone Wars, 136–138, 150
    storytelling and, 150, 153
    transition to writing, 138–141
    writing more/drawing less fix-its, 45, 46, 49, 91

Duranti, A., 43, 172
Dworin, J., 147
Dyson, Anne Haas, xi, 5, 23, 44, 45, 48, 51, 52, 58, 64, 73–74, 80, 85, 90, 106, 113, 115, 117, 130, 135, 136, 139, 141, 145–147, 149, 150, 156, 163, 164, 167–170, 172, 173, 175, 176, 178

Elisha (1st-grade student), in Pine Cone Wars, 138–141
Ella (kindergarten student)
    birthdays and, 115
    coordinated actions and, 110–111
Ellie (1st-grade student)
    birthdays and, 117, 119–120, 173
    complementary relations and, 127, 128
    cross-gender relations and, 123, 127, 128, 130–132
Ellis, R., 133
Encoding words (spelling), 45, 52–57, 62, 165
Eng, H., 169
Engelmann, S., 172
Ernest (kindergarten student)
    birthdays and, 7–8, 115
    coordinated actions and, 108–109
    performance and, 158–159, 160
    situated classroom and, 91
    storytelling and, 77–78, 158, 159, 160
Ethics of writing, 69–81
    copying children in research methodology, 182–184
    individualism in, 69, 75–76, 77–79
    "real stories about you" and, 70–78
    sexism, 139–141
    textual inclusion and, 139–141
    "thick relations" and (Appiah), 88
Ezekial (1st-grade student)
    birthdays and, 119–120
    book fair and, 31, 157
    collegial relations and, 104–106
    complementary relations and, 113–114
    depiction of human voices, 67, 153, 169
    grammatical fix-its, 61–63, 167, 168
    graphological conventions, 65–66, 165
    Halloween and, 30
    introduction, 12–14
    in Pine Cone Wars, 141
    situated classroom and, 31
    social talk with peers, 44

Family love, 79–80, 133–134
Feld, S., 9
Ferreiro, E., 53, 55
Fielder, A. V., 115
First grade. *See* Mrs. Kay's 1st-grade class
    and names of specific students
Fisher, M. T., 8
Fishman, J. A., 166–167
Fix-its. *See* Relational fix-its; Writing fix-its
Format of page, 45
Frames, 70–71

Garvey, C., 146
Geertz, Clifford, 9, 27
Gender relations. *See* Cross-gender
    relations
Genishi, C., xi, 5, 23, 58, 80, 113, 146, 147,
    163, 167, 168, 173, 176
Goffman, E., 95
Golden Rule, 33, 135
Golinkoff, R. M., 5, 173
Goodman, Y., 5, 167
Goodnow, J. J., 165
Goodwin, C., 85, 95, 116, 172
Goodwin, M. H., 85, 95, 116, 128, 146
Gossip, 128
Grammar, 34, 35, 39–40
Grammatical fix-its
    1st-grade class, 59–65
    adjusting sentence structure, 45, 54, 57,
        60, 61, 62
    adjusting usage, 45, 61
    kindergarten class, 64–65
    nonstandard social voice, 63–65
Graphological conventions, 163
    aesthetic judgments, 90, 108
    capitalization and punctuation, 22–23,
        35–36, 45, 59, 60–63, 65–66, 105,
        165
    encoding words (spelling), 45, 52–57,
        62, 165
    page format, 45
    situated, 90
    time/space exigencies, 90
Green, L. J., 147
Greenfield, Eloise, 58, 67, 168
Gregory, E., 147
Grieshaber, S., 33
Group knowledge, as content fix-its, 90,
    104, 105, 106, 128
Gutiérrez, K. D., 172

Haberman, M., 5
Halcon, J., 167
Hall, N., 59, 66
Halloween, 30, 36
Hamilton, M., 5
Hanks, W. F., 23, 59, 95, 114, 115
Hawes, B. L., 100
Heath, S. B., 5, 71, 114
Help, seeking, 53–55, 96–97
Hirsh-Pasek, K., 5, 173
Holland, P., 135
Holquist, M., 59, 88
Honey Love (Greenfield), 168
Hudley, A. H. C., 168
Hull, G. A., 169
Hymes, D., 43, 114, 144, 176

If You Take a Mouse to School (Numeroff), 27
Inclusiveness, 30–31, 33
    sexism and ethics of textual inclusion,
        139–141
    social expectations for inclusion, 90, 91,
        119
Indigenous arrangements. *See* Peer
    relations
Individualism, 23–24
    in approaches to early schooling, 6, 25,
        68
    change in angle of vision, 80–81
    classroom as social community *versus*,
        80–81
    ethics of writing and, 69, 75–76, 77–79
    legal *versus* competitive texts, 77–78
    in mailbox metaphor, 7
    relational dimension of writing *versus*,
        173
    tension with seeking help, 53–55, 96–97
    writing a life story, 78–80, 120–121
Invented spelling, 52–57
Iowa Test of Basic Skills (ITBS), 34–35

Jackson, A., 8
Jackson 5, xi, xii
Jamal (kindergarten student)
    games and, 52
    inclusiveness and, 30–31
    situated content adjustments and, 91–94
    snakes and cookies problem, 48–51, 95
    writing fix-its and, 87–88
Janette (1st-grade student)
    complementary relations and, 124–126

cross-gender relations and, 124–126, 131
   in Pine Cone Wars, 141
Jason (1st-grade student), in Pine Cone
   Wars, 139–140, 141
Jenkins, Henry, 8, 85, 169
Johannesen, B., 95
Johnson, T. W., 13
Jones, B., 100
Jon (1st-grade student)
   birthdays and, 119, 120–121
   complementary relations and, 127, 128
   cross-gender relations and, 127, 128,
      130–132
   storytelling and, 151–152

Kamler, B., 23
Kaplan, B., 170
Katz, A., 27, 157
Kay, Mrs. *See* Mrs. Kay's 1st-grade class *and*
   names of specific students
Kindergarten. *See* Mrs. Bee's kindergarten
   class *and names of specific students*
King, R., 133
Kirkland, D., 8, 67
Kreider, R., 133
Kress, G., 2, 65, 136, 144, 150, 156, 169–170
Kyrastzis, A., 146

Labov, W., 160
Ladson-Billings, G., 172
Lamont (kindergarten student), storytelling
   and, 72–73
Lancy, D. F., 70
Language of Wider Communication
   (LWC), 166–167, 176
La Trell (kindergarten student)
   birthdays and, 7–8, 52, 115
   Boys & Girls Club, 55–57, 175
   collegial relations and, 102–103
   content fix-its, 47–51, 91
   coordinated actions and, 108–109
   encoding fix-its, 52–57
   family love and, 133–134
   graphological conventions, 65
   introduction, 18–19
   performance and, 153, 158, 160
   situated content adjustments and, 91
   storytelling and, 71, 73, 74, 76, 77–78,
      150, 160
   tension between independence and
      seeking help, 53–55

Lego play event, 113–114, 124
Lensmire, T., 91
Levinson, M., 5
Levy, Andrea, xii–xiii
Life stories, 78–80, 120–121. *See also*
   Storytelling
Lindfors, J., 60, 170
Linguistic flexibility, 13, 60–61, 63–65,
   147–149, 166–167, 185
Little, L. J., 58
Loban, W., 62
Long, S., 147
Lonigan, C. J., xi
Love. *See also* Cross-gender relations
   family love, 79–80, 133–134
   Golden Rule and, 33, 135
   kinds of liking, 134
   sibling love, 79–80, 133
Love, A., 176
Luke, A., 33
LWC (Language of Wider Communication),
   166–167, 176
Lyron (1st-grade student)
   birthdays and, 119, 120
   book fair and, 31
   complementary relations and, 113–114,
      124–126, 128
   coordinated actions and, 107
   cross-gender relations and, 123, 124–126,
      128
   introduction, 13
   performance and, 143
   in Pine Cone Wars, 136–138, 139–140,
      141, 173
   situated classroom and, 31, 91
   storytelling and, 74, 148–149
   Valentine's Day and, 30

Mailbox metaphor, 1–2, 3–9
Malaguzzi, Loris, 4, 7
Mallison, C., 168
Mandisa (1st-grade student)
   birthdays and, 119, 120
   complementary relations and,
      124–126
   cross-gender relations and, 124–126
   performance and, 160
   in Pine Cone Wars, 138–141
   storytelling and, 75–76, 148–149, 160
Manipulatives, in Pine Cone Wars, 12,
   135–141

Manny (1st-grade student)
  birthdays and, 117, 118
  cross-gender relations and, 123–124, 135
  in Pine Cone Wars, 136–138, 139, 140
Marginalization of childhood, 174
Marsh, J., 5, 73, 174
Martens, P., 5
Massey, D. B., 9, 174
Matthews, J., 44, 48, 103, 136, 150, 169
Mauer, M., 133
McDermott, R. P., 51
McDowell, J., 52
McKendrick, J. H., 115
McMahon, F. R., 13
Mechling, J., 13
Mermaids, 91–94
Mermelstein, L., 6
Methodology of study, 3, 181–185
Mexican Americans, 11, 13–14, 16
Michaels, S., 173
Miller, P., 22, 147, 165, 172, 173
Minks, A., 146
Mitchell, J. C., 3
Moats, L., 6
Moll, L. C., 147
Montgomery, H., 70
Mrs. Bee's kindergarten class
  basics of writing in case study, 2–3,
    22–23, 34–37
  benchmarks of basics, 67
  birthdays and birthday parties, 7–8
  Boys & Girls Club, 15, 19, 55–57, 175
  collegial relations and, 99–100, 101–104
  content fix-its, 46–52
  coordinated actions and, 108–111
  cross-gender relations and, 124, 126–127,
    134
  demographics of students, 13–14, 187
  encoding fix-its, 52–57
  ethics of writing in, 70
  grammatical fix-its, 64–65
  graphological conventions, 65
  inclusiveness, 30–31, 33
  introduction, 14–19
  mediation of childhood cultures,
    100–101
  official writing lives of children, 37–41
  participation modes of students, 96–97.
    See also Participation modes
  performance in, 149–150, 153–161
  playground, 16–17
  research methodology and, 3, 181–185

rhyming and singing in, 16–17, 157–159
search for relationships and meaning,
    4–5
situated classroom, 32–33
situated content adjustments and, 91–94
situating teacher in, 17, 181–182
storytelling, 27–29, 70–71, 72–74, 76,
    77–81
teacher modeling practice, 39–40
teacher responses to children, 41–42
writing as means of social connection,
    170
writing fix-its, 46–58, 64–65
Mrs. Kay's 1st-grade class
  basics of writing in case study, 2–3,
    22–23, 34–37
  benchmarks of basics, 67
  class picnic, 162
  collegial relations and, 99–100, 101–102,
    104–106
  complementary relations, 113–116
  coordinated actions and, 99–100, 106–107
  cross-gender relations and, 122–135
  daily sharing time, 51, 70, 76, 89, 96, 122,
    127, 138–139, 144–145, 156, 177–178
  demographics of students, 11, 186
  ethics of writing in, 70, 140–142
  grammatical fix-its, 59–65
  graphological conventions, 65–66
  inclusiveness, 30–31, 33
  intensity of child composers, 171
  introduction, 10–14
  mailbox discussion, 1–2
  official writing lives of children, 34–37
  participation modes of students, 96–97,
    135–141. *See also* Participation
    modes
  performance in, 143–149, 150–153,
    160–161
  Pine Cone Wars, 12, 135–141, 150, 173,
    185
  playground, 12
  research methodology and, 3, 181–185
  rhyming and singing in, 157
  search for relationships and meaning,
    4–5, 43–44
  situated classroom, 31–32
  situating teacher in, 12, 181–182
  situational textual choices, 90, 91
  storytelling, 27–28, 70, 71–72, 73, 74–75,
    77–78, 80–81

teacher modeling practice, 34–37
teacher responses to children, 41–42
writing as means of social connection,
    170
writing fix-its, 43–44, 59–66, 83–84
Ms. Hache (student teacher), 21–22, 83, 105,
    107, 145
Multimodality, 5–6, 8, 149–156, 169–171
Music, 16–17, 25, 27, 157–159

Nelson, K., 4, 21–22, 44, 134
Nelson, M. E., 169
Newkirk, T., 5, 6
New London Group, 5
Nicolopoulou, A., 52
Nixon, H., 173
Noguera, P., 10, 31
Nonstandard social voice, as grammatical
    fix-it, 63–65
Numeroff, L., 27

Ochs, E., 76, 101
Odette (kindergarten student), collegial
    relations and, 101–102
Opie, I., 106
Opie, P., 106
Orellana, M. F., 172, 173
Organization
    social organization of writing time, 23,
        25, 26–33
    of text, as content fix-it, 45, 47, 53

Page format, 45
Pahl, K., 136, 174
Paley, Vivian, 52, 74, 91, 135, 170
Paris, D., 67
Park, B., 35, 63
Participation modes, 94–97, 99–161
    collaborative improvisation, 12, 96,
        135–141
    collegial relations, 95, 99–100, 101–106,
        111
    complementary relations, 95–96,
        113–135
    coordinated actions, 95, 99–100, 106–111,
        114
    performance, 71, 96, 143–161
    variation in, 178, 185
Participatory cultures, 8
Pease-Alvarez, L., 173
Pedagogy of poverty (Haberman), 5

Peer relations
    birthdays in. *See* Birthdays and birthday
        parties
    caution about developmental order,
        97–98
    in contextualizing the basics of writing,
        164–174
    cross-gender. *See* Cross-gender relations
    fix-its in. *See* Relational fix-its
    official *versus* unofficial worlds in,
        115–117, 121–122, 133–135, 177–178
    participation modes. *See* Participation
        modes
    play in. *See* Play
    range of influences in, 164–165
    in re-envisioned basic education, 174–178
Performance, 96, 143–161
    linguistic repertoire in, 146–149
    manipulation of sound in, 143–145
    multimodal repertoire in, 149–156
    rhyming and singing, 157–158
    in storytelling, 71, 145–156
    traditional meaning of, 144
Permeable curriculum (Dyson), 178
Philips, S., 95
Piercy, Marge, 4
Pine Cone Wars, 12, 135–141, 173, 185
    curriculum issues, 141
    evolution of symbolic wars, 136–138, 150
    sexism and ethics of textual inclusion in,
        139–141
    spread of textual war, 138–139
Play
    as basis of writing programs, 175
    birthday party. *See* Birthdays and
        birthday parties
    chase games, 12, 122–123, 135–141
    clapping games, 43–44, 99–100, 106, 111,
        114, 157, 161
    dramatic, 116
    frames, 70–71
    Lego play event, 113–114, 124
    Pine Cone Wars, 12, 135–141, 173, 185
    playground, 12, 16–17
    pretend, 70–71, 80
    singing games, 16–17
    Tinker Bell, 74, 104, 108, 111
Powell, A., 100, 106
Pratt, M. L., 143
Prescribed identity, as content fix-it, 90,
    136, 139

Pretend play
    "real stories about you" and, 70–71
    writing a life story and, 80
Prinsloo, M., 23
Process writing pedagogy, 6
Progressive writing pedagogy, 6
Punctuation, 22–23, 35–36, 39, 59, 60–63,
    66, 165

Ra'mell (kindergarten student),
    coordinated actions and, 109–110
Read, C., 38, 52
Reading First grants, 34
Reciprocity
    birthdays and, 7–8
    as foundation for symbolic medium, 4,
    6–9
    reciprocal obligations of content fix-its,
    90, 91, 93, 101, 107, 109
Reder, S., 33
Reggio Emilia schools (Italy), 4, 5
Relational fix-its, 87–94
    content adjustments, 90, 91, 93, 101,
    104–107, 109, 119, 158
    graphological decisions, 90
    relational drama concerning, 83–86,
    87–88
    situated textual choices, 89–91, 93
Repetition, 165
Research methodology, 3, 181–185
Reyes, I., 147
Reyes, M. L., 167
Rhyming, 157–159
Robinson, A., 59
Rogoff, B., 22, 53, 176
Roswell, J., 174

Saez, R., 147
Salvio, P. M., 41
Samway, K., 147
Santa Claus, 71–72, 73
Schieffelin, B., 80–81
Schools-of-choice program, 11
Selective attention, 162–163
Sentence structure, as grammatical fix-it,
    45, 54, 57, 60, 61, 62
Sexism, 139–141
Shanahan, T., xi
Shannon, S., 173
Sharing time, 51, 70, 76, 89, 96, 122, 127,
    138–139, 144–145, 156, 177–178

Shipps, D., 178
Sibling love, 79–80, 133
Siegal, M., 5, 170
Simeon (kindergarten student),
    coordinated actions and, 109–110
Simons, D., 162–163
Singer, D. G., 5, 173
Singing, 16–17, 157–159
Situated practice. *See* Peer relations;
    Relational fix-its
Situated textual choices, 89–91
    aesthetic judgments, 90, 108
    ideological ramifications, 90, 91, 93, 101
    practice expectations, 90
    utterance performance, 90, 158
Slate, J., 37
Small Island (Levy), xii–xiii
Smith, K., 6
Smith, N., 150
Smither, A., 2
Smitherman, G., 63–65, 71, 147, 149, 167,
    175
Social work of children (Dyson), 117
Socioeconomic status, 31–33, 115–116,
    171–174
Sohmer, R., 173
Soto, Gary, 67
Souto-Manning, M., 178
Spacing, 35–36, 39
Spelling (encoding words), 45, 52–57, 62,
    165
Sperry, D., 147, 172, 173
Spider-Man, 72–74
Standard English, 166–167
Steinberg, Z., 167
Sterponi, L., 164
Stetsenko, A., 44, 48, 156, 169
Stires, S., 167
Stock, P., 6
Storytelling, 27–30, 52
    Author's Theater, 170
    dictated stories and, 51–52, 170
    linguistic repertoire in, 146–149
    multimodal repertoire in, 149–156
    performance in, 71, 145–156
    "real stories about you" and, 70–78
    role-playing and, 114
    writing a life story, 78–80, 120–121
Street, B., 5, 22
Sutton-Smith, B., 13
Symbol-weaving (Dyson), 169–170

Take Me Out of the Bathtub and Other Silly Dilly Songs (Katz & Carrow), 27, 157
Tannen, D., 146
Taylor, A., 133
Teacher modeling
  of storytelling, 27–29
  in writing workshop, 35–36, 115–116
Teberosky, A., 53, 55
Telling cases (Mitchell), 3
Thanksgiving, 50–51
Thorne, B., 85, 122
Time/space exigencies, as graphological conventions, 90
Tinker Bell play, 74, 104, 108, 111
Tionna (1st-grade student)
  African American Language (AAL) and, 13, 60–61, 63–64, 147–149, 166–167
  birthdays and, 117, 118
  book fair and, 31
  child *versus* teacher perspective and, 21–24, 178–179
  clapping games and, 99–100, 106
  collegial relations and, 104–106
  complementary relations and, 113–114, 124–126
  coordinated actions and, 106–107
  cross-gender relations and, 124–126, 128, 130–132
  introduction, 12–14
  language flexibility, 44, 166–167
  performance and, 143, 145–146, 147–149, 150–152, 160
  in Pine Cone Wars, 139–141, 173
  situated classroom and, 31, 32
  storytelling and, 21–24, 71, 74, 75–76, 145–146, 147–149, 150–152, 160
  voice as potential resource in fix-its, 67
  writing fix-its and, 43–44, 60–61, 83–84, 88
Tolchinsky, L., 53
Tomasello, M., 4
Toolan, M. J., 160
Tooth fairy, 71

Unofficial cultures. *See* Peer relations

Urciuoli, B., 147
Usage, as grammatical fix-it, 45, 61

Valentine's Day, 30, 91, 132
Varenne, H., 51
Vasquez, O., 173
Voice
  depiction of human voice, 67, 153, 169
  nonstandard human voice as grammatical fix-it, 63–65
  as resource in writing fix-its, 66–68
Volk, D., 147
Volosinov, V. N., 93
Vygotsky, L. S., xii, 6–7, 22, 44, 48, 53, 84–85, 101, 137, 156, 171, 176

War on Poverty, 172
Wenger, E., 51
Werner, H., 170
Willems, M., 165
Williams, V. B., 32
Willo (kindergarten student), sibling love and, 79–80, 133
Wohlwend, K., 174
Wolfram, W., 63, 168
Word walls, 39
Writing basics. *See* Basics of writing
Writing fix-its, 36, 43–68. *See also* Relational fix-its
  content. *See* Content fix-its
  grammatical. *See* Grammatical fix-its
  graphological conventions. *See* Graphological conventions
  hierarchical conception, 45, 163
  importance of, 184–185
  normalizing multimodality, 169–171
  relational drama concerning, 83–86, 87–88
  voice as potential resource in, 66–68

Yung-chan, D., 167

Zeitlin, S., 83
Zentella, A. C., 167
Zickuhr, K., 2

About the Author

Anne Haas Dyson is a former teacher of young children and currently a professor of education at the University of Illinois at Urbana-Champaign. Among her previous appointments was as a long-time professor at the University of California, Berkeley, where she was a recipient of the Distinguished Teaching Award. A fellow of the American Educational Research Association, Dyson studies the childhood cultures and literacy learning of young school children. Among her books are *Social Worlds of Children Learning to Write in an Urban Primary School* (1993), which received the National Council of Teachers of English David H. Russell Award for Distinguished Research, *Writing Superheroes* (1997), *The Brothers and Sisters Learn to Write* (2003), and with Celia Genishi, *Children, Language, and Literacy: Diverse Learners in Diverse Times* (2009).